World History through Case Studies

Published:

Debating New Approaches to History (2018)
Edited by Marek Tamm and Peter Burke

The World since 1945 (2016)
P. M. H. Bell and Mark Gilbert

World Histories from Below (2016)
Edited by Antoinette Burton and Tony Ballantyne

Forthcoming:

Essential Skills for Historians
Edited by J. Laurence Hare, Jack Wells and Bruce E. Baker

History in Practice (3rd Edition)
Ludmilla Jordanova

Writing History (3rd Edition)
Edited by Stefan Berger, Heiko Feldner and Kevin Passmore

World History through Case Studies

Historical Skills in Practice

David Eaton

BLOOMSBURY ACADEMIC
LONDON • NEW YORK • OXFORD • NEW DELHI • SYDNEY

BLOOMSBURY ACADEMIC
Bloomsbury Publishing Plc
50 Bedford Square, London, WC1B 3DP, UK
1385 Broadway, New York, NY 10018, USA

BLOOMSBURY, BLOOMSBURY ACADEMIC and the Diana logo
are trademarks of Bloomsbury Publishing Plc

First published in Great Britain 2020
Reprinted 2020

Cover design by Tjaša Krivec
Cover images: Candlelights (© Smartshots International/Getty Images),
Light bulbs (© Krisikorn Tanrattanakunl/EyeEm/Getty Images)

A catalogue record for this book is available from the British Library.

A catalog record for this book is available from the Library of Congress.

ISBN: HB: 978-1-3500-4260-5
        PB: 978-1-3500-4261-2
        ePDF: 978-1-3500-4259-9
        eBook: 978-1-3500-4262-9

Typeset by Integra Software Services Pvt. Ltd.
Printed and bound in Great Britain

To find out more about our authors and books visit www.bloomsbury.com
and sign up for our newsletters.

Contents

List of Figures

Acknowledgments

Any work of world history is in some sense a collective endeavor, and this book is no exception. Professors, teachers, and the students in my world history classes all provided moments of inspiration, and if I forget any names, I apologize in advance.

This book came into being thanks to the support of Emma Goode. As she moved on to new endeavors, Gopinath Anbalagan, Sophie Campbell, and Dan Hutchins offered invaluable assistance. Some of the ideas contained in this book were presented at the World History Seminar Series at MIT and Wayne State University. Special thanks to Sana Aiyar and Jennifer Hart for organizing these sessions and to Pouya Alimagham, Kate Luongo, Kenda Mutongi, Hiromu Nagahara, and Malcolm Purinton for their comments. Other chapters were presented at the annual meetings of the American Historical Association and World History Association (WHA). Thanks to the audience members for their thoughtful suggestions.

Grand Valley State University has been my home since 2009, and I have been very fortunate to work alongside an incredible range of colleagues. Micah Childress, Matthew Daley, Whitney Dirks, Gretchen Galbraith, Abby Gautreau, Timothy Lombardo, William Morison, Jeffrey Rop, Stephen Staggs, and Sarah Tate helped me come to grips with the enormity of history survey courses in a variety of ways. Several colleagues volunteered their time to read and comment on draft chapters. Thanks to Alice Chapman, Grace Coolidge, Jason Crouthamel, Mike Huner, Chad Lingwood, Louis Moore, Paul Murphy, Andrew Peterson, Patrick Pospisek, Patrick Shan, Tammy Shreiner, David Stark, David Zwart, and the two anonymous reviewers for greatly improving the quality of this manuscript. Needless to say, any remaining errors are my own.

Special thanks are necessary for several colleagues. Mike Huner and I found ourselves teaching world history despite backgrounds in much narrower fields, and our collective efforts to come to grips with this were part of the genesis for this book. He also encouraged me to use sessions at the Great Lakes History Conference as a platform to explore some of the ideas presented here. Tammy Shreiner was an important link to the larger field of history education, and her thoughtful approaches to teaching have been a constant source of inspiration. Her studies of how teachers read and present data inspired the final chapter of this book, and I am grateful that she encouraged me to engage in the vital work of writing high school world history standards. David Zwart introduced me to Stephen Lévesque's *Thinking Historically* through a department teaching circle, and pushed me to think harder about how procedural concepts can be integrated into survey classes. He epitomizes the colleague whose "door is always open," and many of the ideas in this book germinated during conversations with him. Finally, Craig Benjamin was a crucial interlocutor as I began to explore the field of world history. His bubbling enthusiasm for the subject is truly contagious, and when I approached him about how to improve my world history teaching he made the crucial suggestion that I attend "The Read."

"The Read" refers to the once-a-year gathering of teachers and professors to grade the AP World History exams. It represents the largest meeting of world historians on the planet and for a time this course could justifiably claim to be one of the best in the field. I have met countless people here who have gotten me through the excruciatingly long days of marking and changed the way I think about world history, including Eric Beckman, Dawn Bolton, Kristen Collins, Sara Dahl-Wyland, Karen Fry, Karol Giblin, Sam Greene, Rebecca Hayes, Bram Hubbell, Eric Jones, Angela Lee, Suzanne Litrel, Craig Miller, Zachary Morgan, TJ Sakole, Asma Shakir, Bill Strickland, Jennifer Sweatman, Jennifer Wahl, Rick Warner, and David White.

It was also at "The Read" that I met Matt Drwenski. His perspectives on world history transformed my understandings of the subject, and led to the creation of *On Top of the World*, our podcast on world history. This show was designed to bridge the gap between world history teaching and research, and four years later I am delighted with the results. Thanks to our guests including Valeria Alvarado, Andrew Behrendt, Craig Benjamin, Jack Bouchard, Niklas Frykman, Rob Guthrie, Lauren Janes, Eric Jones, Henrik Lohmander, Katey Mayberry, Peter Nicholson, Andrew Peterson, Tammy Shreiner, Mike Vann, Rick Warner, and Molly Warsh for being part of the show.

The ethos of the podcast was shaped by both "The Read" and the WHA. The WHA is one of the few professional organizations that integrates high school teachers and college instructors under a single umbrella, and its annual meetings have always been a wonderful experience. Special thanks to the fascinating world historians I've met here, including Bob Bain, Eileen Baranyk, Mike Burns, Amanda DoAmaral, Ross Dunn, Leah Gregory, Alex

Holowicki, Alan Karras, Gerard McCann, Amy Manlapas, Patrick Manning, Maryanne Meckel-Rhett, Laura Mitchell, Elizabeth Pollard, Jake Pomerantz, Jonathan Reynolds, Louisa Rice, Christoph Strobel, Kerry Ward, and Merry Wiesner-Hanks.

Closer to home, my sister, Heather Eaton, was a constant source of inspiration even if I could barely comprehend her cutting edge virology research. My parents, Dennis and Helen Eaton, have been my biggest fans as I slowly put this book together. I am forever grateful that they did not try to dissuade me when, as a precocious teenager, I decided I wanted to be a history professor. Their steadfast support enabled me to survive the precarity of life as a grad student and contingent faculty member while I struggled to land a tenure-track job. Without that support, this book would not have been possible.

Andrea Melvin, my wife and partner, offered love and patience as this manuscript consumed an ever-growing proportion of my time and energy. Her understandings of gender, material culture, public history, and fashion forced me to recognize my own blind spots on these subjects, and in this book I try to make partial amends. And last but not least, Michael entered our lives just as this book neared completion. We have no idea what the future holds, but in the past four months he has filled our hearts and house in ways that make it hard to imagine how we ever lived without. The sudden experience of parenting has made me more aware of the importance of public education, and my hope is that his world history classes are taught by instructors as passionate as those listed above. All the love in the world to all of you.

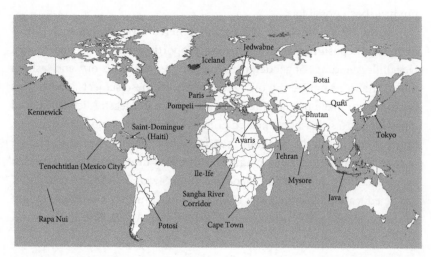

Key Sites from the Book.

Introduction

> Once the problem of historical interpretation makes itself felt in the public culture, it becomes crucial to teach students not just the one best story but the means for assessing interpretations, for weighing the evidence supporting one against another, for comparing different narratives and explanations. If young people are to get a useful history education in this cultural moment, they must not only be exposed to a good historical drama but also be allowed to see the ropes and pulleys behind the curtain.[1]

For many students, their exposure to the discipline of history comes by way of a general survey of the past. This can be a painful experience. They are handed an authoritative textbook, and told that the information contained within is essential to understanding their world. Each week they learn a little more, guided by an instructor who is an expert on only a tiny fraction of the material. After this tedious stroll through the facts, the journey culminates in a test where that information is regurgitated, assessed, and then forgotten.

This approach never worked very well, but its shortcomings have become especially apparent in the age of the smartphone. Content is on the verge of becoming frictionless, subject only to artificial restrictions. Requiring students to memorize facts has been rendered pointless by the smartphone, which offers instant access to (relatively) reliable information on virtually any subject of interest. Stripping students of their phones when they take a test or listen to a lecture simply reinforces that history is out of step with the modern world.[2] At the college level, the number of history majors has entered a precipitous decline.[3] Perhaps rightfully so.

How can historians fight back? By rethinking the survey course. This book takes a new approach to this staple of the discipline. It does not aim to cover everything, and it does not focus on a particular theme. Instead, it is inspired by a specific idea—that historical thinking is badly needed today. Despite the new masses of information at people's fingertips, many struggle to tell the difference between groundless conspiracies and solid evidence, between strong and weak arguments.[4] And as a result of the vast array of sources offering narratives of the past, many students are unable to separate good-faith efforts to present history as it happened from cherry-picked data used to support a predetermined conclusion. In theory, frictionless information should make us smarter. In reality, it has led to conspiracy theories, alternative facts, and a post-truth world.

This book argues that we need to draw back the curtain on disciplinary thinking. All historians engaged in lengthy research projects acquire critical skills at sorting information, skills that are more important now than ever. At the start of my dissertation I feared I would never be able to write 250 pages. After four years of research that left me with 10,000 digital photos, 1,000 pages of archival notes, and over 200 hours of recorded interviews, I feared I would never be able to say what I wanted to in only 250 pages! There are obvious parallels between this and a student Googling the American Revolution. They have access to almost infinite resources, but little idea how to sort them. How do they identify good sources? How should they interpret specific pieces of evidence? What are the best questions to ask about these events? And what lessons can be learned from them? History instructors are well equipped to teach students how to navigate these types of questions.

Five procedural concepts

This book is oriented around case studies, which is not an unusual approach to world history. What makes it unique is that these case studies are chosen because they illuminate specific procedural knowledge of the discipline of history, or "ideas about *how to think historically*."[5] Often referred to as historical thinking skills, these concepts offer students a window into the questions historians ask when tackling challenging topics. Many organizations have produced lists of these skills, but they are often confusing or subject to frequent change.[6] As a result, I have relied upon the five procedural concepts outlined by Stéphane Lévesque in his book *Thinking Historically*. These are historical significance, historical empathy, continuity and change, progress and decline, and evidence.

According to Lévesque, historical thinking means "understanding how knowledge has been constructed."[7] This introduction will not go into as much depth, but will try to illustrate how they can help us make sense of the past:

1   Historical significance: Historians cannot study everything, so how do they identify certain events, individuals, or themes as particularly significant? Having a clear set of criteria for what is worthy of attention and what is not is crucial for historians, but we are often opaque about what shapes this process. Obviously we try to select events that are important, especially to those who were living through them, but every generation believes that the events it experiences are of outsized importance. To get past this, we can look at the ways that events changed people's lives, the number of people affected, the duration of events, or the relevance of events in the present day. But none of these techniques are unassailable, and understanding perceptions of events among those living in the past requires the use of our second procedural concept.

2   Historical empathy: Part of what makes the past fascinating is imagining what it was like. But our imaginations can lead us astray, especially when we rely too heavily on our own framework for perceiving the world. This requires us to ground our imaginings in solid evidence from the time we are studying. We want to be able to understand the beliefs, values, and objectives of past actors without necessarily condoning them. This involves an immersion in past worlds, known as contextualization, in order to comprehend the motives of these individuals. This does not require a suspension of moral judgment. Historians actively judge the past in numerous ways, and we should be clear about how and why we do this. To quote Lévesque, "students should be aware of both their own belief systems and the impacts of these beliefs on historical thinking."[8]

3   Evidence: The meticulous and critical use of evidence is essential to producing good history. Human beings have left traces of the past in numerous ways, and a core element of the historical discipline is interpreting these correctly. We must be able to identify the source, attribute it to the correct author, contextualize the production of this source, and corroborate it through comparison with other relevant information. I would argue that this approach can apply to sources as diverse as written documents, statistical data, archaeological finds, genetic sequencing, and linguistics. This is why I use the term "historian" extremely broadly in this book—anyone engaged in the careful use of sources to illuminate the past is using this procedural concept. Analyzing evidence is a habit of mind that students can develop over time, especially if they are "exposed *gradually* and *persistently* to the practice of investigating the past using sources."[9]

4   Continuity and change: Understanding that events happen in chronological order is important, and it ensures that students have a better sense of cause and effect. But alone this does little to illuminate the more complex processes of continuity and change. Historians are often asked to group events together using a tool known as colligation, and in textbooks this manifests itself in "Eras," "Parts," and "Chapters." These organizing principles implicitly convey continuity for events that are included together as well as pivotal changes when a particular era ends. This can be extremely difficult on the macroscale of a world history survey course, and perceptions of continuity or change may vary dramatically depending on the race, class, age, or gender of the peoples whose views are being discussed. World historians are well aware that there is little agreement in the field on the key moments of change across these world historical narratives, and articulating why disagreements exist helps students understand how perceptions of continuity and change shape understandings of the past.

5   Progress and decline: This procedural concept is essential to the discipline. If changes are frequently taking place, how should historians assess them? By necessity these judgments are subjective, and can be shaped by elements of the other procedural concepts cited above. Indeed, historians may well assess the same evidence from the past differently because of the changing contemporary context that surrounds them. But when trying to determine whether change in the past represents progress or decline, historians must be consistent in their judgments, and only apply criteria that would be relevant. The real danger is that the vast majority of students believe that things simply get better over time, and this implicit narrative drives much of their understanding of the world.[10] While textbooks are far more cautious, they tend to tell a similarly progressive story and encourage this type of thinking. Uncovering the many arguments historians have over this procedural concept helps students understand the importance of historical contingency and the ways that events might have drastically different consequences depending on which group of historical actors one chooses to privilege.

One of the most influential historians of the twentieth century, Fernand Braudel, argued that history "cannot be understood without practicing it."[11] What follows is my attempt to create the scaffolding for a world history survey course that allows students "to do history" using these procedural concepts rather than simply memorize someone else's narrative. Having narrowed down the forms of disciplinary thinking essential for students to learn, it is time to move to the case studies and examine how they were selected.

Twenty case studies

These case studies were designed to support a complete world history survey course from the origins of humanity to the present day, and they were not chosen at random. First, they were selected to ensure geographical balance. This is essential to avoid duplicating an older approach known as Western Civilizations. These courses teach the history of the world as the rise of the West, and often ignore regions like the Americas or sub-Saharan Africa until they come into contact with Europeans. This is based on the racist belief that these people did not experience historical change until visited by more advanced races. One might think that this narrative has been completely discredited, but Western Civilizations courses are still offered in many universities and world history courses often reflect elements of this approach. Even for instructors trying to adopt a more global perspective in the classroom, an enduring problem is that, as Gilbert Allardyce put it, "Eurocentrism is us."[12] When faced with the prospect of teaching the history of the world, we turn instinctively to what we know, and that is often the history of Europeans and their descendants. The result is a course that examines the world primarily as a European story with sections tacked-on dealing with regions like China, described derisively as "Western Civ plus" for its similarities to the old Western Civilizations narrative.[13] This book argues that world history instructors must be conscious of the geographical regions studied in their courses to avoid this problem, and this is reflected in the selection of these case studies. Included are six from Asia, five from Africa, four each from the Americas and Europe, and one from Oceania. Within each region I have tried to avoid major overlap. Thus, the case studies on the Americas include one set in Washington state, one in the Greater Caribbean, one in the Valley of Mexico, and one in the highlands of Bolivia and Peru. No effort is made to isolate these discussions to specific regions, and in certain chapters the material will range widely in order to make essential connections. But the case studies aim to cover a representative swath of the world through a conscious selection process.

Second, I have tried to include case studies that deal with a diverse range of themes. They address topics like race, gender, inequality, labor, religion, spectacle, sport, migration, and the environment. One popular way to make world history comprehensible is to select a specific theme and then follow that thread across time and space. This has been done for almost every conceivable topic, including somewhat esoteric subjects like piracy, salt, and opium. This approach to world history has the advantage of making the past more manageable, but in a survey class I believe it is important to offer students an introduction to a wide range of analytical approaches. Sparking interest in students is always difficult, but casting a wide net offers the best chance at ensuring everyone in the classroom encounters something they find fascinating about the global past.

Last but not least, the case studies were chosen to offer chronological depth. Many historians consider themselves specialists in a particular era. My dissertation covered the nineteenth and twentieth centuries, an exceptionally broad period of time for a recent graduate student! However, most world history courses aim to create a coherent narrative of all human history, and this requires delving into the very distant past. This poses major challenges for historians, who have to engage with unfamiliar fields like archaeology to truly make sense of these eras. These problems are compounded by the lack of a single periodization scheme for the world history survey course. The following table includes four popular ways that textbooks or curriculum materials divide the past into eras:

	AP World History (until 2019–2020)	Panorama	Big History	Traditions and Encounters, 4th Ed.
Era 1	Start to 600 BCE	Start to 1000 BCE	13.8–4.6 bya	3500 BCE–500 BCE
Era 2	600 BCE–600 CE	1200 BCE–300 CE	13.8–4.6 bya	500 BCE–500 CE
Era 3	600–1450 CE	200–1000 CE	13.8–4.6 bya	500–1000 CE
Era 4	1450–1750 CE	900–1500 CE	4.6–3.8 bya	1000–1500 CE
Era 5	1750–1900 CE	1450–1750 CE	3.8 bya–8 mya	1500–1800 CE
Era 6	1900–present	1750–1914 CE	8 mya–8000 BCE	1750–1914 CE
Era 7		1890-present	8000 BCE–1700 CE	1914–present
Era 8			1700–present	

The lack of overlap makes it a struggle to know what to include in a world history survey. I preferred to begin with *homo sapiens* rather than the vast timescale of "big history," a course that begins with the creation of the universe in the crucible of Big Bang. Moving closer to the present, I selected these case studies so that there would be at least two that deal with any of the eras mentioned above. They range from c.16,000 years ago to the present day, and they do not shy away from either the ancient past or the modern era. Finally, in each chapter I connect the issues being discussed to contemporary events. One central contention of this book is that the past and present are in constant dialogue with one another, and events taking place today have an impact on how we interpret our history. These case studies may or may not be timeless, but at the very least they should be timely.

Why not a normal survey?

The history survey course is frequently criticized, often by the same historians who teach it. In a scathing indictment of the traditional survey, Lendol Calder argued that historians "flirt with calamity" by refusing to embrace new approaches in the classroom. But inertia is a powerful force, and despite brutal critiques most professors would tend to sympathize with Calder's colleague who claimed "I may be doing it wrong, but I am doing it in the proper and customary way."[14] One might hope that plummeting enrollment numbers at the college level would encourage instructors to embrace new approaches, but this does not seem to be the case. Instead, coverage-based surveys lurch on, completely out of step with the modern world.

This is an issue because, as Sam Wineburg argues, "the problem with students is not that they don't know enough history. The problem is that they don't know what history is in the first place."[15] Textbooks are an important part of surveys because they not only contain sufficient content to meet the goals of the course, but they also conceal the key debates within the discipline. I would argue that this does students a disservice. By exposing them to the debates that take place behind the curtain, they get a chance to experience the messy and competing narratives that make history such a vibrant discipline. For generations we have tried to hide this disorder behind a façade of authoritative textbook prose. This no longer serves any purpose. By revealing the ways historians think, we can better prepare students for the competing narratives and information that surround them.

So what are some problems with textbooks? First, they make crucial decisions for students. This is especially true with periodization. This crucial skill, which forms an aspect of continuity and change, involves how textbooks select "turning points" in the past. One important example of this can be seen in the four examples described in the table above. The Industrial Revolution is widely considered one of the transformative events in world history, and textbooks usually connect it to urbanization, urban growth, and class consciousness.[16] In contrast, the expansion of cities in the early modern period (1450–1750) receives virtually no attention, with only "scattered signs of what later generations thought of as 'modernity'" visible at this time.[17] According to the textbooks, the Industrial Revolution, urbanization, and modernity are a series of connected events that take place between roughly 1750 and 1914.

In contrast, a vibrant historiographical debate surrounds this subject. As we will see in Chapter 14, many historians would disagree with the argument that the technological shift of the Industrial Revolution preceded urbanization and "modernity." Instead, they would date these changes to the seventeenth century, when cities like Paris experienced both rapid growth and large cultural shifts that helped make future developments possible. By revealing which types of evidence should be prioritized and which definitions of modernity are most meaningful, we can guide students through the process of how historians debate key issues in the discipline. What types of evidence can we use? How should we define the terms? And what changes are most significant?

Second, textbooks are often guilty of hiding the fascinating detective work that goes into reconstructing the past. Take the domestication of plants and animals. These new food sources enabled denser populations, more sophisticated communities, and numerous technological innovations. In *Guns, Germs, and Steel*, Jared Diamond argues that "the availability of domestic plants and animals ultimately explains why empires, literacy, and steel weapons developed earliest in Eurasia and later, or not at all, on other continents."[18] One of the most important animals domesticated was the horse, also known as *Equus caballus*. It was a source of milk, meat, muscle, and mobility, allowing people to travel previously unthinkable distances with astonishing speed. Once coupled with suitable technologies like the wheel, the compound bow, and the stirrup, it offered an important military advantage that would not be fully eclipsed until the First World War. The massive empires of the Persians, Mongols, and Spanish would never have been possible without them.

The above suggests that the domestication of the horse was a turning point in world history, and countless specialists have tried to determine how this happened. But you would never guess it from world history textbooks. *Patterns of World History* scarcely mentions the process—the one line on the subject reads "Shortly after 3000 BCE, in the region around the Ural Mountains in central Asia, local Proto-Indo-European villagers domesticated the horse, using it for its meat and for transporting heavy loads."[19] Other texts discuss the significance of animal husbandry, but information on the process of domesticating horses is scarce.[20] To most authors, the impact of domesticated horses is merely one aspect of the larger Agricultural Revolution, one that is not as significant as the growth of farming and the foundation of settled urban centers. The horse, for all its future importance, receives little attention.

This is a tragedy because archaeologists, anthropologists, geneticists, and linguists have all collaborated and competed with each other in order to piece this story together. Whether it involves bone size, tooth wear, age of death, or pelt color, they have developed a variety of innovative approaches to establish the foundation for that single line in *Patterns of World History*. Obviously it is impossible for textbooks to include this level of detail on every subject, but by ignoring this process students find little of inspiration here, just another date to memorize. Chapter 2 of this book involves a deep dive into this process, one that I hope might give students more to get excited about when looking at the ancient past.

Third, world history textbooks struggle to create a coherent narrative out of the global past. They do so by embracing an argument that seems intuitively accurate—that the story of the world is one of deepening connections and complexity. Jerry Bentley refined this approach, and it now appears in most textbooks. *Panorama*, for example, claims that its story is one of the "growing complexity of human society" as it relates to population, energy, human impact on environment, technology, communications, network density, government, weapons, and the size and elaborateness of systems of faith.[21] From a birds-eye view at 35,000 feet, this argument makes sense. But once we begin delving into specific examples, this can be problematic.

Take the final example from *Panorama* involving systems of faith. The argument that these have become more complex over time is rooted in a particular narrative that claims faiths progress through stages from natural spirits to polytheism to monotheism. The result is that world history textbooks generally address polytheism only before 1500 CE, and do not always do this well. *Ways of the World* has a nice description of Bantu spirituality (*c.*500 BCE–1200 CE) and its notion of "continuous revelation" that separated it, in some ways, from the "major monotheistic religions."[22] But given the vast diversity of Bantu practices, it is perhaps guilty of lumping African forms of spirituality together rather than addressing their specific content and history. Textbooks also struggle with polytheism at a global scale. *Patterns of World History*, for example, argues that the combination of writing and kingship was crucial to the emergence of polytheism in 3500–2500 BCE. While this is an admirable attempt to historicize this development, it is of little use explaining the wide range of polytheistic faiths in sub-Saharan Africa where writing and kingship were absent.[23] And if polytheistic faiths are only discussed in the distant past, doesn't that create an implicit narrative that they are ancient, unchanging, and doomed to be replaced?

Orisa worship, discussed in Chapter 12, provides a valuable counterpoint. This polytheistic faith that originated in Nigeria sometime *c.*100–200 CE has been able to "go global," and today the orisas may be worshipped by as many as 75 million people, a following that dwarfs those of more frequently covered faiths like Jainism, Sikhism, and even Judaism. Crucial to its spread was the Atlantic Slave Trade, when orisa worshippers were forced to move to the Americas. They did not enjoy the freedom to worship openly, so they concealed veneration of the orisas with the veneration of Christian saints. This became the foundation of what are known today as Vodou, Santería, and Candomblé. These forms of worship are briefly mentioned in many textbooks, but the history of this religion, which involved a specific creation myth, its diffusion around West Africa, the incorporation of new orisas into its pantheon, its encounter with Islam, and then its diffusion to the New World, is never mentioned.[24] So too is the case for its modern relevance, made most passionately by Nobel Prize winner Wole Soyinka.[25] The space limitations in a textbook make it difficult to justify a deep dive into the history of a specific polytheistic faith, but the result is an implicit narrative that suggests only monotheistic religions were capable of changing or adapting.

Conclusion

Despite the criticism of world history surveys, we should not be too pessimistic about the future. World history has become a crucial part of the high school- and college-level curriculum, and in 2017, 298,475 students took the AP World History exam.[26] Just as there has been a "global turn" historiographically, there has also been a global turn in the classroom. The problem is that many students only take one history course before they are scared off by outdated and opaque approaches that do little to prepare them for the modern world. There is a real need for concrete steps to reinvigorate the moribund coverage-based survey, and what follows is my attempt to do so.

Further reading

Calder, Lendol. "Uncoverage: Toward a Signature Pedagogy for the History Survey," *Journal of American History* 92, no. 4 (2006): 1358–1370. An impassioned plea for historians to move away from coverage-based surveys toward a pedagogy called "unwrapping the textbook."

Dunn, Ross, Laura Mitchell, and Kerry Ward, eds. *The New World History*. Oakland, CA: University of California Press, 2016. An updated compilation that includes essential writings in the discipline.

Guldi, Jo, and David Armitage. *The History Manifesto*. New York: Cambridge University Press, 2014. Two prominent historians make the case that historians should address essential themes like climate change, inequality, data literacy, and thinking over the *longue durée*.

Lévesque, Stéphane. *Thinking Historically*. Toronto: University of Toronto Press, 2008. An excellent effort to identify and define the procedural concepts used by all historians.

Wineburg, Sam. *Why Learn History (When It's Already on Your Phone)*. Chicago, IL: University of Chicago Press, 2018. An impassioned plea for historians to abandon the traditional memorization-based survey in favor of teaching them critical thinking skills.

1

Urge Overkill

In 1996, a pair of drunken students made one of the most important archaeological discoveries in American history. Stumbling in the shallows of the Columbia River, one of them grasped something solid: it was a skull. The police were called, and the remains were turned over to a forensic archaeologist named James Chatters for examination. Assuming they dated to the nineteenth century, he used skull morphology to identify the skeleton as Caucasoid. The discovery of an arrow lodged in the thigh bone seemed to confirm his suspicions. Perhaps an early settler had been killed in an Indian raid? Chatters was excited: "I thought we had a pioneer."[1]

But the arrow point was made of stone, and resembled the "Cascade" style that was normally found at much older sites. So Chatters sent a fragment of bone from the remains for carbon dating and mitochondrial DNA (mtDNA) sequencing.[2] The sample did not contain enough viable genetic material to conduct an analysis, but carbon dating revealed that the skeleton was approximately 9,200 years old. Responding to media questions about the find, Chatters claimed this long-deceased individual would have resembled Patrick Stewart, a famous white actor. This ignited wild speculation. Was it possible that the Americas had been first settled by whites, who were then exterminated by the ancestors of the modern Native Americans? No historians believed this theory, but there was no disputing that this skeleton offered a treasure trove of information. The research possibilities seemed endless.

These were complicated by the existence of the Native American Graves Protection and Repatriation Act (NAGPRA). Passed by Congress in 1990, this law stipulated that any Native American remains found on federal land had to be surrendered to a culturally affiliated tribe upon request. Less than a week after the radiocarbon dates were made public, five Native American groups demanded that the skeleton be turned over to them for proper burial.

They argued that any 9,200-year-old human remains in Washington State had to be Native American. They also objected to Chatters's decision to name this individual Kennewick Man, after the city in which he was found. The Native American groups preferred "oyt.pa.ma.na.tit.tite," or the Ancient One. The US Army Corps of Engineers (ACE), which controlled the site where the skeleton was found, agreed to return the remains. Chatters then reached out to the academic community, seeking support for his efforts to deny the Native American claim. Eventually eight anthropologists filed a lawsuit to halt the repatriation proceedings. They claimed that Kennewick Man was not affiliated with any living Native American group, and thus the provisions of NAGPRA did not apply.

What followed was an eleven-year legal battle, a temporary resolution, and then a fascinating twist. Kennewick Man is an excellent starting point to examine how historians analyze and interpret evidence. For this chapter, we will start with a single archaeological find and look at how different groups interpreted its significance, the techniques used to uncover its mysteries, and examine how politics can work its way into scientific analysis.

The skull wars

One of the real challenges with regard to Kennewick Man was how to analyze and interpret the evidence about his origins. Historians were already deeply divided over how the Americas were settled. But the political context was even more problematic. The name "Kennewick Man" was coined by a white researcher, and the remains were held at white-run institutions. This tapped into a long history of whites describing the Native American past in racist and offensive ways. Now in 1996 Kennewick Man was being used to suggest that Native Americans were NOT the original inhabitants of the Americas. This political context is crucial to understanding how Kennewick Man became so controversial.

With regard to his origins, the first critical piece of evidence was the carbon dating done on the bone sample, but the same archaeological team also attempted to analyze Kennewick Man's DNA. This can be done using mtDNA, which is located outside the cell nucleus and thus does not undergo recombination from generation to generation. Since it is passed from the mother to child more or less[3] intact, it tells us a great deal about the maternal line far into the past. It can also be done using Y-DNA, which is similarly averse to recombination and is passed directly from father to son. In 1996, however, the age and mineralization of Kennewick Man's bones meant there was insufficient genetic material to say anything one way or another about his origins.

In the absence of any conclusive evidence, sensationalistic theories became popular. Timothy Egan, writing for the *New York Times*, described Kennewick Man as "Caucasian," a provocative statement supported only by Chatters's initial comment that the skull had "Caucasoid features." Craniology can be a helpful tool to determine the cultural affiliation of a particular skull, but only when the remains in question can be compared to an extensive database of similar examples. This is particularly problematic in relation to Kennewick Man because so few skulls have been found from a similar time period. This makes it difficult to know what skull sizes were normal for any Paleoindian population at that time. Craniology is even less accurate when making comparisons from past to present since skull shape changes due to diet, environment, and genetic drift.[4] The facial reconstruction created by Chatters and Thomas McClelland did nothing to clarify the issue. By inserting individually layered muscles and tendons under the skin the face of Kennewick Man looked very "real," but it was impossible to argue that he "looked Caucasian." Depending on one's perspective, one could just as easily see similarities to Native American heroes like Crazy Horse. Nonetheless, this highly subjective form of evidence was cited by Judge John Jelderks in his 2004 decision on Kennewick Man's affiliation.[5]

It may seem innocuous to claim that a skull "looked Caucasian," but this was an explosive assertion that tapped into well-established racial narratives. During the late eighteenth and nineteenth centuries, Native Americans were removed from their land because most whites believed they were too uncivilized to use it efficiently. This casually racist assertion was complicated by the existence of numerous large earthen mounds across these same areas, a sure sign of social complexity. Unwilling to accept that Native Americans were capable of building these monuments, nineteenth-century historians ascribed them to an earlier race of white Mound Builders. These whites, they argued, provided the dynamism necessary for monument building, but were exterminated by the ancestors of Native Americans when they arrived. As Meghan Howey writes, "If Indians had destroyed the white Mound Builders, white Americans were justified in killing Indians and removing them from their lands."[6] This narrative has long since been discredited in academic circles, but it persists among certain white supremacist groups. They interpreted Kennewick Man as evidence that an ancient race had populated the Americas before the Native Americans. It is indicative of the importance Kennewick Man held to them that the Asatru Folk Assembly, a California-based Norse religious group accused of racism, joined the lawsuit.[7] They laid claim to the remains in the same way as the five Native American groups, further complicating an already rancorous legal situation.

It is important to emphasize that the belief Kennewick Man represented an early migration of whites was never shared by the anthropologists involved in the trial, but it is also easy to understand why many Native Americans were skeptical about the motives of researchers in general. After all, anthropology and archaeology had long, tortuous pasts of their own, pasts that were deeply imbued with forms of scientific racism. Samuel Morton, a famous nineteenth-century scientist from Philadelphia, claimed that his mathematical analysis of Native American skulls revealed that they not only possessed an inferior intellect, but were also so deficient in this regard that they could never be civilized. Darwin's theories of evolution were also cited as proof that Native Americans were at an inferior stage of civilization to whites, and as a result doomed to extinction. This led to the belief that those still alive were on the verge of disappearing, and that they should be studied as "living fossils" before they vanished completely. Academics behaved in ways that suggest they shared popular prejudices about Native Americans. Franz Boas, for example, is honored today as "the Father of American anthropology," and played a key role in discrediting forms of scientific racism based on skull shape. But in 1888 he also spent several months looting Native American graves in British Columbia. He later wrote, "It is most unpleasant work to steal bones from a grave, but what is the use, someone has to do it."[8] The looting of Indian graves and the desecration of their corpses was a path to academic fame in the late nineteenth century.

The looting reached such a feverish pitch that Congress passed the 1906 Antiquities Act. This made it illegal to excavate Indian archaeological sites without a permit from the federal government. And while this may have prevented "amateurs" from looting graves, it also excluded Native Americans from involvement in the process. With government officials and academic experts calling the shots, it was possible to get approval for excavations of tombs without ever consulting with living Native Americans. As Walter Hawk-Echo put it, "If you desecrate a white grave, you wind up sitting in prison. But desecrate an Indian grave, you get a PhD."[9]

During the 1960s and 1970s Native American activists, influenced by their role in the civil rights movement, became increasingly critical of their exclusion from their own history. In 1971, the American Indian Movement

(AIM) destroyed an archaeological site at Welch, Minnesota, including field notes and other research materials. Vine Deloria wrote impassioned polemics against the arrogance of academics, imploring anthropologists in particular to "get down from their thrones of authority and PURE research and begin helping Indian tribes instead of preying on them."[10] Some academics held the protestors in contempt, arguing that they were "citified" and just looking for jobs. Others were sympathetic to certain concerns (especially the desecration of graves) but worried about a backlash against scientific research in general.

The passing of NAGPRA in 1990 was the culmination of these tensions. They were evident in the odd coalition that ensured this legislation was enacted; left-wing environmentalists who believed Native Americans had a unique connection to the Earth, civil rights activists who sought equal treatment for all regardless of race, and right-wing culture warriors who perceived the issue through the lens of religious rights.[11] NAGPRA's provisions were sweeping. They required all organizations receiving federal funding to return cultural artifacts to the appropriate Native American group. This process would take decades, but ultimately it was a great success. Many items looted in the nineteenth and twentieth centuries were identified,

Figure 1.1 Members of the American Indian Movement occupy Sacred Heart Catholic Church in Wounded Knee, South Dakota, 1973. Courtesy of Bettman via Getty Images.

linked to an existing tribe, and then returned, often in moving ceremonies that reaffirmed to sovereignty of Native Americans over their past.

Native Americans also began to exert additional pressure on historians interpreting their past. Scholars generally agreed that the earliest Americans (or Paleoindians) arrived here from Asia via Beringia, a land bridge connecting Siberia and Alaska from about 30,000 to 11,000 years ago. However, they struggled to piece together how these Paleoindians managed to reach and settle the rest of the Americas and their theories could be quite speculative. A particular area of frustration for Native Americans was the overkill theory. It originated with the discovery of numerous spear points and mammoth bones at Blackwater Draw, a dry lake bed near Clovis, New Mexico, that had apparently been home to a hunting camp approximately 10,000 years ago.[12] Additional discoveries in the 1930s confirmed that similar hunting societies, called Clovis cultures after the original site, became common all across North America around this time. In 1964, C. Vance Haynes noted that these dates were quite close to those when many scientists believed an ice-free corridor briefly opened between the massive Laurentides and Cordillera ice sheets that isolated Beringia and Alaska from the rest of North America.[13] Paul Martin and H. E. Wright extended this argument three years later by suggesting that when the new migrants reached the warmer plains further south, they rapidly hunted virtually every large mammal to extinction.[14] This not only enabled rapid population growth, but also eliminated numerous species which may have been suitable for domestication. This version of the peopling of the Americas remains popular with many world historians, including Jared Diamond, Yuval Harari, and Neil MacGregor. To them, Kennewick Man was just one of many ancestors of these migrants.

But others were unconvinced by the overkill theory.[15] They noted Haynes had merely demonstrated that a corridor opened just before the expansion of Clovis cultures, not that Clovis peoples had migrated along that route. And Native Americans were wary of the implications of this version of the past. Overkill became popular just as the environmentalist movement was reaching the mainstream, and it seemed extremely convenient as evidence mounted that whites had done irreparable harm to the environment in the process of conquering Native Americans (especially by slaughtering the buffalo in the nineteenth century), academics would now claim that the Clovis peoples were the original perpetrators of mass extinction. Just as the imagined extermination of the white Mound Builders was used to justify the real annihilation of modern Native Americans, the alleged environmental crimes of the Clovis peoples were being used to excuse the much more blatant excesses of nineteenth- and twentieth-century Americans.[16]

The popular alternative to the overkill theory was that Paleoindians arrived by migrating along the coast. Tom Dillehay argues that a number of key archaeological sites in the Americas predate the existence of the ice-free corridor. In the absence of a viable land route, this suggests that the earliest Paleoindians must have traveled along the Alaskan coast, an area that would have been rich with marine life even when the glaciers reached the sea.[17] Initial examinations of Kennewick Man's skull linked him to the Ainu, an indigenous peoples from East Asia, rather than Native Americans. This would fit neatly with Dillehay's coastal migrations theory. Certain migrants from the Kurile Islands and Japan might have reached the Americas by sea, but probably struggled to adapt to this new environment and disappeared from the historical record.

But Kennewick Man revealed that even this alternative was problematic for Native Americans. Numerous smaller scale migrations might be a more realistic representation of the past, but this model also suggested it was possible that people had arrived in the Americas before the ancestors of today's Native Americans, and then disappeared or died. While this seems like a minor detail, it implied that there might be ancient human remains in the Americas that are not related in any way to modern Native Americans, and as a result the provisions of NAGPRA would not apply.[18] If Kennewick Man's morphology did not match that of existing Native Americans, could it be that he belonged to one of these communities instead? Even if rising sea levels would have inundated evidence left by these migrants, could confirmation of the coastal theory be found in the remains of Kennewick Man?

Accurately interpreting Kennewick Man's remains was thus critical. The first key piece of evidence was the intact skull. As we have already seen, craniologists determined that Kennewick Man closely resembles the Ainu or Polynesians more generally. In 2015, the cranial data were reexamined, and it was found that "although our individual-based craniometric analyses confirms that Kennewick Man tends to be more similar to Polynesian and Ainu people than to Native Americans, Kennewick Man's pattern of craniometric affinity falls well within the range of affinity patterns evaluated for individual Native Americans."[19] Kennewick Man's skull does closely resemble that of the Ainu and Polynesians, but if additional evidence were to connect the remains to Native Americans, the skull would not contradict this.

Whether additional evidence could be taken from the remains was an open question. The NAGPRA claim by the five Native American groups precluded additional research on the skeleton, and ACE refused to grant permits to scientists wishing to examine the site where Kennewick Man was found. After the remains were moved to the Burke Museum in Seattle for safekeeping, however, scientists working for the National Park Service examined them in hopes of resolving the controversy. The results were released in September 2000—these scientists linked Kennewick Man to "Asian peoples" just as Secretary of the Interior Bruce Babbitt awarded the remains to the Native Americans. Babbitt felt geographical evidence (where they were found) and oral traditions established "a reasonable link between these remains and the present-day Indian tribe claimants."[20]

However, the legal saga was just heating up. The anthropologists who had filed the original lawsuit in 1996 immediately appealed Babbitt's decision and asked for a chance to conduct additional DNA testing. Three labs were given the chance to solve this puzzle but again the mineralization of the bones prevented them from sequencing Kennewick Man's DNA. Ultimately, the decision would be made by Judge Jelderks. He was sufficiently convinced by the craniological evidence that he ruled the Native American tribes had not proved a cultural link to the remains, and thus Kennewick Man was an archaeological resource deserving full scientific study. This ruling was upheld by the 9th Circuit Court in 2004, and the furor subsequently died down.

Kennewick Man's skeleton remained accessible to researchers, and new studies of the remains by Douglas Owsley and Richard Jantz provided some important information (including revising the age of Kennewick Man to 8,500 years old). However, genetic evidence would ultimately resolve the dispute. Past analyses of Kennewick Man's genetic materials had been foiled by the inability to replicate sufficient DNA to create a complete sequence. This was a major problem in bones, where DNA has a short half-life and the remaining genetic material is mixed with molecules of collagen and hydroxyapatite (a mineral form of calcium). Traditional forms of analysis using polymerase chain reaction (PCR) could only amplify relatively intact DNA, requiring a minimum of roughly ninety base pairs to compare and sequence a complete genome. However, in the early 2000s "massively parallel" next-generation sequencing techniques enabled the inclusion of fragmentary DNA that would have previously been discarded.[21]

Using next-generation sequencing on a single metacarpal bone from Kennewick Man's hand solved the mystery. Researchers at Stanford

University and the University of Copenhagen managed to obtain sufficient genetic material from this bone to connect both the mtDNA and Y-DNA to specific haplogroups, X2a and Q-M3, respectively. These haplogroups represent people with a common ancestor who share a single nucleotide polymorphism, or DNA marker that is unique to them. And both the X2a and Q-M3 haplogroups are found almost exclusively among Native Americans living in the Pacific Northwest.[22] Crucially, the average sequence length used to reconstruct Kennewick Man's genome was 53.6 base pairs, impossible to work with in 1996 but more than adequate for next-generation techniques. With this new information in hand, we can say with confidence that Kennewick Man is more closely related to modern Native Americans than anyone else today. After another group independently verified these findings, ACE agreed to return the remains to the Native Americans, and in September 2016 the legislation had been drafted to make this happen.[23]

Conclusion

The debate over Kennewick Man's origins is a fascinating way to examine how evidence is analyzed and interpreted by historians. The first conclusion is that claims that something resembles something else need to be taken with a huge grain of salt. These assertions are extremely subjective, and often reveal more about the researchers than they do about the past. The second conclusion is that interpretations of the past have a history of their own, and historians need to be conscious of this. Chatters never seems to have been aware that his widely publicized descriptions of Kennewick Man as "Caucasoid" would tap into deeper wells of racism within American society. As we will see in chapters on the Indo-Europeans, Black Athena, and the Vikings, the public often interprets scholarly research through a racial lens.

In this case, the behavior of nineteenth-century archaeologists and anthropologists created deep fissures between Native Americans and the scientific community. But the past does not necessarily determine the future, and academics have proven that they can collaborate with Native Americans while performing cutting-edge research. For example, twenty-two members of the Colville tribe provided DNA to researchers studying Kennewick Man so that they could establish baselines for the Native American population, cooperation that was critical to the successful conclusion of the project.[24] And archaeologists have become more transparent about their methods, reaching out to communities where in the past they might have ignored them. David Hurst Thomas describes a project led by Terry Fifield in Klawock, Alaska, which unexpectedly discovered human remains in a nearby cave. This took place only a few weeks before Kennewick Man was stumbled upon in the Columbia River, but the outcomes could not have been more different. Instead of creating a media circus, Fifield's team adopted a collaborative approach. They informed the community immediately about the find, and asked them how they would like to proceed. Curiosity about the age of the bones led to a community decision to allow further excavations, but they retained control over the information released to the media. They were flown to Denver to visit the lab where bone samples from the skeleton would be carbon dated. And they were given the symbolic authority to name the discovery, a critical form of power that was never given to Native Americans with regard to Kennewick Man.[25]

The controversy over Kennewick Man was not inevitable, but it reveals that researchers never analyze evidence in a vacuum. No doubt some

Figure 1.2 A 1947 photograph of Klawock, a Tlingit village in Tongass National Forest, Alaska. Courtesy of CORBIS via Getty Images.

historians would prefer a world in which they are free to examine evidence without regard for the political context. But that world does not exist. Using craniology and skull reconstruction to "prove" that Kennewick Man was not the Ancient One was not about simply presenting people with the facts; it was an intensely political statement about both the settlement of the Americas and the origins of today's Native Americans. Being conscious of the ways history and politics intersect is critical to doing history well.

Further reading

Burke, Heather, and Claire Smith, eds. *Kennewick Man*. New York: Routledge, 2008. A compilation of writings on the debate over Kennewick Man, with indigenous voices given prominence.

Deloria, Vine. *Red Earth, White Lies*. Golden, CO: Fulcrum Publishing, 1997. This book has significant problems (especially its Young Earth perspective), but it represents a larger Native American skepticism about the overkill theory.

Dillehay, Thomas. *The Settlement of the Americas*. New York: Basic Books, 2000. An effort to revise the argument that the Americas were settled by big-game hunters.

Mann, Charles. *1491*. New York: Vintage, 2006. A synthesis of scholarly literature on the Americas prior to the arrival of Columbus.

Rasmussen, Morten, et al., "The Ancestry and Affiliations of Kennewick Man." *Nature* 523 (2015): 455–464. The definitive statement on the ancestry of Kennewick Man.

Thomas, David Hurst. *Skull Wars*. New York: Basic Books, 2001. A fascinating examination of the relationship between Native Americans and the academic community during the nineteenth and twentieth centuries.

2

Horsing Around

In 1786, a Welsh judge in India announced a fascinating discovery. William Jones was a celebrated linguist, fluent in thirteen languages, including English, Greek, and Latin. As a Supreme Court justice in the new colony of Bengal, he was charged with learning Sanskrit, the ancient language used in Hindu legal texts. It was during this process that he began to see patterns suggesting that all of these languages shared a long-dead ancestral tongue. His presentation astonished the academic world. India, usually seen as exotic and Other, might be a long-lost cousin.[1] Subsequent research validated Jones's findings, and today over 3 billion people speak languages in the Indo-European family. The common ancestral tongue is now known as Proto-Indo-European (PIE). How had people from all across Eurasia come to speak such closely related languages?

For nineteenth-century European scholars, the obvious answer was that this language could only have been spread by the conquering migrations of a "superior race." PIE ceased to be a language and became a peoples who were believed to have been tall, blond warriors.[2] Since the most ancient surviving texts in Indo-European languages were authored by people who called themselves Aryans, this name was given to this invented "race." The world of these ancient Aryans involved chariots and animal sacrifices, which suited the warrior stereotype that European academics had in mind.[3] Racist scholars began to search for the pure ancestral home of the Aryan race. Both the racial term and the use of the swastika as a Nazi icon originated as part of this search.

Racist enthusiasm for the Aryans made them an unpalatable research subject after the Second World War. Even the study of PIE as a language was shaped by this revulsion, with one prominent archaeologist positing that the first speakers of PIE were peaceful farmers rather than chariot-riding warriors.[4] But the linguistic situation was not the same as the racial one. We can reconstruct up to 1,500 words from the PIE vocabulary, and these words are a window into their world. It is because of this lexicon that we know PIE-speakers

Figure 2.1 A portrait of William Jones (1746–94), the English jurist and linguist credited with identifying the Indo-European language family. Courtesy of Hulton Archive via Getty Images.

worshipped a male sky-deity, passed inheritance rights through the male line, and sacrificed animals like cattle and horses. They borrowed some words from non-PIE-speakers, and left their mark on other language families, including Uralic. The question still remains—who were the PIE-speakers, and how did their language spread across so much of Eurasia? This question leads us to an event that might be connected; the domestication of the horse.

This chapter has two aims. The first is to uncover how we know what we know about the domestication of the horse. The second is to explain why we think that the domestication of the horse and the spread of Indo-European languages may be connected. Doing this will require us to once again take a "deep history" approach, one that draws on a wide variety of disciplines to help us better understand the distant past.

Assembling the plausible past

How do we date and locate an event like the domestication of an animal? Historians have developed a number of methods to help answer these questions, but as we will see there are significant challenges in applying these techniques to horses. The key forms of evidence available are the PIE languages, genetic analysis, skeletal remains, and archaeological signs of human control.

A major reason why we believe the horse was domesticated by the PIE-speakers is the existence of a root word for horse, *ek*wo-, in PIE. This tells us that the horse, whether wild or domestic, was a part of the environment in which the PIE-speakers lived. Livestock in a more general sense (i.e., including sheep and cattle) were also an integral part of PIE life, with root words for bull, sour milk, field, and even a term for moveable wealth (*peku-) that became the word for a herd of animals.[5] Most importantly, PIE also contains a number of root words for technologies linked to livestock, including the wheel (*k^{w}ek^{w}los and *rot-eh$_2$-) and the axle (*ak*s-).[6] David Anthony convincingly argues that PIE could only have been spoken between 4500 and 2500 BCE, and given that the horse was present in parts of Europe, the Caucasus, Anatolia, and the Pontic-Caspian steppes during this time, these regions seem like plausible sites of domestication.[7]

Our earliest texts in Indo-European languages confirm that the horse played a crucial role in their myths and rituals. The Rig Veda, the Avesta, and early Greek poetry all describe the sun as a "speedy horse," and compare its rays to a horse's mane. White horses were considered divine in Germanic, Celtic, and Slavic mythology, and in ancient Persia they pulled the sacred chariot of Zeus.[8] Elaborate ceremonies like the asvamedha reinforce this connection. This ritual is described in the Rig Veda, and involved the king releasing a white horse and allowing it to roam. The king's warriors accompanied the horse for a year and prevented it from mating or coming to any harm. After the year was complete the horse was harnessed to the king's chariot and sacrificed to the god of fire.[9] Horses were clearly an important part of the PIE world, but the linguistic evidence can tell us little else.

The second tool, which helped solve the origins of Kennewick Man, is genetic evidence. But what worked so well in that instance is less fruitful with regard to the horse. The variation on the Y-chromosome (for male horses) is so small that it is possible there is only a single ancestral stallion, but the mtDNA is so diverse that at least seventy-seven ancestral mares contributed to it. This means that mares were likely captured or tamed in many different places, while a small number of domesticated stallions were shared between communities for breeding purposes.[10] As a result, modern horse DNA is unhelpful for discerning the date and location of domestication. Sequencing ancient horse mtDNA does offer some guidance—the greatest haplotype variation in the world today can be found in Central Asia, which suggests this location is the source of the modern domesticated horse.[11] Another fascinating study examined pelt colors and their genetic origins. It found that coat coloration rapidly diversified around 3000 BCE in Siberia and Eastern Europe, leading the authors to conclude that humans were selectively breeding horses by this time. While the authors could not identify the exact moment of domestication, they felt comfortable concluding that "horse domestication started in the Eurasian steppe region around at least 5000 years B.P. [before present]."[12] DNA can help us narrow down the most plausible locations and dates for horse domestication, but this evidence remains imprecise.

The third tool is archaeological evidence. Skeletal remains preserve quite well, and this is certainly true for horses. But interpreting this evidence is extremely difficult. Some argue that domestication led to changes in skull shape, particularly by broadening the brain case and the forehead, but the wide range of horse body types (which change markedly in different environmental conditions) make finding a consistent metric impossible.[13] Another possible marker of domestication is a dramatic change in body size. This is often the result of a new diet, human selection, or enclosure in pens. Domesticated cattle, for example, are much smaller than the wild auroch, and analyzing average bone sizes can help us date and place this process.[14] Norbert Benecke and Angela von der Dreisch completed a similar assessment of horse remains on the Eurasian steppes, and found that changes in size variability indicative of domestication first emerged at Csepel-Háros in Hungary in 2500 BCE.[15] This was both later and much further west than expected, and some scholars felt this methodology was not appropriate for horses. They argued that the early stages of horse domestication would not have led to major changes in size since these horses would have continued to eat a similar diet of steppe grasses, and would not have been kept in pens or corrals. If this were the case, size variability would offer few insights, and the change in 2500 BCE might mark the origin of specialized breeds rather than the start of domestication.[16]

Age of death can also be useful. The remains of a domesticated herd will usually contain a different range of ages and genders than the remains of hunted animals. This is because young males (aged 2–4) who have just reached full body size are most likely to be slaughtered in a domesticated herd (since they produce the most meat), but are unlikely to be hunted since they are the strongest and fastest members of the herd.[17] But once again this approach cannot tell us much. The first problem is that determining the sex of horse remains a difficult process, requiring the presence of either a pelvic bone (to confirm a horse is female) or a canine tooth (to confirm a horse is male). Age can be determined through molar teeth, which survive well, but since the process involves average wear patterns it is better at establishing a range of plausible ages than a specific number.[18] Most importantly, it is hard to know what kind of pattern is suggestive of domestication. While Marsha Levine interpreted the remains at Dereivka (25 percent killed before age 5, 50 percent killed before age 8, and 90 percent of viable jaws identified as male) as evidence of hunting stallion bands, V.I. Bibikova noted the age distribution was similar to that of modern domestic herds.[19] The large number of male jawbones may also be a result of ritual sacrifice, which involved the careful burial of stallion crania. This was practiced elsewhere on the Eurasian steppes and would ensure that male teeth were more likely to be found by archaeologists.[20]

Burial practices might be more useful than age or sex. This is evident in Botai, the site of a village c.3700–3300 BCE in modern Kazakhstan. Most houses were located next to pits containing deliberately buried horse skulls.[21] Only two human graves have been uncovered at this site, but one burial site includes the remains of four people and fourteen horses arrayed in a semicircle.[22] Earlier sites in the Ukraine, Russia, and Kazakhstan also contain examples of horses sacrificed at human graves, including in Varfolomievka (c.5000 BCE), Khvalynsk (c.4800 BCE), and S'yezzhe (c.4450 BCE). Since it was extremely rare for wild animals to be buried with humans anywhere in the region, and these horse sacrifices followed elaborate patterns used with other domesticated mammals, it may indicate that horses were domesticated much earlier than anticipated.[23] Even the presence or absence of certain bones within settlements could point to domestication. High weight but low-value bones like the vertebrae and pelvis are unlikely to have been transported long distances without the aid of other (domesticated) horses for transport. The large number of these bones in Botai may indicate that domesticated horses were helping transport hunted wild horse carcasses back to the settlement, or that hunters were culling them from domesticated herds close by.[24] One horse cranium at Botai shows evidence of having been killed by "pole-axing," a slaughter method usually reserved for domesticated animals, but again the wound is not in itself decisive proof of domestication.[25]

The techniques described above are hotly contested. However, there are two generally accepted pieces of evidence which can conclusively show humans had domesticated the horse. The first involves using horses for transportation, and the second relates to the development of milking.

Figure 2.2 A Przewalski's Horse, photographed in Mongolia. Recent genetic evidence suggests that this species descends from wild horses domesticated at Botai in Kazakhstan. Courtesy of DOMENS/FASSEUR/ Gamma-Rapho via Getty Images.

Neither is particularly easy to demonstrate archaeologically. Bitting is a great example of this. Bits are devices inserted in a horse's mouth to help humans control their behavior. Resting on the horse's gums between the incisors and molars, the bit painfully corrects a horse that does not follow instructions. The presence of a bit is clear evidence of domestication. However, the earliest bits were almost certainly made from rawhide or hemp, and would have disintegrated long ago. Antler and bone bits, which are more durable, can be found at Afanasievo (*c*.3600–2400 BCE) and Dereivka (*c*.3600 BCE). These suggest that riding horses began in the Ukraine, spread east to the steppes south of the Urals, and from there to Kazakhstan and beyond.[26] But even this evidence is not fully convincing, since the antler bits might just be rounded, perforated pieces of bones. The small number of examples is also a weak base from which to extrapolate. Physical evidence of bitting would be more convincing.

Since bits irritate horses, they often chew on them. With metal bits, this chewing creates abrasions visible on the surface of the P_2s molar when held under an electron microscope.[27] Since the earliest bits were likely made of organic materials like leather, horsehair, bone, or hemp, would they have left any visible traces on horses' teeth? In 1985 David Anthony and Dorcas Brown began investigating this problem. In a series of experiments they attached organic bits to previously unbitted horses, fed them a diet approximating that on the steppes, and then measured wear on their P_2s molar every 150 hours. This experiment revealed that organic bits created bevels on the P_2s molar. After comparing these data with data derived from horses that predated contact with humans, they were able to arrive at a metric that suggested a tooth beveled to a specific level had been bitted. This number was 3 mm. Any P_2s molar with that amount of beveling or more was certain to have been domesticated.[28]

This method encountered considerable skepticism. One of the first uses of it was on the Dereivka Cult Stallion, a horse found at stratigraphic layers dating to roughly c.4200–3700 BCE. The one surviving P_2s molar had bevels of 3.5 and 4 mm, and deep abrasions in the enamel. Even though they only had one tooth, Anthony and Brown were confident enough to publish their findings in *Scientific American* and *Antiquity*. Clearly this horse had been domesticated. But they were immediately challenged because the bit wear was similar to that created by metal bits. Since metal bits did not exist until much later, scholars suggested that the tooth might have been from a more recent time period than the layer in which it was found. Radiocarbon dating of the skull confirmed this suspicion—the horse was from c.800–200 BCE.[29] Anthony and Brown subsequently retracted their finding.

However, they felt this method was still useful so long as the teeth could be accurately dated. The main problem was the need for a specific molar, and even in large finds these were relatively rare. The teeth also had to be sufficiently intact to examine. The most promising location was Botai, where over 300,000 animal bones had been found, all dating to approximately 3700–3300 BCE. Even here, however, the total number of P_2s molars suitable for study was only nineteen. Anthony and Brown discovered that five of these molars had significant bevels that measured between 3 and 6 mm. Unlike in Dereivka, the wear on these teeth was polished smooth, suggesting that they had been bitted with organic materials. Anthony and Brown argued that the people of Botai were horse hunters and gatherers who successfully learned to ride horses in order to more effectively hunt them.[30]

Organic residue analysis of ceramics recently enabled scholars to determine if they were filled with certain substances in the past. At Botai, given the overwhelming presence of horse bones (99.9 percent of all bones found there), the presence of milk fats on the interior of ceramics would confirm that horses were being used for secondary products, and thus domesticated. Alan Outram and others succeeded in isolating equine milk fats from equine flesh fats through the use of a deuterium isotope analysis, and were able to conclude that mare's milk had been processed in ceramics at Botai. This confirmed Anthony and Brown's conclusion that the domesticated horse was present at that site.[31] The horse was probably domesticated even earlier than that, possibly around 4,000 BCE, somewhere on the Pontic-Caspian steppe.

Horse domestication is a critical moment in world history. But it stands for far more than just the human capacity to harness its environment to its own ends. Part of the debate over PIE is that the spread of this language must be linked to some sort of innovation by the people who spoke it. Colin Renfrew argues that PIE was spoken first in Anatolia and the Balkans as early as 6500 BCE, and then spread eastward into the steppes. He believes that these PIE-speakers brought a suite of domesticated foods and animals with them, and subsequently transformed the societies on the steppes. He argues that the PIE-speakers were not fierce warriors, but peaceful farmers. Their language spread via trade, not war.[32]

This version of PIE history is a reaction against nineteenth and early twentieth centuries racist interpretations of the PIE-speakers as an Aryan master race. What better way to counter Nazi mythology about a superior race than to discover that the Aryans were peaceable farmers who happily interacted with nearby hunter-gatherers? But the linguistic evidence for PIE originating in Anatolia is extremely weak due to the presence of non-Indo-European tongues like Hurrian and Hatti that seem to have been "older, more prestigious, and more widely spoken."[33] The much earlier origin date for PIE is also problematic because it posits that the language changed very slowly from 6500 to 3000 BCE across the entirety of the region, a suggestion that is at odds with linguistic behavior and the archaeological evidence.[34] The arrival of PIE from Anatolia and the Balkans also does not fit the archaeological evidence, which provides ample evidence of material cultures moving from east to west but far less from west to east.[35]

The domestication of the horse is an extremely plausible cause of the spread of PIE languages. If the horse were domesticated on the Pontic-Caspian steppe between 4500 and 3500 BCE, this would match up with patterns of language diffusion at that same time. And since no earlier evidence for domesticated cattle or sheep has been found at Botai, the domestication of the horse likely took place in isolation, and then spread rapidly across the steppe along with PIE. Environmental pressure during a cool and dry period led to increased combat near the Ural Mountains, and it was the society of Sintashta *c.*2100 BCE that offers us our first evidence of the chariot, distinguished by its spoked wheels. Their funerals involved horse sacrifices very similar to those described in the *Rig Veda*, and by 2000 BCE Anthony argues they had begun trading horses with settled peoples in exchange for metals, especially tin. Central Asian charioteers brought their Indo-European languages with them, and since these languages were used in important rituals relating to horses, some settled people may have gradually adopted them across the region.[36] As Gojko Barjamovic claims, "In Anatolia, and parts of Central Asia, which held densely settled complex urban societies, the history of language spread and genetic ancestry is better described in terms of contact and absorption than by simply a movement of population."[37]

Conclusion

Despite the plausibility of Anthony's argument and our increasing mastery of a variety of new kinds of historical evidence, the limits of "deep history" must be acknowledged. Asya Pereltsvaig and Martin Lewis, for example, observed that the spread of PIE-speakers can also be plausibly connected to their dominance of the drug trade. Hemp, which was useful for its fibers as well as its mind-altering tetrahydrocannabinol (THC), is well attested in Indo-European languages, and it was the focus of many ritual activities at the same time that the horse was being domesticated. *Soma* is also mentioned in many early Indo-European texts, and was used by priests to achieve ritual intoxication. Whether *soma* was fly agaric (a mushroom), ephedra (a stimulant), or harmel (a seed used to create a red dye), expertise in drugs might be plausibly connected to the diffusion of certain Indo-European language branches![38] Such are the margins of error when studying the ancient past.

However, historians are becoming more adept at assessing the evidence at their disposal. In Anthony and Brown's argument we can see how the fragments of the past can be pieced together to create a representative picture of the ancient world. Whether it involves processing horse DNA to date the spread of new pelt colors, determining how to identify bit wear on 5,000-year-old molars, or reconstructing the vocabulary that no living person has used for millennia, "deep history" has opened up the past to historians in extraordinary ways.

Further reading

Anthony, David. *The Horse, the Wheel, and Language*. Princeton, NJ: Princeton University Press, 2007. A sweeping overview of the archaeological and linguistic evidence pertaining to the origins of the Indo-European language.

Kelekna, Pita. *The Horse in Human History*. New York: Cambridge University Press, 2009. A sweeping history that argues the domestication of horses triggered cultural changes across the world's steppes and deserts.

Olsen, Sandra, Susan Grant, Alice Choyke, and László Bartosiewicz, eds. *Horses and Humans: The Evolution of Human-Equine Relationships*. Oxford: Archaeopress, 2006. A collection of field reports from numerous leading archaeologists studying the domestication of horses.

Pereltsvaig, Asya and Martin Lewis. *The Indo-European Controversy*. New York: Cambridge University Press, 2015. A devastating critique of a 2012 article that used a Bayesian analysis to reinterpret the origins of the Indo-European language.

Renfrew, Colin. *Archaeology & Language*. New York: Cambridge University Press, 1992. An important but flawed study of the Indo-European language that argues it emerged in Europe well before most scholars supposed.

3

#AncientEgyptMatters

Many professors aim to write a book during their career. These painstakingly researched monographs usually sell a couple hundred copies, mostly to university libraries and other experts in the field. But occasionally an academic publication resonates with the public. One of the most stunning examples of this is *Black Athena*, a book on the ancient Mediterranean written by Martin Bernal. In it, he argues that the early Greeks were deeply influenced by ancient Egypt and Phoenicia. He also suggests the Greeks freely acknowledged this debt at the time, but racist nineteenth-century-CE scholars rewrote the past in order to make Greece appear "whiter" than it actually was. When *Black Athena* was published (part 1 in 1987, part 2 in 1991, and part 3 in 2006) it ignited a firestorm of controversy. Over 70,000 copies of the first book have been sold, and it has been the subject of numerous reviews, several documentaries, and a series of internet chats (in the early 1990s!). Several other monographs have been written either supporting or debunking his claims. *Newsweek*, a popular weekly magazine, included Bernal in an article entitled "Was Cleopatra Black?"[1] The idea that many Greek accomplishments had been stolen from the Egyptians was not new, but *Black Athena* was arguably the first time that it triggered a response from the academic community.[2] During the late 1980s and early 1990s, Bernal's book was an extremely significant cultural battleground.

But Bernal's success irritated many scholars, especially within the field of Classics. They were stung by his accusations that their nineteenth-century predecessors were racist, and they criticized Bernal's work for what they believed were shameless factual errors.[3] Martin Bernal once ruefully noted that "with the exception of *of*, I have been criticized for every word in my title, *Black Athena: The Afroasiatic Roots of Classical Civilization*."[4] The sheer volume of academic criticism directed his way is truly staggering.

One of the biggest challenges when studying the ancient world is the scarce evidence. As we have seen with the settling of the Americas, historians can only analyze a tiny fraction of the distant past. Bernal's study of the ancient Mediterranean speaks directly to this issue. If we can only examine a small percentage of the past, don't we rely on our own assumptions to fill in the gaps? And if many of the foundational nineteenth-century texts on ancient Greece were imbued with scientific racism, isn't it possible that some elements of these beliefs might remain embedded, not only in the texts, but also in those who study them? Much like the more recent Black Lives Matter movement, the argument that even well-meaning academics might be unintentionally racist provoked an extremely hostile response.

Ancient culture war

Why did so many people consider Bernal's argument significant? The procedural concept of historical significance is a tricky one. On the one hand, we need to understand why historians choose to study particular moments of the past. On the other, we must try to make sense of why certain historical arguments resonate with contemporary audiences. In the case of *Black Athena*, let's divide this issue into three sections. The first analyzes why Bernal chose to study ancient Egypt. The second examines the evidence that the Greeks were directly influenced by Egypt and Phoenicia. And the third looks at Bernal's claim that racist nineteenth-century scholars covered this up.

Martin Bernal was heavily influenced by the 1960s and '70s. During these tumultuous decades, American universities were the sites of student protests over the Vietnam War, the civil rights movement, gender inequality, and the environment. Academia responded by becoming more inclusive, and created new departments that remain ubiquitous today, including Area Studies, African-American Studies, Women's Studies, Ethnic Studies, and Interdisciplinary Studies. Many of these incorporated aspects of traditional disciplines like history, political science, economics, and sociology. Historians responded by trying to diversify their offerings, with courses like African history being offered for the first time. They also moved away from a focus on political leaders, and tried to incorporate the voices of ordinary men and women of all backgrounds. Staple history courses like "Introduction to Western Civilizations" began to face criticism for focusing only on white men.

Bernal certainly saw himself as part of this new wave of scholarship, and he wrote *Black Athena* in response to the conservative backlash these new ideas generated. Bernal was particularly worried about the influence of Allan Bloom. Bloom was a conservative philosopher who had a devoted following at Cornell University, the place where Bernal would start teaching in 1972. In *The Closing of the American Mind*, Bloom dismissed the civil rights movement and protests against the Vietnam War as modern manifestations of Nazi Socialism, and suggested that universities teach a curriculum based on the Great Books of Western civilization.[5] Suffice it to say, this curriculum did not include many of the "new voices" so important to the scholars of the 1960s. In a later interview, Bernal claimed that Bloom's influence "made me realize the reactionary potential of the Romantic interpretation of Greece. I had been brought up in Cambridge, where the classicists were stuffy liberals … But here, though this was the mid-seventies, I suddenly saw a potential for the extreme right-wing intellectual movement that didn't actually take power until the 1980's."[6] While *Black Athena* originated when Bernal began to investigate his Semitic heritage, its interdisciplinary and multicultural thesis was intended as a rebuke to those who believed the Greek past belonged to whites alone.

Bernal argues that the ancient Greeks took it for granted that their civilization owed a great debt to the rest of the Eastern Mediterranean world. One critical source is Greek mythology, including the story of Danaus, where fifty virgins arrive in Greece after fleeing Egypt. The myth suggests that the ruler of Argos may share blood ties with the Egyptians. As a way of confirming the substance of this myth, Bernal quotes Herodotus (*c.*490–425 BCE), the famous Greek historian, who wrote "How it happened that Egyptians came to the Peloponnese, and what they did to make themselves kings in that part of Greece, has been chronicled by other writers; I will add nothing, therefore, but proceed to mention some points which no one else has touched upon" (5.60). Herodotus also describes the Egyptian pharaoh Sesōstris who he claims settled a group of soldiers along the coast of the Black Sea in roughly 2000 BCE. Herodotus met the descendants of this colonial venture and describes them as black skinned and woolly haired. To Bernal, this reveals that Egypt can be treated as a "black" civilization. And he notes that evidence for Egyptian influence can be found not only in Herodotus but also in the linguistic record. His most memorable example of this is the Greek word "Athena," which he argues is derived from the Egyptian *Ht Nt*, meaning temple of the goddess Neit. He ultimately claims that as much as 50 percent of the Greek language stems from the tongues of Egypt and Phoenicia.[7] Bernal again cites Herodotus who wrote that the Phoenicians "introduced into Greece, after their settlement in the country, a number of accomplishments, of which the most important is writing" (5.58). While most scholars agree that the Phoenicians contributed to the development of Greek writing, Bernal argues this cultural borrowing took place more than a thousand years earlier than is generally accepted.[8]

Bernal labels this evidence "the Ancient model," and he argues that its basic premises of cultural exchange and cosmopolitan contact were widely accepted until the late eighteenth century CE. After the 1786 discovery of the Indo-European language family, European scholars became convinced that speakers of these languages (called Aryans) had invaded Greece around 2300 BCE. They believed these people were white, and that they borrowed little from the rest of the Mediterranean world. Their civilization flourished, and by virtue of its superior language and technology became the ancestral home of the modern nations of Europe.[9] If the ancient Greeks

Figure 3.1 Bust of Herodotus (c.484–425 BCE). Interpreting his writing remains a challenge for historians to this day. Courtesy of De Agostini via Getty Images.

like Herodotus thought that they were deeply indebted to Egypt and Phoenicia, early-nineteenth-century scholars felt they were wrong. After all, it was widely accepted in European universities that African and Semitic peoples were inferior. New historical techniques like "source criticism" were used to discredit Herodotus, whose work was discovered to be littered with exaggerations and outright lies.[10] Rather than serving as an example of flourishing cosmopolitan civilization, scholars argued ancient Greece developed in isolation. Romantic ideas that were popular at the time posited that childhood was essential to the growth and development of a person, and that racial purity was a highly desirable trait. Bernal argues that nineteenth-century scholars applied these concepts to civilizations.[11] Ancient Greece had its past scrubbed of outside influences, and it became the pure racial origin of modern European dominance. Bernal calls this new scholarly understanding of Greece "the Aryan model," and argues that it became the accepted baseline for future scholarly understandings of the region. This makes it possible for new interpretations to be dismissed because they aren't decisively proven true even though the established wisdom is equally prone to imperfections. To Bernal, modern scholars who argue that Greece developed in isolation are inadvertently mimicking this racist narrative, and *Black Athena* is his effort to restore, albeit in revised form, the ancient model to prominence.

To say *Black Athena* received mixed reviews is being exceedingly generous. To the vast majority of scholars, regardless of political affiliation, it was poorly researched and fundamentally flawed. Scholars noted that stories of Danaan colonization of Greece may well have been created hundreds of years later than Bernal believes, and as such are not proof of Egyptian influence between 2000 and 1500 BCE.[12] Herodotus's account of Sesōstris was challenged on the basis that Egyptian military campaigns rarely lasted as long as he suggests and that a more likely source for the story is a combination of the adventures of Amenemhet II (r.1914–1879 BCE) and Senwosret III (r.1878–1839 BCE). Both were skilled military leaders who campaigned briefly in Asia and more extensively to the south of Egypt in Nubia. The colonies that Herodotus seems to have seen were far more likely to be groups of Kushites and Egyptians captured during Assyrian campaigns in the 600s BCE. The Assyrians had a long-standing policy of deporting peoples defeated in battle in order to facilitate occupation, and the Hittites may even have done this to a largely Kushite force captured in the fourteenth century BCE. When Herodotus visited the region, perhaps these foreign deportees had forgotten their origins, and told him a more speculative and stirring tale of ancient kings and former glory. Egyptologists acknowledge that Bernal's story of colonization by Sesōstris cannot be decisively disproven, but argue that it is "the least attractive possibility."[13]

Even Bernal's titular claim that the Greek goddess Athena stems from an Egyptian counterpart called Neit is called into question. Jay Jasanoff and Alan Nussbaum note that the words share only one common feature; an "n" proceeded by a "t." They feel Bernal ignores the issue that the "n" and "t" are in direct contact in Egyptian but separated by a vowel in Greek whose presence is unexplained. They also suggest that Bernal's characterization of the goddesses Neit and Athena as "virgin divinities of warfare, weaving and wisdom" is extremely misleading, and suggest an equally plausible alternative that Athena might derive from the Carthaginian goddess Tanit, whose name would have been preceded by the Greek feminine article "ha" to become *Hathana. While they admit that they cannot offer a conclusive explanation for the etymology of Athena, they are adamant that Bernal's hypothesis is "suspect."[14] Even the idea that Egyptians were "people whom one might usefully call black" has come under attack.[15] Frank Snowden remains unconvinced, and observes that black Africans were generally referred to as *aethiopes* by the Greeks and Romans while Egyptians were considered distinct, particularly due to their "non-woolly" hair.[16]

The extent of racism in eighteenth- and nineteenth-century European universities may also be overstated by Bernal. Robert Palter, a specialist on these intellectuals, wrote an impassioned defense of their thinking. Describing the influential University of Göttingen in the eighteenth century, he writes that "there were significant antiracist and universalistic (antichauvanistic) elements in German culture as a whole, and in Göttingen higher education in particular."[17] He rebukes Bernal for his specific criticism of Johann Friedrich Blumenbach as a Eurocentrist who relied on race as the foundation of his research. Palter notes that Bernal's citations miss several of Blumenbach's most important writings, including some very sympathetic biographies of black individuals who had relocated to Europe at that time.[18] To Palter, it is grossly unfair to describe Blumenbach as racist. Bernal's critique of racist eighteenth-century scholarship has generally been the most widely accepted part of his argument. That even it is under attack is striking testimony to the breadth of the academic assault on *Black Athena*.

So what are we to make of Bernal's argument? His key premises are as follows: (1) that Egypt and Phoenicia had a massive influence on the development of ancient Greece through direct colonization, (2) that the ancient Greeks freely acknowledged this debt, (3) that the Egyptian visitors were "usefully black," (4) nineteenth-century scholars found the culturally mixed origins of the Greeks impossible due to their views on race, and (5) they rewrote the history books to erase Greece's multiculturalism, allowing whites to claim exclusive credit for Greek accomplishments. Every aspect of this argument has been challenged. Archaeology and linguistics suggest it is very unlikely that Egypt and Greece had direct, long-term contact with one another. Ancient authors may have been guilty of anachronism when crediting Greek accomplishments to ancient Egypt. The ancient Egyptians are unlikely to have resembled people we would consider "black" today. Nineteenth-century scholars probably were not as racist as Bernal suggests. And modern classicists remain adamant that they are open to the general idea that ancient Greece borrowed from numerous other cultures, primarily through trade and diplomacy. Indeed, they suggest that they embraced this idea long before Bernal appeared on the scene.

But *Black Athena* remains significant despite these problems. When studying the ancient world any useful argument will contain errors. Some will be more egregious than others. But a single mistake does not necessarily discredit an entire contribution. Bernal's belief that Egypt colonized Greece was probably an error, but Egypt certainly was in contact with Greece, and the discovery of Minoan frescoes in Avaris suggests that this contact was not just casual. Meaningful cultural exchange was taking place, something now widely accepted by prominent scholars like Eric Cline.[19] Ancient Greeks certainly had a healthy respect for ancient Egypt by the sixth century BCE, and clearly viewed it as a source of inspiration. Ancient Egyptians were probably not considered black by ancient authors, but by modern American standards (one drop of black blood makes someone black), there is no doubt that ancient Egyptians could be "usefully considered black." Bernal may not grapple with the "complexities and tensions" of the thought of late-eighteenth- and early-nineteenth-century scholars like Johann Friedrich Blumenbach, but there is no question that Blumenbach's research was entirely predicated on race and racial hierarchy. His early writing was obsessed with ideas of racial degeneration due to climate, with Blumenbach claiming that the "Mongolians" and "Ethiopians" had "degenerated furthest from the human form."[20] While Palter is correct to note that his later views were strikingly more humanist, Blumenbach's students like Samuel Taylor Coleridge readily used his teaching to support a Romantic understanding of race that placed Caucasians at the top as a "master race [which] would dominate humanity, improve the others, and leave them in their own distinctive inferior orbits."[21] And even though Bernal surely overstates his case that classicists continue to cover up Egyptian and Phoenician influence over Greece, he is just as surely correct to note that academics still care deeply about who receives credit for historical accomplishments. As Frank Yurco points out, while "many scholars acknowledge the cosmopolitan nature of the Late Bronze Age ... Bernal is [also] quite correct that *some* classicists have been slow to accept this evidence, or have even sought to deny it."[22]

Mary Lefkowitz writes that "teaching the myth of the Stolen Legacy as if it were history robs the ancient Greeks and their modern descendants of a heritage that rightly belongs to them."[23] The suggestion that ancient Greek accomplishments pass in an unbroken line from the 2000s BCE to their white ancestors today denigrates later groups like the Byzantines, and Ottoman Turks, peoples who also made significant contributions to modern Greek culture. Lefkowitz's belief that ancient Greek history should inspire modern national pride is also deeply problematic, since she implies that if Socrates happened to be black it somehow hurts today's Greeks. As David Konstan points out in his review of the debate, can't the accomplishments of the ancient Greeks (and the ancient Egyptians for that matter) simply represent part of a common history of humanity? If not, how do we link ancient peoples to modern groups; by similarities in race, language, and the land they occupy, even if these connections waxed and waned during the intervening centuries?

Figure 3.2 A painting from the tomb of Senmut (Senenmut) showing figures from the Aegean bringing goods to Egypt. It dates to the reign of Hatshepsut/Thutmose III (1473–1425 BCE). Courtesy of Universal History Archive via Getty Images.

He argues that both Bernal and Lefkowitz fall into the trap of attributing particular historical accomplishments to modern peoples, whether they are black or Greek. Konstan argues that both are guilty of anachronism, or superimposing modern concepts of race and nationality into the past.[24] These concepts were significant to the world in which these scholars lived, but it is not entirely clear that anything comparable existed in the ancient world. This is not only a major historical error, but is done in service of the present political views of each scholar. On both counts, it is not good history.

Conclusion

Too often, history is taught as a form of "gotcha" politics. Like a presidential candidate who struggles to answer a question during a debate, the assumption is that a historian caught in a mistake is completely discredited. This is simply untrue, particularly with regard to ancient eras where our knowledge will inevitably be incomplete. Those seeking a perfect theory of the ancient past will always be disappointed.

Black Athena is an imperfect text that has been attacked on numerous points. Many of these criticisms are substantial. For example, Bernal's third volume draws heavily on Greek lexicon lacking PIE roots to posit substantial borrowings from Afroasiatic tongues, despite the much more plausible consensus being that these words are remnants of an indigenous language spoken in the region before the arrival of Indo-European speakers.[25] These criticisms matter. But *Black Athena* has also made significant contributions to our understanding of the Eastern Mediterranean world. Today we freely acknowledge the multicultural milieu of the region, and most textbooks do not hesitate to suggest that this was responsible for its vibrancy. Bernal also inadvertently revealed the truth of his key assertion; that some classicists still defend uncomfortably racialist assumptions about the ancient Greeks, specifically that their accomplishments belong to their modern, white ancestors. Black Lives Matter, as a movement, is committed to uncovering and confronting implicit racism in modern American society, a society that generally believes these tendencies were eliminated during the civil rights movement. *Black Athena*, for all its faults, served a similar purpose within the Classics discipline; as an uncomfortable warning that for all the changes in academia over the past two hundred years, we may not have made as much progress as we would like to assume.

Further reading

Berlinerblau, Jacques. *Heresy in the University*. New Brunswick, NJ: Rutgers University Press, 1999. An intellectual history of the debate over *Black Athena*.

Bernal, Martin. *Black Athena*, vols. 1, 2, 3. New Brunswick, NJ: Rutgers University Press, 1987, 1991, 2006. Bernal's three-volume series which argues that racist scholars concealed the Egyptian and Phoenician roots of Greek civilization.

James, George. *Stolen Legacy*. New York: Philosophical Library, 1954. An Afrocentric scholar whose argument closely resembles Bernal's and predates it by over three decades.

Lefkowitz, Mary. *Not Out of Africa*. New York: Basic Books, 1997. An angry response to Bernal from a trained classicist.

Lefkowitz, Mary and Guy Rogers, eds. *Black Athena Revisited*. Chapel Hill: University of North Carolina Press, 1996. The definitive collection of experts challenging key points of Bernal's argument.

4
Stretching the Past

In 2010 the Hindu American Foundation (HAF) initiated a campaign to "Take Back Yoga." They argued that yoga was an ancient Hindu practice, but that this legacy had been stolen by the rest of the world. The aim of "Take Back Yoga" was not to have instructors start teaching Hinduism, or to ask practitioners to become Hindu, but merely to make more people aware of the practice's Hindu origins.[1] Siding with the HAF was Albert Mohler, President of the Southern Baptist Theological Seminary. In a blog post, he argued that yoga could not be separated from its Hindu essence, and as a result led to "theological confusion" among Christians.[2] To Mohler, the spread of yoga and the de-Christianization of America were inexorably linked, something that he even connected to First Lady Michelle Obama's decision to add yoga to the events of the annual White House Easter Egg Roll.[3]

On the surface, the claim that yoga is essentially Hindu does not seem controversial. Classes often begin and end with a long "OMMMM," a Hindu mantra, and participants greet one another by saying "Namaste," a Sanskrit phrase meaning the divine in me recognizes the divine in you. One of the earliest texts on yoga is Patanjali's *Yoga Sutras*, written in India during the second century CE. Virtually all yoga participants in America recognize the spiritual primacy of India in the practice—leading gurus are almost always from there, or spent years honing their craft on the subcontinent.

But the claim made by the "Take Back Yoga" campaign is controversial precisely because it is historical. What proponents of this view are saying is that yoga can trace an unbroken lineage from its Hindu origins to its contemporary form. This provides us with an opportunity to test out a crucial historical skill; patterns of continuity and change over time. The key to this skill is accurately assessing connections across time and space. In this case, is yoga today similar in essence to yoga practiced hundreds or even thousands of years ago in India? Are there sufficient continuities to justify the claims of the "Take Back Yoga" campaign? Or has yoga changed so dramatically that it has become something different?

Into the yogaşala

In order to understand if yoga is essentially Hindu, we need to know more about yoga in the distant past. The first possible reference dates back to the second millennium BCE. At this time an enigmatic civilization was flourishing on the Indian subcontinent, usually referred to as the Harappans or the Indus Valley Civilization. While we know little of their language, the archaeological record has preserved a number of what we think were personal seals. And at the ancient city of Mohenjo-Daro, a seal was found depicting a god-like figure in what appears to be a yoga pose. However, the famous Pashupati seal is unlikely to have any connection to yoga, with Geoffrey Samuel arguing that such an analysis is "so dependent on reading later practices into the material that it is of little or no use for constructing any kind of history of practices."[4] Second, in ancient texts the term yoga "has a wider range of meanings than nearly any other word in the entire Sanskrit lexicon."[5] These meanings include yoking animals to a chariot, a constellation of stars, or a mixture of various substances. The word can also stand-in for a recipe, a strategy, or the work of alchemists. For example, the Mahabharata, written between 200 BCE and 400 CE, mentions that dying warriors are connected (*yoga-yukta*) to a supernatural chariot that will deliver them to heaven.

By the third century BCE, yoga had begun to acquire a new meaning—the suppression of breath. The Shvetashvatara Upanishad directs one aspiring to a higher state of consciousness to suppress his breaths and control his body. Through these practices, "the wise one should restrain his mind like that chariot yoked with vicious horses."[6] In the second century CE, the practice of yoga was outlined in far greater depth by Patanjali. The *Yoga Sutras* included 195 aphorisms on yoga, and emphasized meditative training with a goal of transcending the material world (prakriti) in order to allow one's consciousness (Atman) to merge with the divine (purusha). The *Yoga Sutras* are fascinating because they include the "eight limbs" of yoga, two of which are postures (asanas) and breath control (pranayama).[7] When Patanjali uses the term asana, however, he explicitly means any posture that is "comfortably steady" for the body during meditation, and "pranayama" refers to "cutting off the movement of breathing in and breathing out."

Many yoga instructors today are taught Patanjali as part of their training. But David Gordon White, who wrote a biography of the text in 2014, is skeptical of its value to modern yogis. First, the *Yoga Sutras* is a deliberately opaque text that is very difficult to translate. One element of this is that the entire original text contains only four verbs! This forces modern translators to rely on later commentators to fill in the missing links. For example, Patanjali's second sutra uses a verb-less aphorism to define the subject, writing "yoga + citta + vritti + nirodha." This fits the form of an apposition, and is better translated as yoga = citta + vritti + nirodha. Citta likely refers to thought, vritti to turning (and is connected to the modern English introvert, meaning turning inward), and nirodha to stoppage or restraint. White argues that the simplest definition of yoga from Patanjali is thus "yoga is the stoppage of the turning of thought," but he notes that one can find twenty-two different English translations of the phrase.[8]

More problematic is how the text was preserved. Key commentators like Vyasa were involved, but they had very different philosophical backgrounds and may have objected to some of the content in the *Yoga Sutras*. We know very little about Patanjali, but his writing espouses a dualist philosophy that suggests the goal of yoga is aloneness (*kaivalya*) through the separation of the spirit from the material self. Patanjali also cites *ahimsa*, or nonviolence, as a universal principle for all yogis. Transcending the physical self to achieve communion with the divine, along with a focus on nonviolence, closely resembles the tenets of Jainism. Indeed, many early commentators on the Yoga Sutras were aware that Patanjali's text sharply disagreed with Vedantic thought, which advocated animal sacrifice and the absolute perfection of the Vedas. It is fascinating that Shankara, the philosopher often credited with unifying Hindu thought, wrote a highly critical commentary on Patanjali's *Yoga Sutras*. This opens the possibility that the Yoga Sutras were NOT exclusively a Hindu text, but rather a more general product of the rich spiritual discourse of first millennium CE India. It might be more fruitful to think of yoga as "open-source software" accessible to all religions in ancient India.[9]

This can be seen in the extreme variety of yoga practice in medieval India. One example of this is the appropriation of yoga into tantra, where it was used as a way of communing with the divine. Hatha yoga, a system based on the Shaiva Tantras, developed in the tenth to eleventh century CE. It used a variety of postures called asanas to help transform the body by unleashing Shakti, in the form of a serpent (called *kundalini*), from the base of the spine. As the serpent awakens and passes through various bodily seals, it penetrates the eight chakras and activates the *prana*, or breath, that lies within. Eventually, Shakti and Shiva will copulate, creating union that results in *samadhi* (the final meditative state of intense concentration). The erotic element of this is seen not only in the imagery but also in the methods used by yogis to unleash one's *prana*, which include consuming forbidden substances (semen, menstrual blood) or transgressive sexual encounters (usually with lower caste women believed to embody Shakti's divine feminine energy).[10]

These yogis became known as the Gorakhnathi order (or Naths). And in practice, they used mantras, alchemy, and transgressive behavior to achieve *siddhis* (supernatural powers), and were a frequent feature of medieval Indian literature.[11] The Gorakhnathi order even managed to influence the practice of Islam, with Sattari Sufi texts describing how to use chakras, mantras, and postures to achieve supernatural powers like levitation.[12]

The Gorakhnathi order, however, was extremely controversial. While they have always been described as yogis, Mallinson argues that they did not really do hatha yoga, and Nath yogis were never represented among the adepts of the practice. Instead, to many Indians they were self-indulgent magicians pursuing sex, pleasure, and supernatural powers. A consequence of this is that the term yogi became a slur, and was used as a name for mystical low-caste groups like snake charmers or Muslim devotional singers. Those practicing the philosophies of Patanjali like the Dasanamis and Ramanandis generally did not call themselves yogis to avoid the negative connotations of the term.[13]

At the end of the nineteenth century, Swami Vivekananda sought to take back yoga as a respectable philosophical system. A student of Western philosophy as well as a devotee of Sri Ramakrishna, he was part of the Hindu Renaissance movement that rejected British rule in India but also embraced Western science. In the 1890s he traveled around the world, a journey which culminated in a visit to the 1893 Columbian Exposition in Chicago to attend the World's Parliament of Religions. Here he aggressively attacked American stereotypes of Hinduism as polytheistic, and stated that "holiness, purity, and charity are not the exclusive possessions of any church in the world."[14] He argued that all religions should be tolerated; indeed, he stated that all religions were true. Three years later, he wrote a famous overview of the *Yoga Sutras* called *Raja Yoga*. This text argued that yoga and Vedantic principles could be applied by members of any faith to better know the divine. It also contended that yoga was rational and scientific, but while Vivekananda argued the practice did provide some health benefits (through the subtle energy channeled by meditation), these were not as significant as the spiritual benefits for the practitioner. In a famous statement he dismissed physically demanding hatha yoga techniques, including asanas, since they "do not lead to much spiritual growth." He likely downplayed what he felt were the "irrational" elements of hatha yoga since he feared they would hinder "the global diffusion and universal application of Hindu [and Vedantic] thought."[15] Vivekananda's contempt for the physical elements of hatha yoga loomed large over practitioners in both India and the West. Throughout this period postural yoga was "ridiculed so much that only a few select people were practicing it."[16] Vivekananda (and many Orientalist scholars) defined yoga as a textual rather than embodied practice.

What is interesting about yoga prior to the twentieth century is its extreme diversity. Yoga as a literary term designated a wide array of religious practices that range from meditation to semen-retention to alchemy. And even during this earlier period there is little "essentially Hindu" about yoga. The *Yoga Sutras*, the purported origin of the practice, seem to have been shaped as much by the ascetic orders as by Vedantic thought and Hinduism more generally. But even more interesting is the lack of any order resembling forms of modern postural yoga prior to the twentieth century. I would argue that specific global forces transformed the practice in ways that would have been utterly unfamiliar to earlier yogis.

The first global force was nationalism. As people began to see themselves as part of larger "imagined communities," they began to think about health as a collective responsibility. Especially for men of military age, good health was seen as a patriotic endeavor, and this led to unprecedented enthusiasm for fitness systems. Books like Walker's *British Manly Exercises*, published in 1834, provided instructions on strength-building exercises suitable for patriotic young men. Under the posthumous influence of Pehr Henrik Ling, physical training shifted toward gymnastics which were understood to be healthful. This fitness culture reached colonial India through missionary schools and the YMCA. Retired Indian soldiers trained by the British often led gymnastics classes for young Indian boys, yelling out instructions in a manner akin to a drill sergeant issuing orders.[17]

The second global force was imperialism. Britain began directly administering India in 1858, and the colonial rule offered contradictory lessons to Indian subjects. On the one hand, it represented in tangible form the power of industrial technology, understood more broadly as Western science. Many Indians happily embraced this hegemonic discourse, and even began experiments to demonstrate that India possessed its own ancient body of scientific knowledge.[18] But on the other hand, the colonial rulers positioned themselves as strong and masculine in opposition to their weak and effeminate subjects, a notion Indians fiercely rejected. One way to visibly display masculinity without risking persecution was through weightlifting, which was seen as a particularly masculine form of exercise and became extremely popular in early-twentieth-century India. Pratinidhi Pant, the ruler of a small princely state and an early enthusiast of Eugen Sandow, both lifted weights and created sequenced movements known as the *suryanamaskar* (salutation of the sun) system as a technique to enhance his bodybuilding routine.[19] Sun salutation remains an integral part of most yoga classes today.

It was against this backdrop that Timulai Krishnamacharya (1888–1989) created modern postural yoga. Born into a Brahmin family of scholars, he was tutored at a young age on the philosophy of yoga. Fascinated by the subject, he headed to Mount Kailash in Tibet to learn from the sage Ramamohana Brahmachari. After seven years (likely 1911–18) of tutelage, he returned to Mysore and spent five years promoting yoga across the state. This caught the attention of the Maharaja Krishnaraja Wodiyar IV, who invited Krishnamacharya to teach at a Sanskrit *Pathaṣala* in the city in 1931. Two years later, the Maharaja gave Krishnamacharya a wing in the royal palace to found a *yogaṣala* (studio). While this studio would close soon after independence, it was the site of dynamic innovation.

Figure 4.1 The sequence of poses known as *suryanamaskar* (sun salutation). Popular in yoga classes today, these poses were likely created by Pratinidhi Pant, Raja of Aundh, in the early twentieth century CE. Courtesy of kaisphoto via Getty Images.

Figure 4.2 A portrait of Krishnaraja Wadiyar (Wodiyar) IV (1884–1940), the ruler of Mysore who sponsored Krishnamacharya's yoga studio. Courtesy of Hulton Royals Collection via Getty Images.

Maharaja Wodiyar's contribution was essential. A strong advocate for physical culture, he was described by the YMCA's World Committee President as a man with "reverential regard for the great traditions of ancient India, and yet with up-to-date contacts with modern progress the world over, and responsiveness to new visions and plans; one, therefore, who has successfully blended the priceless heritage of the East with much that is best in the Western world." Thanks to the Maharaja, the spirit of physical culture in Mysore at this time was one of "radical fusion and innovation."[20]

Krishnamacharya's studio fully embraced this ethos. His position involved providing physical and spiritual education for the male children of palace residents. But he quickly ran into a challenge—the weightlifting classes held just down the hall attracted more students. Part of the problem seemed to be that yoga had a reputation as esoteric and effeminate, and did not build muscles the way bodybuilding did. So Krishnamacharya spent time chatting with the weightlifting instructor, K.V. Iyer. It may have been here that Krishnamacharya incorporated the flowing *suryanamaskar* movements into yoga. This new, more physical yoga developed through a process of trial and error, with one former student recalling that Krishnamacharya was "innovating all the time." If students could do poses easily, he would add new elements to make them more challenging for that person. There was no specified order of poses, just personal programs shaped by the flexibility of the individual.[21]

While the *yogaşala* did well, Krishnamacharya never stopped promoting yoga around Mysore. This was necessary since yoga still struggled to match the popularity of weightlifting. One strategy he used was to take his students on the road and use them to demonstrate particularly difficult poses. These feats of strength, which Krishnamacharya cheerfully referred to as "propaganda work," were often dismissed as circus tricks by students. Larger demonstrations involving dozens of students were hard to coordinate, so Krishnamacharya suggested that each pose be held for five audible breaths, and that student's move through a sequence in tandem. This ran counter to his early instructions at the *yogaşala*, where he recommended students hold their poses for three minutes or more, but it was more effective at handling large numbers of students. Certain critical elements of postural yoga today, *ujjayi* breath and sequenced poses, may well stem from Krishnamacharya's promotional tours in Mysore during the 1930s.[22]

Two other influences likely shaped Krishnamacharya's yoga. First, both the YMCA and British Army adopted a new form of rhythmic exercise in the 1920s called Primitive Gymnastics, created by the Dane Niels Bukh. It contained sequences of moves graded into six series, each designed to be done vigorously in order to generate heat in the body. The movements were coordinated by an instructor, accompanied by deep breathing, and flowed from one pose to the next. Based on a manual published in 1925, at least twenty-eight of Bukh's exercises are virtually identical to postures now found in *ashtanga yoga*. While it is unlikely that Krishnamacharya borrowed directly from Bukh, his system definitely reflects common elements of physical culture practiced in India at this time.[23]

Second, Krishnamacharya also visited Sri Kuvalayananda's research institute that was engaged in creating a scientific form of physical education based on yoga. He had combined asanas found in hatha texts with the type of drill instruction found in Ling gymnastics in order to create Yogic Physical Education. Kuvalayananda had come to see asanas as a form of gymnastics to be used pragmatically to improve fitness. While some of the poses may well have originated as ritual prostrations during pilgrimages, by the 1930s they had become part of physical culture. These poses, including *caturanga* and *tadasana*, likely entered Krishnamacharya's yoga practice at this time.[24]

So why are these nineteenth- and twentieth-century innovations so important to the history of yoga? In essence, they shaped what Mark Singleton called "globalized modern yoga." Several crucial elements were necessary. Vivekananda's translation of *Raja Yoga* offered an introduction to the discipline that fused Western esotericism, religious universalism, and classic "yoga" philosophy in ways that were accessible to audiences beyond the subcontinent. Yoga's accessible spirituality contributed to its popularity the West, especially after the Beatles paid a visit to the Maharishi Mahesh Yogi during the 1960s. Here they sought to learn more about Indian metaphysics and yoga.[25] But the physical benefits of yoga, first studied by Sri Kuvalayananda, also contributed to its popularity, especially in the more recent past. Krishnamacharya's students were critical to this process. Both Pattabhi Jois and B.K.S. Iyengar established new types of yoga based on their training in Mysore. Jois's *ashtanga yoga*, in particular, was incredibly influential due to the perceived fitness benefits of this vigorous athletic practice. Even if you have never done the *ashtanga* sequences (which are popular with celebrities like Gwyneth Paltrow, Sting, and Madonna[26]), any class called "power yoga," "power vinyasa," or "vinyasa flow" was shaped by Jois, and through him Krishnamacharya and his studio. Recruiting attractive celebrities as participants was another way yoga became popular in the United States, with both Indra Devi and Bikram Choudhury teaching Hollywood icons like Marilyn Monroe and Shirley MacLaine. As these studios grew in popularity in the 1990s and early 2000s, an entire consumer culture developed around yoga. At times, this culture enabled behavior seemingly out of step with yoga's philosophical roots, including sexual assault allegations leveled at Bikram and the toxic "boy's club" at leggings company Lululemon.[27]

Krishnamacharya was never a historian. While students fondly remembered his postural innovations, Krishnamacharya rarely brought up the philosophies of yoga in class.[28] This reflected his perception that students were not interested in those ideas, and it is striking that his son felt a need to explain Krishnamacharya's lack of philosophical engagement with the *Yoga Sutras* in a recent biography.[29] Earlier biographies focus on how Ramamohana Brahmachari revealed a 5,000-year-old text called the *Yoga Kurunta* to Krishnamacharya during his apprenticeship. While this text purportedly contains the exact sequences later found in *ashtanga yoga*, it was allegedly destroyed by ants in a Calcutta library after Krishnamacharya transmitted it orally to Pattabhi Jois. And it is fascinating that this text, supposedly an elaboration on the *Yoga Sutras*, is not mentioned in either of Krishnamacharya's major published writings, *Yoga Makaranda* (1935) and *Yogasanagalu* (1941). In all likelihood, the *Yoga Kurunta* was invented to endow modern postural yoga with an antiquity it never possessed. Singleton is likely correct to describe Krishnamacharya's innovations as "less an indication of a historically traceable 'classical' asana lineage than of the modern project of grafting gymnastics or aerobic asana practice onto the Yogasutras, and the creation of a new tradition."[30] This physical variant, more popular in the West, has become the dominant version of the globalized modern yoga today, but as we have seen, the meanings of yoga are constantly in motion.

Conclusion

Yoga is often presumed to possess great antiquity—after all, the *Yoga Sutras* of Patanjali date back almost 2,000 years! However, the assumption that yoga as we understand it today resembles yoga as it was practiced thousands of years ago needs to be interrogated. Did yogis in the past behave the way yogis do today? Does the fact we use the same word mean that it retains the same meanings? These questions are at the heart of establishing patterns of continuity or change over time. And to return to the introduction, the "Take Back Yoga" campaign argues that an unbroken thread of ancient Hindu thought is present in forms of the practice today.

This chapter argues that yoga experienced a transformation during the early twentieth century. The *Yoga Sutras* of Patanjali, in particular, describe a system of yoga with only a passing connection to that practiced today. While breath control and comfortable postures were a part of Patanjali's yoga, the active asanas practiced today were not. The text also reflects a philosophical school that predates and in some ways contradicts later forms of Hinduism. Yogis from the first millennium CE were generally part of the Gorakhnathi order. This group sought supernatural powers through the transgressive tantras, but did not really practice yoga as often supposed. Other orders like the Dasanamis and Ramanandis did practice forms of yoga (especially *bindu* in an effort to achieve *samadhi*), but they never resembled the modern postural practice. Finding a single definitive version of yoga in the middle of such a spiritual mélange is impossible, and nowhere do we find physical poses similar to those practiced today.

Modern postural yoga becomes recognizable only in the twentieth century. Thanks to influences as diverse as Indian nationalism, muscular Christianity, Danish Primitive gymnastics, and the medicalization of hatha yoga, new forms of yoga appeared on the subcontinent. These dramatic changes manifested themselves in places like Krishnamacharya's *yogaṣala*. Here yoga was transformed from a philosophical system to a fitness activity, one with flowing sequences of poses orchestrated by instructors. And while Hinduism certainly played a role in shaping modern postural yoga, it is not at all clear that its influence is significantly larger than that of the ascetic orders, Western science, or even of Christianity. Given what yoga has become, it hard to imagine that yoga ever belonged to any one religious group.

Further reading

Iyengar, B.K.S. *Astadala Yogamālā*. New Delhi: Allied Publishers, 2000. A compilation of numerous lectures, articles, and interviews on yoga produced by a student of Krishnamacharya.

Jain, Andrea. *Selling Yoga*. New York: Oxford University Press, 2015. An examination of the ways yoga has changed in the twentieth century through its encounter with consumer culture.

Samuel, Geoffrey. *The Origins of Yoga and Tantra*. New York: Cambridge University Press, 2008. An effort to contextualize the origins of yoga and tantra, both in terms of philosophical understandings and the rhythms of day-to-day life.

Singleton, Mark. *Yoga Body*. New York: Oxford University Press, 2010. A crucial new interpretation of the history of yoga that focuses on the innovations of Krishnamacharya while teaching in Mysore.

White, David Gordon. *The Yoga Sutra of Patanjali: A Biography*. Princeton, NJ: Princeton University Press, 2014. This biography of Patanjali's text examines the different lenses through which it has been understood in the past.

5

Whose Key to China?

In 1966, a wave of violence swept through China. Known today as the Cultural Revolution, the Red Guards targeted symbols of the Four Olds which included old ideas, old customs, old habits, and old culture.[1] In November, they turned their attention to the descendants of the famous sage Confucius. After declaring their intent to "annihilate the Kong family business," they attacked the temple complex in Qufu. They destroyed countless statues, sacred relics, and desecrated the grave of Confucius himself. His corpse had likely been removed millennia earlier, but others buried at Qufu were unearthed, strung up on trees, and left to rot.[2] The Communist Party of China (CCP), by rejecting the Confucian traditions that had guided its Imperial predecessors, was making a clean break with the past.

However, the CCP and Confucius quickly reconciled. In 1984, Communist leaders began hosting an annual ceremony celebrating Confucius's birthday in the same Qufu compound the Red Guards had damaged. Twenty years later, when deciding to name their foreign language centers around the world, they called them "Confucius Institutes." Despite its small population, Qufu received a stop on the high-speed rail line connecting Beijing and Shanghai in order to receive millions of tourists wishing to see the same sites the Red Guards had damaged.[3] At the 2008 Summer Olympics, the CCP made Confucian philosophy a part of the opening ceremony, and Professor Yu Dan's recent reflections on the subject have sold millions of copies.[4] Former President Hu Jintao's (2003–12) stated political goal was a "harmonious society," (*hexie shehui*) a phrase borrowed from Confucius. The relationship between the Communist state and Confucius has been completely transformed.

Confucius is perhaps the most famous Chinese individual in history. Understanding his thought is often believed to be crucial to understanding the culture of this powerful nation—that it is, in some way, "the key to China." In a world history class, Confucianism will often appear as China's

Figure 5.1 The stone stele and burial mound marking the grave of Confucius at his former home in Qufu. Courtesy of Universal Images Group (UIG) via Getty Images.

defining cultural trait. Samuel Huntington goes so far as to call China a "Confucian civilization."[5] But is this an accurate assessment? The CCP's embrace of Confucius is part of a longer pattern of elite enthusiasm for the ideas of this sage, but does their enthusiasm reflect China as a whole? This chapter will investigate the significance of Confucius to Chinese culture, and why it might be overstated.

The life of Confucius

Confucius lived from 551 to 479 BCE during an era of seemingly endless disorder, and his main intellectual contribution was a theory of governance shaped by this turbulent age. It reflected the optimistic belief that human beings were driven toward ethical behavior and that certain fundamental patterns (known as Dao, or "The Way") should govern their communities. The relationship between a child and parent, marked by obedience from the former and restraint from the latter, was viewed by Confucius as a model for good governance. Cultivating ethical behavior was a fundamental obligation of the elite, and one who was kind, humane, and behaved correctly toward others became a *junzi*, or "superior man," regardless of their status at birth.[6]

His ideas were not influential until after his death. His students, including Mencius, collected and preserved his teachings, which gradually became popular among scholars. After the persecutions of Qin Shi Huangdi (r.247–220 BCE) discredited Legalist approaches to state-building, Confucian ideas grew in significance. Under the Han Emperor Wudi (r.141–87 BCE), Confucian principles were upheld as a state doctrine. Gradually, the Five Classics (*Book of Change, Book of Documents, Book of Odes, Book of Rites*, and *Spring and Autumn Annals*) became the curriculum for civil service exams. These texts were largely written before Confucius lived, but were associated with his name and considered to contain the classical Confucian traditions, or *ru*. *Ru* referred to the traditional Confucian creed including sacrifices honoring the sage and his disciples, as well as a conceptual scheme for ideal behavior.[7] As Han Dynasty emperors began making these sacrifices, the imperial cult and Confucian worship became intertwined.

It is important to note that these sacrifices were restricted to members of the imperial family and the scholarly elite, defined as those who had passed the exams, examination candidates, students at private academies studying Confucian texts, and members of the gentry who had failed exams but still aspired to behave according to this moral code. *The Book of Rites* explicitly indicated that "ceremonial rules do not extend to the common people."[8] Chinese peasants generally relied on more mystical rituals that involved amulets, exorcism, and sacrifices to local spirits. Daoism was an important source of inspiration for "popular religion," but it was far from the only one.[9] After the collapse of the Han, Buddhism spread rapidly across China, and monasteries grew with extraordinary speed. Pure Land Buddhism, which involved invoking the name of Amitabha ten times in order to achieve salvation, was especially popular. Despite the disapproval of many Confucian scholars, Daoism and Buddhism came to occupy significant places in the China's religious milieu. Together, they were known as the three teachings.

When the powerful Sui dynasty (589–618 CE) and Tang dynasty (618–907 CE) consolidated their authority, they required civil service candidates to take written exams. This was accompanied by an expansion of state schools that helped prepare students for the grueling exam process. The curriculum was based heavily on the Confucian classics, and accompanying each new academy was a Confucian temple. These were the first Confucian temples constructed outside Qufu. The impact of the exams on the scholar-elite was evident to the Tang Emperor Li Shimin who observed that "the heroes of the Empire are all in my pocket!"[10]

The final crucial change in Confucian thought took place during the Ming dynasty (1368–1644) but had its roots in earlier intellectual developments. Neo-Confucianism, based on the writing of Cheng Yi (1033–1107), Cheng Hao (1032–85), and Zhu Xi (1130–1200), became the dominant interpretation of *ru* across the empire. Neo-Confucianism adopted meditative approaches from Buddhism and focused more on the internal cultivation of ethical behavior, but Zhu Xi was also dedicated to purging Daoist and Buddhist elements that he believed had infiltrated Confucian rites.[11] This was expressed in his compilation entitled *Family Rituals*, which was a compendium of orthodox Confucian practices for important rituals. During the centralization of power that marked the early Ming dynasty, symbolized by the construction of the Forbidden City, the state also ordered the construction of countless Confucian altars across rural China. This was the first time that Confucian ritual practices became a regular part of life for most Chinese peasants, and it would have important consequences in the future.

The scholar-elite and Chinese culture

If Confucian ideas were the subject of such heated debate, why is there reason to doubt his significance across China? It really comes down to whose voices are privileged. If you focus on the China in which the scholar-elite believed they lived, his ideas appear vitally important. But if you take the perspective of Chinese peasants, Confucius's impact was less meaningful. This is why the skill of significance matters. By choosing to amplify particular voices, historians can shape perceptions of the past. The rest of this chapter will look at why elite voices may have been given an undue prominence in accounts of Chinese history, and then examine how an alternative perspective reveals important insights into everyday religious practice.

The two individuals who shaped early Western perceptions of China were Matteo Ricci and Michele Ruggieri, a pair of Italian Jesuits. They fervently desired to convert the Ming dynasty to Christianity, and they founded a mission at Zhaoqing in 1583 to expedite this purpose. It was here that they put into practice a conversion strategy that would come to be known as "accommodationism." In effect, they sought to become Chinese through mastery of the local language and culture. Their extraordinary commitment to this goal was buttressed by their relative autonomy from other Jesuit orders. Within a year, Ricci would write "in our clothing, in our books, in our manners, and in everything external we have made ourselves Chinese."[12]

What is most fascinating about this moment is that Ricci and Ruggieri initially adopted the appearance of Buddhist monks. Ricci noted that the monastic members of China's vibrant Buddhist sects numbered in the millions. If they wished to preach to the largest possible audience, being recognized as Buddhist was probably the best path forward. For twelve years they participated in Chinese life as Buddhist monks.[13] But they never received the official respect that they recognized as essential to converting this geographically immense state. In 1592 they began the process of presenting themselves differently, first by traveling in palanquins favored by China's scholar-elite rather than on foot. Three years later they began wearing the ornate robes of this class, and became admirers of *ru*.[14] Their linguistic skills, honed over years of translating Christian concepts into Chinese characters, allowed them to participate in disputes over Confucian doctrine, and they rapidly gained respect at the Chinese court.

Ricci and Ruggieri never convinced China to embrace Christianity, but they did have a massive impact on Western understandings of this region. First, they suggested that China had a single language known as *guanhua* (lit. "speech of officials"). Had they become Buddhist monks, they likely would have been more aware of the importance of regional dialects, but as members of the scholar-elite, they shared the view that China had achieved linguistic unity. Second, they argued that Buddhism was a foreign infection that was "weakening the original vitality of Chinese culture."[15] The Jesuits believed that Buddhism was riddled with idolatry, a view that likely developed during their close interaction with Confucian scholars. Scholar-elite perceptions of Buddhism were most famously epitomized by Han Yu's claim that it was "no more than a cult of barbarian peoples."[16] Third, the Cheng brothers and Zhu Xi had reformed *ru* in ways that Ricci and Ruggieri respected. The Neo-Confucians were staunch opponents of involving physical representations of Confucius in sacred rituals since these were not mentioned in the most ancient Confucian texts, something with which the Jesuits heartily agreed.[17] Zhu Xi's focus on self-cultivation through contemplative prayer, reading, and meditation also closely resembled monastic life in the Catholic tradition.[18] This combination of factors led to considerable Jesuit sympathy for the views of China's Confucian scholar-elite.

Jesuit perceptions were critical to shaping the place of Confucian thought in world history. Ricci in particular felt that *ru* was a singular and ancient tradition that had been corrupted by Buddhism and Daoism. He also believed that the original Confucian tradition was conducive to monotheism, with Confucius representing a vehicle for divine awareness in China. This resulted in his belief that *ru* was "theologically compatible" with Christianity.[19] Ricci was so convinced by this argument that he suggested a variety of Chinese ritual practices should be tolerated by Christians since they were not based on the idea that ancestral ghosts existed or that Confucius was a God.[20] Those rituals that were too mystical to fit this framework were quietly edited out of Ricci's works.

Ricci's perceptions not only shaped how Europe perceived China, but also received support from the Chinese scholar-elite. The sixteenth- and seventeenth-century literati shared a desire to minimize the prominence of Buddhist and Daoist forms of worship in China. In particular, they wished to eliminate Confucian rituals that borrowed too heavily from other religious traditions. This confluence of interests meant that the scholarly consensus in both Europe and China focused on *ru* as a singular and ancient tradition that was best understood as an ethical way of life, perhaps as a result of past contact with a singular divine. And this tradition remains the one that dominates most world history textbooks.

There are several problems with this interpretation of *ru*. The first is that it overstates the unity of the Confucian tradition. Debates over appropriate canonical texts, forms of worship, and figures of veneration were all quite vibrant among Confucian adherents, but this is often forgotten today. These debates began with the struggle to find agreement on which texts were suitable for inclusion as canon. Emperor Wudi established the core of the Five Classics in 136 BCE, but this did little to resolve debates since certain texts contradicted others. It also did not help resolve the core debate between the Modern Text tradition and the Ancient Text tradition. The former were supposedly written from memory after the Qin emperor destroyed the Confucian classics, but the latter claimed that originals were hidden during the Warring States period and discovered much later.

These debates during the Han dynasty speak to an uneasy relationship between those who saw Confucius as someone endowed with cosmic power and those who saw him as a gifted philosopher. The Modern Text tradition claimed that Confucius was directly responsible for altering and rewriting the Six Classics (the Five Classics plus the lost Book of Music), and that these texts contained "esoteric meanings." To them, Confucius was an uncrowned king blessed with mystical sources of knowledge. The Ancient Text tradition countered that Confucius himself denied "innovating" when he compiled the Six Classics, and that they were best understood as ancient historical documents.[21] The Ancient Text tradition became dominant under the unified Tang dynasty in the 640s CE, but adherents of the Modern Text interpretation lived on in the south of China, albeit with greatly diminished influence. These two versions of Confucius would be important during the sixteenth century. The scholar-elite that Ricci and Ruggieri became a part of was the product of hundreds of years of Ancient Text tradition, and this led the Jesuits toward a view of Confucius as a sage rather than a mystic.

Another significant division emerged over the position of the Four Books including *The Analects*, perhaps the best known Confucian text today. During the Han and Tang periods the Four Books were considered less important than the Five Classics. This began to change in the early 1000s, when Wang Anshi added *The Analects* and *Mencius* to the civil service exams. Mastering these works, along with *Great Learning* and *Doctrine of the Mean*, became essential for any student of the Confucian classics. Zhu Xi, who wrote the famous *Collected Commentaries of the Four Books* in 1190, continued to push the significance of these works. Despite facing initial persecution, Zhu Xi's *Commentaries* became part of the core curriculum assessed on exams.[22]

The final problem with the Jesuits' interpretation of Confucian thought is that they saw *ru* as a singular entity. This was problematic even when the Jesuits were active. *Ru* was never isolated from other aspects of China's religious mélange, and the lack of a fixed form for sacrifices to Confucius ensured there was heavy borrowing from other practices. This was true even at the highest levels. The Tang emperor Taizong established the first network of state-funded Confucian temples alongside government academies. Scholars borrowed from the liturgy for sacrifices to the Gods of Soils and Grains, an official state cult that predated Confucius, for use in these rituals. The use of portrait icons, common in Chan Buddhism and the worship of bodhisattvas, also became a part of Confucian rites at this time.[23] This caused issues related to iconoclasm throughout the fifteenth and sixteenth centuries, with the worship of Confucian icons being banned in the 1530s. The most famous sculpture of Confucius at the temple in Qufu was left undisturbed, but when it was destroyed by a fire in 1724, it was rebuilt with sacred objects like bronze mirrors and ancient texts hidden inside. This closely resembled a similar Buddhist practice that was believed to endow the image with special powers.[24]

Innovations like this continue to the present day. The most recent innovation to Confucian rituals involves prayer cards. Based on Shinto *ema* found in temples around Japan, these cards are inscribed with the name of a god or temple on one side and a written wish on the other. According to Anna Sun, these were invented in 2002 after a visit to Japan by the director of the Shanghai Confucian Temple, and have subsequently spread across China. Unlike "paper offerings" common in Chinese rituals, these prayer cards are not burned, but displayed in public until there are so many that they must be moved to private storage on the temple grounds.[25] Confucian ritual often appears ancient and unchanging, but it is better understood as a product of constant innovation.

Figure 5.2 Shinto *ema* wish plaques at Ueno Toshogu Shrine in Tokyo, Japan. This practice was integrated into Confucian worship in the early twenty-first century CE. Courtesy of Education Images/UIG via Getty Images.

An in-depth look at the history of Confucian worship among ordinary people reveals the diverse range of popular practices. During the Ming and Qing eras, most community rituals were led by *lisheng*. *Lisheng* were government officials or degree-holders who had been trained in Zhu Xi's *Family Rituals*. They performed sacrifices to patron gods or distant family ancestors, participated in community festivals, and conducted appropriate rites at events like weddings and funerals. *Lisheng* were expected to compose, recite, and burn written texts at these rituals. These generally praised a supernatural being, asked them to enjoy the sacrifice, and beseeched them to aid those who were making this offering.[26] They were part of a larger project by Neo-Confucians to spread orthodox forms of worship beyond the scholar-elite to ordinary people.[27]

Compilations of ritual texts composed by *lisheng*, known as *jiwenben*, reveal important evidence of syncretism long after the Neo-Confucian reforms began. For example, Yonghua Liu discovered that several Ming and Qing-era *jiwenben* mentioned amulets. They were present at weddings, were part of rites performed when the foundation of a house was laid, or even used to repel white ants. Many of these charms were thought to derive their power from Pu'an, a Daoist exorcist who later converted to Buddhism. Similar syncretism was evident at *jiao* festivals. These were the site of communal offerings overseen by the *lisheng*, and were performed to alleviate drought, disease, or problems with wild animals. *Lisheng* and Daoist priests likely performed these rituals together at official altars, with the latter taking the leading role.[28] To Liu, "*lisheng* functioned as mediators not only between official and gentry culture and village world but also between Confucian rituals and the rituals of other traditions, in particular those of the Daoism."[29]

Another example of the complexity of Confucian rituals relates to the cult of *She*. It dated to the Western Zhou (*c.*1046–771 BCE), and was incorporated into Imperial worship as *sheji*, or the cult of the Gods of Soil and Grain. During the Tang, Song, and Yuan eras, this cult became popular across China, with people making sacrifices asking for good harvests or to aid orphaned souls. The Ming made a conscious effort to propagate this cult by asking all communities to construct altars for these sacrifices. This was likely the first time that Chinese peasants became deeply involved in a state-approved religious ritual, and was part of a larger Ming project of centralizing authority. The results suggest active resistance to Confucian rituals. Across Fujian, legends sprung up that the real god worshipped at these altars was Shegong, a malevolent figure who demanded human sacrifices from the villagers. Many versions of these legends indicate that Shegong was thwarted when someone in the village learned the secrets of Daoist exorcism. As a result, Shegong was expelled and the villagers no longer worshipped him. The individuals who supposedly drove off Shegong often became the founders of prominent lineages.[30] The scholar-elite disliked these legends, so they created their own versions of the story that acknowledged the prior existence of a demon demanding these sacrifices in the name of Shegong. But the fact that villagers believed a key figure in Confucian rituals was exploitive and illegitimate suggests that efforts to enforce orthodoxy were fiercely resisted.[31]

The examples listed above suggest that describing China as "Confucian" is a major oversimplification. Part of the problem is the sources, which tended to privilege the views of China's scholar-elite. Prior to the Ming, this group was divided on key issues. The Neo-Confucians were able to resolve these disputes among the literati, but their efforts to standardize ritual practices met with stout resistance. By looking at rites from the bottom-up, one discovers that, as Tim Barrett argues, "Chinese heritage is far more complex than the description 'Confucian' can convey."[32]

Conclusion

In 1918 Lu Xun wrote "The Diary of a Madman." He wrote at a time when China was subject to ruthless exploitation by Western powers, and the collapse of the Qing dynasty had led to the division of the nation between a number of warlords. Distraught by what he had witnessed, Lu Xun inverted a typical scholarly trope; instead of China's Confucian character being the essence of its civilization, he argued it made China barbaric. To him, the endless discussion of etiquette, morality, and rituals benefited only one group of people—cannibals who exploited others.[33] In a telling excerpt, he writes "Almost all of those who praise the old Chinese culture are the rich who are residing in the concessions or other safe places … Those who praise Chinese culture, whether they be Chinese or foreigners, conceive of themselves as belonging to the ruling class."[34] To Lu Xun, it was better for people to live for themselves than their ancestors, better to worship Darwin and Ibsen than Confucius or Guan Yu.

Lu Xun's work reveals two important things. The first is that Confucian traditions were sometimes perceived as a hegemonic project, one imposed on China by the scholar-elite. The second is that Lu Xun was susceptible to the same error that we sometimes see in world history textbooks; namely, that of equating Chinese history with Confucianism. Even as he recognized that Confucian traditions were used as a weapon by China's literati, he took for granted their main claim. In this he was similar to the Jesuits described earlier in this chapter. They too viewed China's history through the lens of Confucian scholars. And they too saw a past shaped by Confucius. They missed the stubborn resistance across rural China that prevented Confucian traditions from becoming fully standardized, despite the best efforts of Neo-Confucians like Zhu Xi. Elements of Daoism, Buddhism, and other local forms of worship remain an active part of this spiritual milieu to the present day.

The resurrection of Confucius in the eyes of the CCP, mentioned in the introduction, may well shape future understandings of Chinese history. Especially for world historians, it is tempting to follow their lead and offer up Confucius as the benevolent "key" to understanding this extraordinarily complex region. But this is not nearly as accurate as it might seem, and needs to be tempered with an awareness of how it privileges certain voices at the expense of others.

Further reading

Elman, Benjamin, John Duncan, and Herman Ooms, eds. *Rethinking Confucianism*. Los Angeles: University of California Press, 2002. An edited volume that challenges generalizations about Confucianism and argues that it can only be understood in its local context.

Jensen, Lionel. *Manufacturing Confucianism*. Durham, NC: Duke University Press, 1998. A pathbreaking monograph that suggests much of what the West knows about Confucius was actually constructed by Jesuit scholars in the seventeenth century.

Liu, Yonghua. *Confucian Rituals and Chinese Villagers*. Leiden: Brill, 2013. This book examines how Confucian rituals and local traditions became intertwined in Sibao (Fujian Province) from the Ming dynasty to the Communist Revolution.

Sun, Anna. *Confucianism as a World Religion*. Princeton, NJ: Princeton University Press, 2013. A brilliant analysis of how Confucianism came to be understood as a world religion even though it is not officially considered a religion in China.

Wilson, Thomas. *Genealogy of the Way*. Palo Alto, CA: Stanford University Press, 1995. A detailed examination of different internal debates over the nature of Confucianism.

6

Making Waves

Today we take it for granted that everywhere in the world has a history worth uncovering. Sadly, this is a very recent development. In the 1950s Hugh Trevor-Roper, the Regius Professor of Modern History at Oxford University, casually dismissed Africa's ancient past as "the unedifying gyrations of barbarous tribes in picturesque but irrelevant corners of the globe."[1] This remark is frequently cited as evidence of the arrogance and Eurocentrism of an earlier generation of scholars, but at the time it reflected the dominant view. Trevor-Roper argued that history was "essentially a form of movement ... We study it ... in order to discover how we came to where we are." And since Europe had come to dominate the world and colonize Africa, Europe's story was considered history while events in Africa were considered irrelevant.

Cracks in this façade became apparent around the same time. In 1950, Kenneth Dike received his PhD from King's College London, becoming the first African to complete a dissertation in African history.[2] Seven years later, the British colony of Gold Coast became the first of what would become dozens of African nations to win their independence. The decision by the Gold Coast to take the name Ghana, evoking the ancient empire that had flourished just to its north, reflected a newfound fascination with Africa's past. By the 1960s a vibrant community of African historians had been born, one that was active in universities across Africa, North America, and Europe.

Initially scholars focused their attentions on the powerful states of Africa's pre-colonial past. These were mostly located along the savanna belt of West Africa, and Central Africa remained "the ahistorical region of black Africa, for no important state developed there."[3] But there was an awareness of one dramatic event in the region which had taken place in the distant past. During the mid-nineteenth century, Wilhelm Bleek identified three different tongues that he classified as "Bantu" due to their

Figure 6.1 Kenneth Dike (1917–83) became the first African to receive a PhD in history from a European university in 1950. His dissertation marked a turning point in the study of Africa, which began to incorporate African academics after this time. Courtesy of Bettmann via Getty Images.

shared—ntu root for the word "person." He believed these languages were related to an original "proto-Bantu" tongue, and that the speakers of this language had likely migrated across the continent before settling in South Africa.[4]

The Bantu migrations were subsequently integrated into world history narratives as an example of the Agricultural Revolution. The Bantu-speakers possessed a suite of crops that included yams and oil palm that gave them an advantage over the hunter-gatherers (known as the Batwa) they encountered in Central African rainforests. These crops did not produce significantly more calories, but a combination of ceramics (for cooking) and disease resistance (to malaria, which was more common near yam fields) may have given the Bantu-speakers a demographic edge over the indigenous peoples they encountered.[5] How historians have used different types of evidence to both reconstruct and deconstruct the Bantu migrations is the subject of this chapter.

The problem of the Bantu migrations

The Bantu migrations never received the level of scholarly attention that was directed at the Indo-Europeans, and this allowed past interpretations to exert disproportionate influence. This is evident in the writing of Harry Johnston, a British colonial official who was stationed in Uganda during the early twentieth century CE. In a 1913 paper he placed the original Bantu homeland in Bahr-al-Ghazal (in modern Sudan). He believed that they subsequently migrated south after acquiring the guinea fowl from Egypt in 300 BCE.[6] He describes them "penetrating," "conquering," and "invading" the Batwa as they rampaged across sub-Saharan Africa, leaving no doubt that this process involved considerable conflict. Thanks to their iron-working skills and superior weapons, the Bantu were able to displace and assimilate non-Bantu-speakers with astonishing speed.[7] This narrative was imbued with racism—Johnston believed that the presence of "more dynamic" races in Egypt (just to the north of Bahr-al-Ghazal) provided the impetus for the Bantu migrations. And this story was transparently self-serving. Johnston, as a British colonial administrator, saw himself as part of a superior and more dynamic race that had conquered Central Africa thanks to its advanced weaponry.[8] If the Bantu could conquer and dispossess the inferior Batwa, weren't the British entitled to do the same to them?

It should come as no surprise that racial explanations for the Bantu migrations fell out of favor after the Second World War. Instead, scholars turned to new research methods like glottochronology. Glottochronology involved compiling lists of 100 words from a wide range of languages, and then using the number of cognates to calculate the degree of similarity. A series of abstract calculations can then estimate how long ago the languages separated. Margins of error are extremely large, especially due to problems caused by multiple cognates with similar meanings, but in Central Africa there were few alternatives. Glottochronology enabled linguists like Joseph Greenberg to successfully place the ancestral proto-Bantu language in southwest Cameroon, and general rules of linguistic change suggested it had first been spoken roughly 5,000 years ago (3000 BCE).[9] Roland Oliver felt an appropriate analogy for Bantu success was the settlement of Australia and North America by Europeans; "of course the European migrants of modern times were better armed than the Australian aborigines or the North American Indians, but ... the main reason for their success was that they brought with them from Europe a way of life which was capable … of producing population explosions which provided the main dynamic of their settlement."[10] The arrival of the banana from Southeast Asia (which he placed between 0 and 500 CE) and its rapid adoption in Central Africa transformed the Bantu into powerful farmers, and offered an important "alternative to a conquest theory."[11] By necessity, the migration he was describing was much more gradual, with movement measured in generations. The term scholars use for this is *demic* migration.

This image of the Bantu migrants emphasized the environment but told readers little about what these people thought or believed. Jan Vansina sought to go beyond the environment to flesh out the intellectual world of the Bantu migrants in the Congolese rainforests. Synthesizing anthropological and linguistic data from over 200 distinct societies in his book *Paths in the Rainforest*, he argued that the rates and causes of immigration varied enormously. In some places, it may have been a product of the need to move villages to new sites every ten to twenty years. In others, purposeful movement into more amenable environments played a role. Everywhere they went, they encountered the indigenous peoples known in proto-Bantu as *-tua*, the root of the more recent term Batwa. Vansina speculated that a combination of population growth, trade dominance, and perhaps increased disease (spread by the *anopheles* mosquito) gradually eroded the autonomy of the indigenes.[12] The villages established by the Bantu were united by common traditions. Village leaders were generally chosen on merit, but their power was circumscribed by the ability of family units (called Houses) to join other communities. Natural spirits and charms to placate them were a key part of Bantu understandings of the world, and witchcraft was used to avoid excessive accumulation by elites.[13]

Vansina's *Paths in the Rainforest* was about a "Bantu migration" in the singular. Five years later he used new linguistic data to show that a "single continuous migration" was impossible. While he acknowledged that "straightforward migration may indeed have occurred" in certain instances, he argued that people and languages generally did not move in unison. And most importantly, scholars were studying events that took place over thousands of years as an integrated whole. He felt the entire narrative was flawed. The Bantu-speakers did not suddenly emerge due to overpopulation in the Sahara. Their root crops did not give them a massive demographic advantage over foragers. And the wide distribution of ceramics, bananas, and pottery suggests that they were never monopolized by any one group. Only five years after writing what many world historians considered the definitive book on the Bantu migration, Vansina claimed it had never happened.[14]

Vansina's alternative explanation was that numerous, much less dramatic migrations had happened, generally involving single languages. He identified nine examples over the course of 2,000 years, and suggests the history of each of these events needs to be written. His explanation ultimately focused on processes that were familiar—sedentarization and population growth, albeit with foragers being incorporated into the Bantu communities rather than being exterminated by them.[15] But others borrowed from Vansina and took his ideas even further.[16] John Robertson and Rebecca Bradley suggested that the suite of Bantu technologies spread across the region through a process of gradual diffusion that did not involve the large-scale movement of people. Using four sites in the Mulungushi region of Zambia, they noted that Iron Age technologies like domesticated plants, iron and slag, and permanent dwellings were all present by 100 CE. However, the quantities of *daga* (the clay-fired remains of a wattle-and-daub dwelling) found at the sites did not rapidly change. One site dated *c.*450 CE had roughly the same amount of *daga* present as a site that was 2,000 years older. But after 500 CE the quantity of *daga* increased exponentially, reflecting dramatic population growth.[17] This fascinated Robertson and Bradley. Almost everywhere around the world the adaption of agriculture leads to rapid population growth. Why the 500-year delay in Mulungushi?

They pointed to a tiny culprit—the *anopheles* mosquito. Prior to the spread of agriculture, highly mobile foragers would have been at low risk of contracting malaria. But as people sedentarized, *anopheles gambiae* became endemic. This mosquito is a highly efficient malaria vector, but a variety of predators keep its population in check along rivers and swamps. Cutting holes in the forest canopy allowed rain to pelt the ground, creating large puddles of water that served as nurseries for this mosquito.[18] The other issue for the spread of malaria is the need for a person to be bitten twice to transmit the disease; first by a mosquito to become infected by the disease and second by another mosquito while the human is sick to transmit the parasite to a new insect host. From the perspective of malaria parasites, hosts needed to stay in place for at least ten to twenty days to complete a full cycle of the disease. Hunter-gatherers enjoyed a degree of protection from the disease by virtue of their mobility. But sedentary farmers were vulnerable, especially women and children who likely remained in a single place during the rainy season. The spread of falciparum malaria by *anopheles gambiae* would have triggered a dramatic increase in infant mortality combined with a reduced birth rate. To Robertson and Bradley, this explains the 500-year gap between the arrival of Iron Age technologies and the start of explosive population growth. Sedentarization could not bring about the latter until the spread of genetic traits (including the sickle cell trait) that protected people from the worst ravages of falciparum malaria.

So what does this mean for the Bantu migrations? They noted that there was no evidence for the arrival of migrants when the suite of Iron Age technologies appeared in 100 CE—no new ceramic traditions, for example, that developed elsewhere. And in the absence of evidence for people in motion, they argued the "the default assumption should be internal development."[19] Perhaps what looked like migration was actually the more mundane process of sedentarization, something that did not require large-scale population movements. Linguistic terms might have been borrowed from neighbors when new technologies arrived. Were the Bantu migrants sweeping across the continent just a figment of our imaginations?

Robertson and Bradley were cognizant of the racist history of the Bantu migration. They observed that physical anthropologists continued to take for granted certain assumptions about the peoples of Africa inherited from the racial theories of the late nineteenth century.[20] But were Robertson and Bradley correct to completely discard migration as an analytical model

Figure 6.2 A Batwa pygmy hiking near the Bwindi Impenetrable Forest, Uganda. The Batwa likely became forest specialists after centuries of contact with Bantu-speakers. Courtesy of Andrew Aitchison/Corbis Historical via Getty Images.

for this period? After all, the linguistic evidence is quite clear that Bantu languages are connected to one another, and they often contain similar cultural concepts. Migration might not apply in Mulungushi, but this is not necessarily true everywhere.

New scholarly approaches are beginning to shed light on critical elements of the Bantu migrations. Kairn Klieman's remarkable look at the history of Bantu interactions with the indigenous Batwa is one fascinating example. Klieman suspects proto-Bantu-speakers began to migrate into the rainforests of Gabon and southern Cameroon around 4500 BCE. Klieman suggests that they were then incorporated into already extant communities of hunters and gatherers. The Bantu-speakers believed these indigenous peoples had a unique connection to their ancestral homes, and that their knowledge was essential to ensuring the fertility of the land and the people who lived on it. Bantu-speaking leaders thus maintained close ties with the Batwa in order to placate the spirits of the land and ensure the survival of the community.[21] At the site of Obobogo, for example, there is evidence of domesticated plants, ceramic pottery, stone tools, and large rubbish pits that testify to sedentarization by 1500 BCE. However, linguistic evidence suggests that Bantu-speakers arrived in the area one thousand years earlier.[22] This gap is crucial. As Bantu-speakers formed new communities they relied heavily on Batwa hunters and gatherers to survive. Once agriculture became more viable, however, the indigenous peoples had to either fully assimilate into the Bantu communities (losing their language in the process) or continue to live in the forests. Klieman argues that those who took the second choice were considered spiritually powerful, and became the ancestors of the Batwa who still live in the forests of Central Africa today. They stayed in contact with Bantu-speakers and traded items like ivory, medicinal bark, or hunted animals for iron and bananas. This assimilative process became a common cultural thread that continued as Bantu-speakers moved into new regions and as their languages became mutually unintelligible.[23]

A second finding of potentially great significance is the discovery of pearl millet at two sites in southern Cameroon c.400–200 BCE. Today this region is dense rainforest, and cultivating this crop is impossible because it requires an extended dry season for the grain to ripen. But the rainforest today is not the same as it was 2,500 years ago. Pollen records demonstrate that the seasons were more distinct, with the dry season in particular becoming hotter and drier. This changed the forest, reducing the number of large evergreen trees and replacing them with faster-growing and more sun-tolerant species like *trema orientalis*.[24] This "disturbed" rainforest was helpful to farmers in several ways. It enabled the cultivation of high-yield crops like pearl millet, boosted yam production, and was much easier for farmers to clear.[25] It seems that the rainforest was never totally replaced with savanna along this corridor, but it changed enough to enable the cultivation of this valuable grain.[26] The simultaneous arrival of human settlers with ceramic technologies suggests that the millet-growing corridor may have been a path for one group of Bantu migrants.[27] Recent linguistic research using phylogenetic trees strongly supports the existence of this path, which they call the Sangha River Corridor.[28] This may finally settle the question of where the most puzzling Bantu migrations happened—a single migration south along the corridor, followed by another migration eastward across the savannas just to the south of the Congo rainforest.[29]

Another important crop continues to baffle scholars. Bananas were far more productive than yams, were easier to tend, and did not create a suitable environment for *anopheles gambiae*. For scholars who believed the migration was a slow and steady wave, the date of the arrival of bananas was critical. Oliver used 500 CE as a rough estimate, with the banana arriving in East Africa with migrants from Southeast Asia.[30] This remained the scholarly consensus until 1999 when a team of archaeologists led by Christophe Mbida identified a single phytolith from bananas in charred organic matter attached to a piece of pottery. Dating to 840–370 BCE, this was the earliest evidence for the cultivation of bananas. But it was found in Cameroon on the western side of the continent, far from its presumed ancestors in Southeast Asia. Sadly this remains our only find of such antiquity, and this species rarely leaves any trace in the archaeological record.[31] Linguistically, almost all Bantu languages share a common word for plantain (*-konde*), but 5,000 years ago it likely referred to the bark of certain medicinal plants, giving us little indication when Bantu-speakers first encountered the crop.[32] Regardless, we have no idea how plantains first reached the region. They were clearly domesticated in Southeast Asia, and their appearance much earlier than expected in West Africa, without leaving any traces in other parts of the continent, continues to baffle scholars.[33]

Last but not least, iron remains crucial to understanding the Bantu migrations. Iron smelting likely developed separately in two places between 800 and 400 BCE; first, at Taruga on the Adamawa plateau in Nigeria, and second in the Great Lakes region at Rwiyange and Mabuga. From these locations knowledge of iron spread quickly, although this does not prove that people moved along with it. By the last century BCE iron was available virtually everywhere across the Central African rainforests.[34] Loanwords like

(*-(i)o#ndo), meaning "sledgehammer," entered Bantu languages at roughly 400 BCE and gradually spread to the Great Lakes region. A combination of linguistics and archaeological finds reveal early iron was shaped into jewelry, agricultural tools, arrow points, knives, and ceremonial razors.[35] Ehret argues that iron was most important as a trade item and that exchange of this metal triggered a Commercial Revolution in the Congo Basin.[36]

The combination of pearl millet, bananas, and iron transformed the region. Populations in villages grew rapidly, long-distance trade boomed, and empty spaces between communities shrank as newcomers arrived to establish their own communities. Batwa hunter-gatherers who lived alongside the Bantu-speakers generally decided either to adopt this new agricultural lifestyle or to leverage their reputation as first-comers and become forest specialists. As Vansina points out, the delicate balance between centralization and autonomy was an integral part of the Bantu tradition.[37] But the details of the Bantu migration remain vexing. One frustrated scholar compared teaching precolonial Africa to being immersed in thick fog, "most of the time seeing nothing, but hearing, perhaps, an occasional blast of a distant horn or the bell on some unseen buoy."[38] Sadly, little has changed.

Conclusion

Textbooks generally struggle with the Bantu migrations. In place of careful analysis of linguistic, genetic, and archaeological evidence, they show arrows "scything" across the continent in ways that look uncannily similar to maps of world wars. Why anyone was moving and who these migrants encountered is generally left to the reader's imagination. What sticks is that the Bantu migrations were linked to the Agricultural Revolution. This neatly aligns with world history periodization and allows it to become an African example of a larger process. People domesticated crops, smelt metals, and conquered their more primitive adversaries. The outcome seems inevitable.

There are two problems with this narrative. First, it borrows heavily from racialist interpretations of the settlement of Africa. These ideas, popular in the nineteenth century, rested on the assumption that historical change was triggered by the arrival of more racially developed people. When Jared Diamond writes that the Bantu engulfing the Batwa was analogous to British settlers annihilating the Aboriginal Australians, it is painfully clear that this racist perspective remains popular to this day.[39]

Second, this perspective might have some value if it added anything to our understanding of the Bantu migrations. But it does not. The first 2,500 years of diffusion involved the Bantu-speakers settling alongside the indigenous inhabitants of the rainforests. This amicable coexistence was marked by mutual respect, and it is clear that neither the Bantu nor the autochthons possessed a significant technological edge. When millet, bananas, and iron arrived, the Bantu-speakers and the original inhabitants had comingled for so long that they were virtually indistinguishable. Those with ancestral links to the autochthons had the option to join sedentary villages or live as forest specialists who remained an integral part of village life. Either way, knowledge of Bantu languages seems to have gradually supplanted what prior alternatives existed. In all likelihood, this process was entirely peaceful, and involved only small groups of people moving relatively small distances. Less dramatic than the arrow covered map, perhaps, but also more accurate.

Further reading

Ehret, Christopher. *The Civilizations of Africa*, 1st edn. Charlottesville: University of Virginia Press, 2002. A comprehensive history of Africa before 1800 from a leading proponent of integrating archaeological and linguistic data.

Klieman, Kairn. *The Pygmies Were Our Compass*. Portsmouth, NH: Heinemann, 2003. A complete rethinking about the relationship between the Batwa and Bantu-speakers, one that centers on cooperation and exchange.

Mbida, Christophe et al. "Evidence for Banana Cultivation," *Journal of Archaeological Science* 27 (2000): 151–162. An archaeological report that suggests bananas/plantains may have been present in West and Central Africa over 1,000 years earlier than believed.

Robertson, John and Rebecca Bradley. "A New Paradigm." *History in Africa* 27 (2000): 287–323. An important challenge to the entire concept of a Bantu migration, although this approach might only be applicable in the Zambian region where this research was based.

Vansina, Jan. *Paths in the Rainforest*. Madison: University of Wisconsin Press, 1990. A classic account of the Bantu expansion across the basin of the Congo River. Vansina revised his own conclusions in a 1995 article, but his attempts to reconstruct the Bantu cultural landscape using traditions remain vitally significant.

7

Bread and Circuses

In 2012, *The Hunger Games* became a worldwide hit. Set in the fictional nation of Panem, it featured a brutal contest in an opulent Capitol that pitted young "tributes" against one another in a battle to the death. *The Hunger Games* was a clear critique of the modern world's fascination with sport and spectacle. But it also harkened back to ancient Rome, another society that has often been interpreted in a similar fashion. Suzanne Collins made this allusion clear in a number of ways.[1] The name Panem means bread in Latin, the language of Rome's ruling class. The Capitol is a reference to the Capitoline Hill in the ancient city of Rome. And the tributes refer to *tributa*, or taxes, paid by outlying provinces to the Roman capital in exchange for protection. Characters were named after famous Romans, including Cinna, Caesar, Plutarch, Coriolanus, Octavia, Flavia, Seneca, and Cato.[2] Collins weaves ancient Rome, modern America, and a dystopian future together to devastating effect.

The Hunger Games is the latest example of using the Roman past to settle contemporary scores.[3] The term Panem is important, once again, because it was part of a famous line from Juvenal's *Satire*, written at the height of Roman power in 100 CE. Bemoaning what he believed was declining popular interest in performing civic responsibilities, he wrote "already from long ago, from when we sold our vote to no man, the People have abdicated our duties; for the People who once upon a time handed out military command, high civil office, legions—everything, now restrains itself and anxiously hopes for just two things, bread and circuses [*panem et circenses*]" (*Satires* 10.11). Part of why *The Hunger Games* resonated was because of the pressing relevancy of its central narrative—that people could be pacified, at least for a time, through elaborate spectacles. In Rome, these were the gladiatorial combats. In Panem, they were *The Hunger Games*.

But is this an accurate depiction of Roman games? Were they really just a tool to placate the seething masses? Or did they represent something else? In the introduction to *The Roman Triumph*, renowned classicist Mary Beard writes that "the study of the ancient world is as much about *how* we know as *what* we know. It involves an engagement with all the processes of selection, constructive blindness, revolutionary reinterpretation, and willful misinterpretation that together produce the 'facts' ... out of the messy, confusing, and contradictory evidence that survives."[4] Constrained by the limited evidence, historical empathy is crucial as we try to avoid bringing too much of our present into the Roman past.

The lure of the arena

The remainder of this chapter will include what Clifford Geertz called a "thick-description" of the Roman games on the Italian peninsula during the early imperial period. By describing not only the games but also the context in which they took place, we can better understand what they meant to people at that time. Having done this, we can then assess the various scholarly interpretations of the games.

To begin with, we need to examine three key aspects of Roman life that shaped the games: warfare, inequality, and the spread of Roman culture. The Punic Wars, fought between Rome and Carthage, led to an almost constant state of war between 264 and 146 BCE. The eventual triumph of Rome was marked by the brutal sacking of Carthage's capital. The legions, comprised of free farmers known as *assidui*, were responsible for the victories of the Roman republic. But these victories enabled the capture of hundreds of thousands of slaves, and their cheap labor led to the expansion of plantation agriculture at the expense of small-scale farmers. As Michael Crawford claims, "A part-time peasant army conquered the Mediterranean; that conquest then facilitated its destitution."[5] After the frequent civil wars of the first century BCE, roughly 40 percent of the population of the Italian peninsula was enslaved.[6] This made many Romans nervous, and draconian sanctions were applied to any slaves showing a hint of rebelliousness.[7] Nonetheless, major rebellions took place on Sicily from 135 to 132 BCE and from 104 to 100 BCE, and in Capua and Campania from 73 to 71 BCE. The leader of the latter war, the escaped gladiator Spartacus, later became a "symbol of just resistance to oppression."[8]

As Rome conquered additional territory, they often established military garrisons that became permanent. This process, known as "cultural Romanization," can be seen in the North African town of Timgad. Built in the early second century CE, Timgad was a military colony that became a major urban center. At its peak it included "temples, theaters, baths, palatial homes, and a triumphal arch."[9] Towns like this became locations where local elites could learn Latin, mimic Roman culture, and demonstrate their loyalty to the emperor.[10] In many cases, becoming Roman involved attending gladiatorial games.

These spectacles took place on a massive scale. The Roman Colosseum, a magnificent marble stadium and sports arena opened in 80 CE, provided seating for about 50,000 spectators. The floor area (called the *arena*) was designed for gladiatorial games, but it was also the site of elaborate animal hunts, and even mock naval battles. Smaller stadia were located in urban centers across the Roman Empire. While today we may think of large stadiums as "ordinary and normal," nothing similar existed in the contemporary Han dynasty in China, where elites used private hunting parks for their own amusement. Gladiatorial games, by incorporating the public into town life, were a distinctive part of what it meant to be Roman.[11]

Figure 7.1 The interior of the Colosseum in Rome, originally constructed *c.*70 CE. Courtesy of De Agostini via Getty Images.

The first gladiatorial games attested in the sources took place in 264 BCE, and they continued until the collapse of the Roman Empire in 476 CE. Numerous historical changes took place during that time. The most important, and one that had a major impact on the games, took place in 27 BCE when Rome ceased to be a republic with forms (albeit imperfect) of representative rule. Octavian was recognized as *princeps* (first citizen) and granted sweeping new powers. This effectively made him an emperor, and marked the beginning of the Roman Empire. It would endure for another 503 years, and thanks to its more centralized form of rule the games became somewhat different.

Most of our written evidence deals with extravagant or unique spectacles, such as the fourteen days of games held by Commodus in 192 CE.[12] But thankfully the archaeological record offers us an unparalleled glimpse into the daily life of early imperial Rome. The sudden eruption of Mount Vesuvius in 79 CE rapidly covered and preserved the city of Pompeii under layers of volcanic ash. After its rediscovery in 1748 and subsequent excavations, it has offered a snapshot of Roman life.

On one of Pompeii's walls is an inscription that reads as follows:

Twenty pairs of gladiators of D. Lucretius Satrius Valens, priest for life of Nero Caesar, [adopted] son of Augustus [the Emperor Claudius], and ten pairs of

Figure 7.2 The colonnade of the portico of the gladiator's barracks in Pompeii, originally constructed in the first century BCE. Courtesy of De Agostini via Getty Images.

gladiators of his own son D. Lucretius Valens will fight at Pompeii from April 8 to 12. There will also be a proper beast hunt and awnings. Aemilius Celer painted this all by himself by the light of the moon.[13]

While this inscription isn't long or especially detailed, in combination with other evidence it offers a window into a typical day at the Roman games.

The first step to hosting games was to find a patron, known as an *editor*. This individual would be responsible for procuring the gladiators and wild beasts that attracted the crowds. Hosting games had long been a way for the Roman elite to transform private wealth into political capital.[14] During the Republic ambitious individuals like Julius Caesar went deeply into debt in order to sponsor magnificent spectacles. In 22 BCE, three years after the hugely successful private games of P. Servilius, the new emperor Augustus passed legislation giving responsibility for the games to public officials.[15] He seems to have perceived private games as a threat, but also recognized that they were suitable for "performing" imperial rule. In our example from Pompeii, the patron was a priest of the local imperial cult, and thus part of the Roman administration.[16]

The patron would advertise the games ahead of time using a brief painted inscription like the one mentioned above. The final line of the translation indicates that Aemilius Celer painted this at night. This was done deliberately so it would be read by surprised citizens in the morning. Advertising was taken very seriously, and Celer cunningly incorporates his name into the inscription twice—any other patrons would know who to call if they wanted to have their own shows announced![17]

The most important element of the show was the gladiatorial pairings. Lucretius was clearly proud that he had mustered thirty pairs for this spectacle, a large number for games taking place outside the city of Rome. No individual names are included, but elsewhere in Pompeii we find public inscriptions announcing the results of fights.[18] Cicero (*Fam.* 2.8.1) and Ovid (*Ars Am.* 1.167) also mentioned pamphlets with information on the gladiators that were distributed in advance. Spectators and gamblers could buy these to get background information on the specific combatants.

Another absence in this inscription was the introductory parade. Called the *pompa*, it may have been such a common feature that mentioning it was considered unnecessary. Led by the patron, it snaked its way through town to the stadium on the opening day of the spectacle. It offered the audience a chance to express their gratitude for the games, and also to take a look at the gladiators. A bas-relief elsewhere in Pompeii includes a *pompa*, complete with the patron, trumpeters, armorers (likely to ensure the sharpness of the weapons), and arena attendants. Gladiators usually took part as well, and they might even have visited town forums for several days to drum up interest before the games began.[19]

The inscription does provide valuable information about the arena. The indication that the games will take place "under awnings" suggests that Lucretius was a wealthy patron. Hoisted on large wooden mastheads at the top of the amphitheater, they provided shade for the audience during the hot summer months.[20] The stadium in Pompeii was constructed in *c.*70 BCE and a painting of it during riots in 59 CE shows the awnings fully deployed.[21] Lacking the elaborate trapdoors and basement corridors of the more famous Colosseum in Rome, Pompeii's amphitheater still had seating for 22,000. And perhaps surprisingly, the audience "was heavily weighted toward the top half of society." Elite spectators included religious leaders who were ushered to their seats first. Jerry Toner claims that this reflected an imperial fascination with rank and hierarchy. The "well ordered, rigidly arranged crowd was how [the emperor] wanted his empire to be seen."[22] Reflecting their subaltern status, freedmen, slaves, and women were restricted to the upper tiers of amphitheaters, but it is interesting that they were still welcome to attend.[23] Roman amphitheaters always included prominent seating for the patron.[24]

Once the spectators had filed into their seats in the morning, Lucretius's games would have begun with a "proper beast hunt," or *venatio legitima.* The adjective *legitima* was added to confirm to fans that these games were of sufficient quality that they would include animals from across the Roman Empire. Deer, boar, bears, bulls, and large cats were particular favorites. By 79 CE professional arena hunters known as *bestiarii* (heavily armed and closely resembling gladiators) and *venatores* (much more lightly armed and agile) were responsible for killing these animals.[25] For most of the audience, the amphitheater was the only place they would ever see these exotic beasts. Representing imperial control over natural forces and the extent of the patron's connections within the empire, *venatio* became an integral part of the games at approximately the same time that Rome transitioned from republic to empire.[26]

During the heat of the day a lunch break gave the spectators a chance to stretch their legs. Thanks to the awnings, those wishing to keep their seats could stay in the shade and watch the *meridianum spectaculum.* These centered on the execution of condemned criminals, often in elaborately staged productions. Some were killed by carnivorous animals, something which led to agonizingly bloody deaths if the predators cooperated. Other *damnati* might be forced to fight one another with swords, although they were not provided with the armor and shields that protected gladiators. The terrified combatants also lacked the skills of professional gladiators, and elite spectators rarely showed anything but disdain for the participants. Torturing the condemned was common, and being burned alive in a combustible tunic, roasted while sitting in a red-hot iron seat, or torn apart by horses were all considered appropriately painful and humiliating for the victims.[27] One inscription on a Pompeii tomb notes that at games to be held in nearby Cumae "there will be *cruciarii*," a reference to criminals condemned to die by crucifixion.[28] Seneca heaped scorn on the audience, writing "what is the need of defensive armour, or of skill? All these mean delaying death. In the morning they throw men to the lions and the bears; at noon, they throw them to the spectators" (*Ep.* 7.3–4). But it is important to note that the majority of those in the amphitheater with Seneca were quite enthusiastic during the noonday spectacle.

Once the executions had finished the gladiators would take their places and fight in matches that lasted until someone was killed or forced to beg for mercy.[29] They were equipped with different weapons and armor, and at the time of Lucretius's games the most common pairing involved a *secutor* and a *retiarius*. Thanks to the tomb of Aulus Umbricius Scaurus in Pompeii, we have a fresco that includes depictions of this pairing. The focus is on a *retiarius* named Nepimus who wields a trident but has no shield or armor covering his torso. The *secutor* he has defeated is recognizable due to his short sword and distinctive helmet. The latter was made of smooth metal with only two tiny eye holes. It offered complete protection from the *retiarius*'s trident but also severely limited the *secutor*'s field of vision and ability to breathe. The contrast between the light but agile *retiarius* and the heavy but ponderous *secutor* was essential to the drama of this pairing, which usually involved the *secutor* trying to corner and kill the *retiarius* before exhaustion (or the entangling net also carried by the *retiarius* but not pictured in this fresco) reduced his mobility and left him vulnerable.[30]

Cowardice was every bit as dangerous as incompetence in the arena. Death in combat was not uncommon, but in many cases a badly wounded gladiator gave a signal (usually by discarding a weapon or shield) to concede defeat, and appealed to the patron for release, or *missio*. Once the signal had been given the referee would step in and restrain the victor while the patron made his decision. If release was granted, the defeated fighter would leave the amphitheater alive, and popular fighters might receive support from the crowd in the form of a thumbs-down gesture.

Patrons might consider the opinion of the crowd, as Emperor Titus did during an epic match between Priscus and Verus; they were both granted their freedom.[31] But whatever the decision the defeated gladiators were supposed to accept it without hesitation and receive the deathblow from their opponent without flinching. Roman slaves were viewed with extraordinary contempt. Cicero described them as "a talking sort of tool," and displayed more empathy for animals killed in games than gladiators (*Verr.* 2.5.170). Writing later, Florus noted that slaves "are still a type of human being, albeit an inferior type."[32] That people viewed with such contempt could occasionally demonstrate courage and heroism was another essential part of the spectacle.

What were the odds that the gladiators in Lucretius's show would have died? While it is important to keep in mind this is just an estimate, they seem to have been roughly one in six.[33] The odds of surviving were probably better for skilled or veteran gladiators, whose reputations ensured they retained value to their owners even after a defeat. Overall, the average age of death for gladiators was likely in their mid-twenties, although this was hardly unusual for Romans—three in five Romans died before reaching age twenty without ever fighting in the amphitheater.[34] Gladiators received prizes for victories, including palm leaves, laurel crowns, money (usually divided with the gladiator's owner), and the *rudis* that signified they had earned their freedom. Many gladiators who received *rudis* served as trainers or referees at gladiatorial schools, but others continued fighting as freedmen. Famously popular with Roman women and the public more generally, the life of a gladiator had some appeal.

Thanks to our "thick-description" of Roman games, we can now examine some of the ways scholars have interpreted them. Until the twentieth century, the most popular explanation approached the topic from a moral perspective. Ludwig Friedländer, writing in 1890, described the games as an infection "that did not just occupy the masses, for whom they were intended … [they] fascinated all, infected the intellect of Rome, even the highest and most cultured circles, and especially the women … when they drew breath, they breathed in the passion for the circus, the stage, and the arena, 'an original evil begotten in the womb.'" To him, the appearance of noble men and women in the games was a sign of Rome's "decay" and "decadence."[35] Many scholars agreed with this interpretation.[36] It closely replicated the views of elite Romans like Juvenal, who felt that the games were useful for placating the poor, but was deeply uneasy about members of his class who became too enamored with them.

This widely held interpretation was challenged by Keith Hopkins in 1983. His essay "The Murderous Games" argued that these spectacles reflected Rome's origins as a "warrior state." As the conflicts of the republic waned and a lengthy period of internal peace began, the Romans "recreated battlefield conditions for public amusement." Romans became less likely to serve in wars and lost the right to vote, and Hopkins believed the games become a safety valve for social tensions and a martial spirit. Indeed, the amphitheater "provided an arena for popular participation" in Roman politics.[37] While Hopkins's argument was weakened by the obvious popularity of games during the wars of the Republican period, his contention that the arena was a venue for political expression has proven durable. Toner's recent book, for example, argues that "the games sat at the heart of the imperial political process," with Commodus using them as a way to connect directly with the people at the expense of the traditional elite.[38] This is a long way from Friedländer's argument that emperors who loved the games were corrupted by bloodlust.

Hopkins opened the door for more interdisciplinary approaches to the games at the same time that a broader global turn was taking place in historical research. These elements can be seen in the writing of Alison Futrell. She used a cross-cultural anthropological approach that compared gladiatorial combat to similar spectacles in Mesoamerica, and argued that part of the significance of the Roman games lay in their purported origins as human sacrifices.[39] Garrett Fagan's *The Lure of the Arena* took an explicitly psychological approach to explain the attraction of gladiatorial combat to audiences. He noted that being part of the crowd created "sensations of connectedness, validation, purposefulness, agency, and empowerment." The uncertain outcomes of combat also generated excitement comparable to modern sports, and "affective dispositions" encouraged the audience to cheer for the more appealing competitor.[40] He noted that certain contextual factors can help explain the popularity of blood sports in Rome, including slavery, an obsession with hierarchy, and the casual frequency of violence, death, and pain. But he did not believe these were enough to explain the games.[41] Instead he included an entire chapter on blood sports around the world, and argued "what unites all these violent spectacles … is the readiness of people to watch."[42]

But other scholars have eschewed the comparative approach to delve more deeply into the specifically Roman dimensions of the games. Katherine Welch, writing in 2007, focused on archaeological evidence drawn from the amphitheaters themselves. To her, the ancient Romans were too different from us for comparisons to be meaningful, and that focusing on the "contextual factors" that Fagan dismissed is more useful. The specific Roman contempt for competitors and the ways these cultural factors were built into the amphitheater is a fascinating approach to the vexing question of what the games meant to Romans on their own terms rather than in our own.[43] Toner's chapter on "How to Be a Roman" reflects a similar ethos, one that centers on how the games were an ideal medium to deliver messages about what Romans valued, with an emphasis on masculine and military virtue.[44] While there has been a broad global turn in the historiography, specific local factors remained crucial to understanding the games.

Conclusion

Interpreting the past is a complex task, one that requires a detailed understanding of events as well as the possible theories that might help make sense of them. As times change, the ways we make sense of the past are often transformed. This was certainly the case with regard to approaches that prioritized the writings of Roman elites. The "sneering elitism" of Seneca and Juvenal shaped our understanding of gladiators for centuries. Only recently have new approaches developed. One element of this change reflects a willingness to make larger-scale comparisons, and draws on our own obsession with crowds and spectacles. It asks if maybe we are not that unlike the Romans. But as is clear in *The Hunger Games*, this view can ultimately replicate the earlier approach, one that links obsession with spectacle to imperial decline.

The other reflects a desire for a deeper understanding of the Romans on their own terms, one that incorporates a version of their worldview that is constructed from a variety of evidence. Archaeological evidence in particular has allowed us, in tandem with written accounts, to create a "thick-description" of the Roman games. This process of contextualization enables us to use the skill of historical empathy to reconstruct what the games meant in their original context, but as is often the case the evidence can defy easy interpretation.

Further reading

Dunkle, Roger. *Gladiators*. New York: Pearson Longman, 2008. An excellent overview of gladiators and the Roman games.

Fagan, Garrett. *The Lure of the Arena*. New York: Cambridge University Press, 2011. A comparative analysis of the Roman games using social psychology to better understand the spectators.

Futrell, Alison. *Blood in the Arena*. Austin: University of Texas Press, 2001. A reinterpretation of gladiatorial games that focuses on their religious and sacrificial meanings.

Hopkins, Keith. *Death and Renewal*. New York: Cambridge University Press, 1983. A book that aims to uncover what it meant to be Roman, with an influential chapter on gladiators that argued their popularity was due to Rome's militaristic nature.

Toner, Jerry. *The Day Commodus Killed a Rhino*. Baltimore, MD: Johns Hopkins University Press, 2014. A short book that attempts to explain the Roman games through an examination of Commodus's epic spectacle in 192 CE.

Welch, Katherine. *The Roman Amphitheatre*. New York: Cambridge University Press, 2007. This book argues that gladiatorial combats were popular long before the amphitheater became the distinctive monument of the Roman Empire.

8

Veiled Meanings

1979 was a tumultuous year in Iran. In January the Western-backed dictator Mohammed Reza Pahlavi fled the country. In April Iranians voted to establish an Islamic Republic. In December Ayatollah Khomeini became Iran's Supreme Leader. It took less than a year to transform this powerful Middle Eastern state.

Among the iconic images of the protests were photos of women fighting alongside the male revolutionaries. These women often carried guns and wore *chadors*, a long black outer garment that wrapped around the body and head.[1] On the deadliest day of the Iranian Revolution, over 700 women lay among the dead.[2] This was so striking because Iran had been one of the most progressive nations in the Middle East with respect to gender. Women could be found at the highest levels of Mohammed Reza's government, including as cabinet ministers, senators, professors, engineers, and judges. At a grassroots level, roughly 2.5 million girls attended elementary schools. Iranian women were free to wear what they wanted, and despite being a predominantly Muslim nation, veiling was "a real hindrance to climbing the social ladder, a badge of backwardness, and a marker of class. A headscarf, let alone the chador, prejudiced the chances of advancement in work and society."[3]

There were many reasons for women to protest Mohammed Reza's regime, which was corrupt, oppressive, and propped up by its Western allies. It was also not surprising that women who fought to establish an Islamic state did so in traditional dress. However, it is fascinating that when Ayatollah Khomeini issued orders forcing Iranian women to wear veils, they protested in the streets and he was forced to back down.[4] This familiar item of clothing offers an excellent entry point into the procedural concept of progress and decline. To many Westerners, the veil represents Islam's inherent misogyny and backwardness, and removing it is often seen as a step toward women's liberation and, presumably, modernity. But this progressive narrative does not do justice to the complex reasons why Iranian women, and Muslim women more generally, hold such a variety of views of the veil.

Uncovering the truth

To understand the history of veiling and how it has been connected to narratives of progress and decline, we will first need to establish two things. The first is that veiling has never been an exclusively Islamic practice, and was common in Mesopotamian societies long before being adopted by Muslims.[5] The second is that the English word "veiling" conceals the wide variety of terms that refer to specific forms of Islamic head-coverings. These include *chador* (mentioned above), *burqa* (a full-body veil with crocheted eye-holes), *niqab* (a face veil), simple head-scarves, and many more. The closest synonym to the English term "veil" is probably *hijab*, but in Arabic this term is more of a reference to general modesty in women's dress than to a specific item of clothing.[6] For simplicities sake I will use "veil" throughout this chapter unless quoting a source that is more specific.

The historical origins of veiling in the Middle East can be traced back to the thirteenth century BCE, when it was mentioned in an Assyrian legal text. The context suggests that veiling was used as a form of class distinction.[7] Wives and daughters of noblemen had to veil, as did "sacred prostitutes" who had married. But any peasants, unmarried prostitutes, and slaves caught wearing the veil might be flogged, covered in pitch, or have their ears removed.[8] This use of clothing to publicly demonstrate a woman's respectability became common around the Mediterranean world. The Babylonian Talmud stipulated that Jewish women dress modestly, and that those who were married should only reveal their hair in private.[9] The Greeks of the Classical Era practiced almost complete gender segregation, with women restricted to the house for most of their lives. Those women who were forced outside by necessity wrapped themselves in a shawl called *himation*, a cloth wrap that they used to cover their face.[10] These traditions continued under the Romans, the early Christians in Syria and eventually around the Byzantine Empire.[11] They were formally enshrined in the Bible, and the verses below are the basis for many Christian forms of the practice:

> But I want you to know that the head of every man is Christ, the head of woman *is* man, and the head of Christ *is* God. Every man praying or

prophesying, having *his* head covered, dishonors his head. But every woman who prays or prophesies with *her* head uncovered dishonors her head, for that is one and the same as if her head were shaved. For if a woman is not covered, let her also be shorn. But if it is shameful for a woman to be shorn or shaved, let her be covered. For a man indeed ought not to cover *his* head, since he is the image and glory of God; but woman is the glory of man. For man is not from woman, but woman from man. Nor was man created for the woman, but woman for the man. For this reason the woman ought to have *a symbol of* authority on *her* head, because of the angels. (1 Cor. 11:4–11)

The Bible is clear that women should wear head-coverings while worshipping, and is explicit that the reason for this is women's inferiority to man. According to Leila Ahmed, veiling was just one of many "reductive and controlling" patriarchal practices in the region.[12]

The rise of Islam had a variety of impacts on women. Bedouin society prior to the birth of Muhammad may have been "rigidly patriarchal" due to its acceptance of female infanticide and unrestricted polygyny. The Quran's ban on the former practice, its explicit endorsement of marriage only with the woman's consent, and its insistence that wives directly receive and manage the dowries they bring into their families all expanded women's rights.[13] But the patriarchal norms of the Mediterranean world worked their way into Islam as well. The Quranic verse on modesty is worth quoting at length:

Say to the believers, that they cast down their eyes and guard their private parts [*furujahum*]; that is purer for them. God is aware of the things they work. And say to the believing women, that they cast down their eyes and guard their private parts [*furujahunna*], and reveal not their adornment [*zīna*] save such as is outward; and let them cast their veils [*khumur*, sg. *khimar*] over their bosoms [*juyub*], and not reveal their adornment [*zīna*] save to their husbands.[14]

Unlike the Bible, this verse never explicitly requires women to conceal their head or face. The Quran certainly suggests that modesty is a virtue for all believers, but the main distinction between men and women is that women should not reveal their adornment. Defining the term has preoccupied Muslim theologians for centuries.

The reports of the words and actions of Muhammad, or *hadith*, were a crucial part of this process. Compiled in the ninth century CE, the thousands of Sunni *hadith* included a single reference to veiling. Reported only by Abu Dawud almost 200 years after the life of the Prophet, this *hadith* described an

Figure 8.1 A Greek sculpture of a woman veiled in the *himation*. Veiling was common around the Mediterranean Sea long before the rise of Islam. Courtesy of UIG via Getty Images.

encounter between Muhammad and Asma, the daughter of Abu Bakr. She was wearing a transparent gown, and Muhammad supposedly turned away and said "Asma, if a woman reaches the age of menstruation, it is not fit that anything be seen of her except this and this." Abu Dawud reports Muhammad then pointed to his hands and face, and conservative commentators used this to define women's adornments as every other part of her body.[15] Subsequent reinterpretations were even more sweeping. For example, in the thirteenth century the Sunni jurist Ibn al-Jawzi argued that women should also be circumcised, beaten, and forbidden from leaving the home.[16] This reflected a long history of misogyny in the Eastern Mediterranean world and placed severe limits on Muslim women's ability to participate in the public sphere.

So why might a Muslim women choose to veil? The reasons are as diverse as Muslim women themselves, but they can be arranged into a number of categories. The first, prominent during the earliest days of Islam, was safety. The following Quranic verse was revealed to Muhammad in 627 during a series of battles in the city of Medina:

> Prophet, tell your wives, your daughters, and woman believers to make their outer garments [jalabib] hang low over them so as to be recognized and not insulted. God is most forgiving, most merciful.[17]

The context is crucial; Muhammad's supporters were under attack in Medina, and all women were in constant danger of assault and sexual violence. This verse should be understood in this context, one where elite women were at risk and their clothing could be used to signify that they were part of a protected class.[18] Wearing a veil could also offer concealment. A fascinating series of thirteenth century laws in Cairo indicate that the authorities felt a need to repeatedly ban women from wearing male cloaks and headdresses. This example reveals that women used veiling to travel to places supposedly reserved for men.[19] The use of veils for privacy remained an important rationale for the practice much later during the colonial period. Veiling allowed subject women to see without being seen, and to use their invisibility as a weapon that could potentially undermine the state.[20]

The colonial era reshaped perceptions of the veil. Europeans overwhelmingly viewed veiling as an indication that Islam was inherently patriarchal. When the British took control of Egypt in the nineteenth century, the Consul-General Lord Cromer claimed that only by ending veiling and the seclusion of women could Egyptians attain "that elevation of thought and character which should accompany the introduction of Western civilization." However, he was no feminist. Cromer simultaneously curtailed

Egyptian women's access to education, and in Britain he was a founding member of the Men's League for Opposing Women's Suffrage. To Cromer, "feminism directed against white men was to be resisted and suppressed," but in Egypt it could be used as a weapon to enhance colonial control.[21] Frantz Fanon feels the real reason for colonial fascination with the veil was that they believed "unveiling this woman is revealing her beauty; it is baring her secret, breaking her resistance, making her available for adventure."[22]

Colonial calls to remove the veil received support from certain Muslim subjects, especially those with an upper-class background who had spent some time in the West. Qassim Amin, an Egyptian lawyer educated in France, wrote in 1899 that the veil was "a huge barrier between women and her elevation, and consequently, a barrier between the nation and its advance."[23] Amin's argument stemmed from his exposure to Western stereotypes that considered Muslim men inferior and "uncivilized" because their women were veiled.[24] His own views on Muslim women bordered on contempt, and in the same book, he describes them as ignorant, lewd, and obsessed with gossip. By internalizing the contempt for Islam held by men like Cromer, Amin called for the symbolic removal of the veil without ever confronting his own misogyny.[25] It is not a surprise that many Egyptian women questioned the motives behind calls to unveil.

However, some elite women embraced unveiling as part of the anti-colonial movement. Huda Sha'rawi was a famous example. After attending the 1923 International Women's Alliance Conference in Rome, she returned to Egypt and tore off her face veil.[26] This represented the start of a feminist movement among upper- and middle-class urban women in the Middle East. She credited her friend Eugénie Le Brun, a Frenchwoman, with teaching her that "the veil stood in the way of their [Egyptian women's] advancement."[27]

Elite calls to unveil accelerated as Europeanized elites took control of Middle Eastern states. Mustafa Kemal Atatürk, the founder of the first Republic of Turkey, was one example of this top-down approach. In 1925, he made a speech expressing his contempt for traditional Muslim women's clothes, saying "in some places I have seen women who put a piece of cloth or a towel or something like that over their heads to hide their faces ... Gentlemen, can the mothers and daughters of a civilized nation adopt this strange manner, this barbarous posture?"[28] While he did not explicitly make the veil illegal, it was strongly discouraged in all public spaces across Turkey. Women from Turkey gained the right to vote in 1934, a decade earlier than French women, and they were forbidden from wearing veils in Turkish universities.[29] Veils became a symbol of backwardness and women's oppression.

Reza Shah Pahlavi actually did make veiling illegal in Iran in 1936, and women who continued to cover up were harassed in the streets. Women's lives were changed overnight, and those who felt uncomfortable appearing in public without a veil found themselves ironically confined to their homes.[30] For them, the veil was not a symbol of backwardness but a sign of propriety. Other Iranian women were cognizant of this ambiguity, and as they began to occupy more powerful positions in the Shah's state, they focused on reforming other laws that affected women, such as those related to marriage, divorce, and voting rights. Ultimately the ban on veiling was overturned after Reza Shah's death in 1941. Tacit forms of disapproval limited women's ability to wear it, however, and when the Iranian Revolution began in the late 1970s, women seeking to wear veils for religious reasons were joined by others who wore them as a symbol of resistance to the Shah.[31] Forced unveiling, whether performed by a colonial power or an independent state, was (and remains) deeply unsettling for many Muslim women. Understandably, some resisted these policies.[32]

Figure 8.2 Iranian women guard a square in Tehran during the Iranian Revolution in 1979. Courtesy of Hulton via Getty Images.

New enthusiasm for veiling as a political statement developed in the 1960s and 1970s. The crucial event was the defeat of the Arab states by Israel during the Six Days War in 1967. Many Arab men and women from all classes were already skeptical about the headlong rush to embrace European norms. After this war, embracing Islam became a popular way to demonstrate discontent with these secular, modernizing states, and when the Egyptian army destroyed the Bar-Lev line during the month of Ramadan in 1973, its soldiers made very public use of Islamic signs and slogans. One result of this Islamic Movement, as Fadwa El Guindi terms it, was a resurgence of veiling across the Middle East.[33] Religious conservatives leaped at the opportunity, and a new edition of the writings of Al-Jawzi (discussed above) was published in 1981 by religious authorities who were "concerned for the future of Islam."[34] In some cases, this new conservative theology was aided and abetted by Western governments, who were comfortable working with Islamic fundamentalists like the Wahhabis in order to ensure a profitable and stable oil supply.[35] State efforts to forbid women from veiling continued into the 1980s. Baathist Syria actually sent paratroopers into Damascus in 1982 to strip women of their veils at gunpoint, but this was so unpopular that they had to issue a humiliating apology a week later.[36] Across the Middle East, patriarchal rationales for veiling won the day.

Women resisted this wave of religious conservatism. Some did so from an explicitly secular perspective. Mona Eltahawy, an Egyptian civil rights activist during the Arab Spring of 2010–2011, places the blame on a "toxic mix of culture and religion." In a scathing piece for *Foreign Policy*, she writes that "even after these 'revolutions,' all is more or less considered well with the world as long as women are covered up, anchored to the home, denied the simple mobility of getting into their own cars, forced to get permission from men to travel, and unable to marry without a male guardian's blessing—or divorce either." After describing a litany of misogynistic behaviors like sexual harassment, virginity tests, and child marriage across the Middle East, she observes that politics are still dominated by men "stuck in the seventh century ... who believe that mimicking the original ways of the Prophet Muhammad is an appropriate prescription for modern life."[37] Ayaan Hirsi Ali, in her wrenching autobiography *Infidel*, notes that while the West may be "money-grubbing" and "soulless," "there is far worse moral corruption in Islamic countries. In those societies ... women are policed by both the state and by their families whom the state gives the power to rule their lives."[38] In Mogadishu, she found herself torn between two groups of women at her university—one wearing short skirts and high heels and the other wearing the *jilbab* (a long, loose-fitting garment common in Somalia).[39] To Ali, the type of clothing worn by Muslim women symbolized the divide between modernity and backwardness. There are echoes of Huda Sha'rawi in Eltahawy and Ali's uncompromising feminism.

Other women were more willing to work within the Islamic religious context. The experiences of Ziba Mir-Hosseini are instructive in this regard. Writing for *Critical Muslim*, she recalled her despair after returning to Iran in 1980. She had an Anthropology PhD from Cambridge University, but her life abroad led to her being labeled "not a good Muslim" and ineligible for an academic job. Her seemingly liberal husband used their *shari'a* marriage contract to forbid her from leaving the country or getting a divorce. After escaping in 1984, she continued her research and began identifying as "a feminist, an Iranian, and a Muslim." She conducted an ethnography "of the entire edifice of gender inequality in Muslim legal tradition," and concluded that it had no sacred basis. In this way, she argued it was not contradictory to be a feminist and a Muslim. Indeed, she felt that progress toward healthier gender relations required challenging *shari'a* norms "from within," especially through a focus on Quranic verses emphasizing "justice, passion, and equality." Most importantly, she provides a lengthy description of her activist work through *Sisters in Islam* (SIS), a Malaysian-based NGO committed to challenging patriarchy in Islam. She never mentions veiling, and she does not seem to have viewed it as oppressive.[40]

This is likely because religion was not the only cause of renewed enthusiasm for veiling. Its popularity was also driven by the expansion of the Arab middle class and the rise of consumer culture during the 1980s and 1990s. Women sought veils as a symbol of piety or modesty, but unlike clerics they also wanted to be stylish. The result was the creation of the industry of Islamic fashion, one now worth roughly $100 billion annually. The "hijabistas" were able to choose from an incredible array of headscarves, and the veil gained a reputation as a trendy accessory even as it simultaneously demonstrated religious devotion.[41] As Mohja Kahf pointed out, the new veil is "tailored for getting out *into* the modern world, not … retreating from it."[42]

Muslim women adopting the veil during the past twenty years were more likely to have university degrees than any generation before them. And their reasons for veiling went beyond just a political turn to Islam. That is certainly an important part of the context for their actions, but other factors are at play as well. Sahar Amer provides an excellent summary of these reasons:

Thus veiling, far from confining women, as many non-Muslims might hastily assume, instead sometimes allows Muslim women to assert themselves as active individuals and citizens, to compete with men on equal terms in the workforce, and to exercise their human right to a satisfying public and personal life. If veiling is on the rise in Muslim-majority societies today, and it certainly is, it is because for many the veil is a sign of and means to female autonomy.[43]

While many Westerners assume that the veil signifies religious fundamentalism and gendered oppression, this is not necessarily the case. At times, a Muslim woman may consciously decide to adapt the veil for convenience or modesty in ways that are not that dissimilar from a Western woman choosing to wear a wedding ring.

This element of conscious decision-making can be seen in a number of cases of veiling in France. In 1989, three Muslim school children refused to unveil for school, and were expelled for this. The principal cited French laws that made religious displays in public schools illegal, but in the context of growing migration from Muslim nations to France, the veil quickly became a major political issue. Many French politicians seized on the veil as a form of patriarchal oppression brought to France by these migrant communities, even though the girls expelled from school claimed they sought "to distinguish themselves from their parents (who did not veil) and to claim their own identity as Muslims."[44] Eventually a compromise was reached that permitted "light" headscarves, but the debate resumed in 2003, when two Muslim women were expelled from high school for wearing elaborate veils. This debate was especially contentious because their father was an atheist Jew and their mother a Catholic from Algeria. They were not recent arrivals from a Muslim nation or under any parental pressure to wear veils; they were French teenagers exploring aspects of their identity. In the end France passed a draconian new law banning all ostentatious religious displays at school, including Islamic veils, Jewish skullcaps, and large Christian crosses. French Muslims were the true target of this law, however, and France even banned publicly wearing the *burqa* and *niqab* in 2010. Most Europeans assumed the women wearing veils were recent immigrants with misogynistic male relatives, even though many were second-, third-, or even fourth-generation Frenchwomen.[45] Claiming that Muslim women wear veils because of religious fundamentalism dangerously oversimplifies a complex phenomenon.

Conclusion

In 2017, a variety of protests began in Iran. Upset about mandatory veiling, a social media campaign (*#whitewednesdays*) showed women enjoying private moments of freedom from this draconian imposition. This spread to the streets, and during the first five months of 2018 over thirty-five women were arrested. A recording of a female morality police officer harassing a woman for a loose headscarf was seen 3 million times on Instagram, and received over 30,000 comments. Masih Alinejad, one of the coordinators of the *#whitewednesdays* movement, observed that "for forty years they have been saying that it is not the right time to talk about women's rights, but now they cannot control women."[46] In this context it is easy to see unveiling as a symbol of liberation, freedom, and progress.

But as historians, we need to understand the complexity of narratives of progress or decline. In some cases states have tried to use the forcible removal of veils as a tool to justify imperial authority or dictatorial power. The act of unveiling derives its power from the individual agency being exercised by the woman involved, and means nothing in isolation. Likewise, wearing a veil does not necessarily represent religious fanaticism or patriarchal authority. In an atmosphere where simply donning a headscarf can lead to expulsion, like modern French public schools, choosing to wear a veil can be a form of resistance or rebellion. Veiled women are hardly brainwashed or passive, but crafting an identity in which the veil can mean almost anything.

Further reading

Ahmed, Leila. *Women and Gender in Islam*. New Haven, CT: Yale University Press, 1992. A classic study of gender and Islam, with a particular focus on Egypt.
Amer, Sahar. *What Is Veiling?* Chapel Hill: University of North Carolina Press, 2014. This book aims to challenge common misconceptions about veiling, including that it is exclusively Islamic.
El Guindi, Fadwa. *Veil: Modesty, Privacy and Resistance*. New York: Berg, 1999. A provocative book that argues veiling is often a symbol of resistance to colonialism and at times even a feminist statement.
Eltahawy, Mona. "Why Do They Hate Us?" *Foreign Policy* 193 (2012): 64–70. An important account of misogyny in the Middle East written by a Egyptian activist during the Arab Spring.

Heath, Jennifer, ed. *The Veil*. Berkeley: University of California Press, 2008.
   A collection of papers that look at veils as sacred objects, the relationship
   between the veil and the physical body, and the sociopolitical context for
   veiling.

Mernissi, Fatima. *The Veil and the Male Elite*. New York: Basic Books, 1991. A
   Moroccan sociologist argues that the Muslim male elite manipulated sacred
   texts in order to justify oppressive forms of veiling.

9

Going Berserk

On May 26, 2017, Jeremy Christian boarded a MAX train in Portland, Oregon. Seeing two African American women wearing *hijab*, he started yelling obscenities at them. When three men tried to get him to stop, he stabbed them with a knife, killing two and seriously injuring the third. A long-time white supremacist, pictures emerged of him giving a Nazi salute and shouting "Hail Vinland."[1] Anders Behring Breivik, a Nazi sympathizer who massacred 77 people in 2011, "championed the Vikings as heroes of the Aryan race." During the Second World War, Germany sought recruits from Norway for a unit they named the SS Viking division.[2] In the "Urge Overkill" chapter, the white supremacists who claimed Kennewick Man's remains were part of a Norse religious organization called the Asatru Folk Assembly.

White supremacists have a long-standing fascination with the Vikings. For Nazis, they represent a white, non-Christian, warrior race that they believe aligns with Aryan ideals. The Viking raids that were common along the Atlantic coast of Europe throughout the 800s and 900s CE are the best-known example of the Vikings military prowess. For American racists, the Vikings represent a European claim to the Americas due to their landing in Newfoundland *c.*1000 CE. This claim is nonsense since Native Americans clearly settled in the area first, but it remains popular with a subset of white supremacists to this day. After Jeremy Christian's attack, David Perry wrote "As we mourn the martyrs in Portland … we shouldn't ignore the danger that racist appropriation of the medieval past presents. American white supremacists want to make Vinland great again, laying out an imagined past in which Vikings are the rightful conquerors of North America, locked in eternal battle with the Skraelings, the Viking slur for indigenous people."[3] For historians, this was a call for action. But if the Vikings weren't the brutal warriors beloved by white supremacists, then who were they?

The academic community has struggled to offer a coherent answer. After the Second World War, many Scandinavians were embarrassed by the appropriation of the Vikings by Nazi sympathizers. This led historians to create a new image of the Vikings, one that downplayed their martial prowess. Noting that most accounts of Viking raids were written by their victims, Peter Sawyer suggested in a famous 1962 monograph that the attacks were merely "an extension of normal Dark Age activity."[4] In a study of a Viking market in Birka, Wilhelm Holqvist argued "the foremost task of the fleets of armed traders was not to raid or to plunder. It was the very opposite. Their task was to establish and maintain the peaceful exchange of trade. It was the era of the peaceful Vikings."[5]

The Vikings certainly were important players in world history. They connected the Baltic and Black Seas by trade, became early converts to Orthodox Christianity, were the first Europeans to cross the Atlantic Ocean, and established long-lasting settlements on the remote islands of Iceland and Greenland. But in each case there is a link to violence; the trade route between the Baltic and Black Seas was known to Arabs as "the Highway of the Slaves," the Vikings encountered Orthodox Christianity in Constantinople as mercenary bodyguards, their impact on North America was limited by constant conflict with the indigenous peoples, and Iceland and Greenland were settled by migrants fleeing blood feuds. While it is easy to sympathize with historians' desire to reinvent the Vikings as pacifistic, is this image truly representative? And if the warrior narrative was so wrong, why has it persisted to the present day? In this chapter, we will examine changing perceptions of the Vikings. Perhaps the most important historiographical debate about the Vikings is whether they were uniquely violent for their era. And as we investigate this question, we will try to assess the past on its own terms using the skill of historical empathy.

Lost in translation?

Why do we casually assume that the Vikings were uniquely violent people? The answer is embedded in the forms of evidence that survive from this period. The three main types are the medieval chronicles, the Norse sagas and skaldic poetry, and various types of archaeological evidence. The chronicles, usually written by Christian monks who lived in areas targeted for raids, describe the Vikings as barbaric opponents of civilization. The sagas might appear to offer an "insider" view that can correct the image of the Vikings from the chronicles, but they were composed centuries after the events they describe, and were written by Christian converts unfamiliar with Norse religion. And while archaeology can support alternative hypotheses about the Vikings, historians often prefer to rely on written accounts. In many cases, one's perception of the Vikings as either violent raiders or peaceful traders depends on which type of evidence one prioritizes—the biased but fascinating written sources, or the more enigmatic archaeological finds. This ambiguity provides a veneer of legitimacy to the white supremacists' deeply problematic views of Viking history.

Christian chronicles are a key source for historians of eighth to tenth-century Europe. In certain cases they provide only a bare-bones account of events. The famous Anglo-Saxon Chronicle, itself a compilation of nine different manuscripts, is typical in this regard. The first Viking raid is described as follows: "On the sixth day before the Ides of January of the same year [8 January], the miserable raiding of the heathens destroyed God's church on the Isle of Lindisfarne through plundering and murder."[6] Some are more informed than others, with the *Royal Frankish Annals* (741–829 CE) standing out for its sophisticated understanding of events in Denmark.[7] But speaking generally, these documents paint a consistent picture of the Vikings; as heathens who arrived by sea, were extremely skilled in battle, and who committed numerous atrocities. A typical example from the *Annals of St-Vast* describes a series of Viking raids in northern France in 882:

> From there they [the Northmen] devastated with fire and sword the entire kingdom up to the Oise. Defenses were pulled down, monasteries and churches were demolished, and the servants of the [Christian] religion were killed by the sword or by hunger or they were sold abroad, and the inhabitants of the countryside were killed. No one resisted them.[8]

There is no question that the Christian chroniclers viewed the Vikings as an unusually violent people, and there is likewise no doubt that they often attacked key Christian sites. For many alive at the time, the history of this age simply involves compiling when and where the Vikings struck.

But just how significant were these raids? And can we always depend on these accounts? The medieval chroniclers were often guilty of "massively exaggerating" the number of attackers, and may well have deliberately overstated the amount of damage and disruption done by the raids. A closer look at these accounts reveals that the chroniclers had a variety of motives for exaggerating the Norse impact. One example comes to us from the *Annals of St-Bertin*, which describes the church of Saint-Hilaire-le-Grand being destroyed by the Vikings in 863. According to Ademar of Chabannes, this destruction was so complete that Saint-Hilaire was abandoned by the monks who had lived there, and the church was not restored until 937.[9] But this record is problematic for a number of reasons. The first is that we know from other sources that Saint-Hilaire stopped housing monks and became a house of canons sometime before 808. The second is that the charter records of Saint-Hilaire resume in 876 when a man named Adraldus donated land, vineyards, and serfs to the church so that canons could resume living on the site. The region was not left desolate for seventy-five years; the church was rebuilt within fifteen years, and canonical life resumed under the guidance of an abbot. It is possible that Ademar sought to exaggerate the extent of the destruction in order to serve his more personal frustration with what he perceived to be a decline in the area toward inferior canonical observance. To him, Viking raids had triggered this decline, and as a result he may not have believed that the area had recovered from Viking raids until monastic life had resumed.[10] Suggesting that religious life was badly disrupted by the Vikings also glorified Bishop Ebles, a person who may well have been Ademar's close friend. This account seems to have dramatically exaggerated the destruction wrought by the Vikings.

Similar problems with the chronicles come from issues of translation. The Vikings have become synonymous in pop culture today with "raping and pillaging," and the inclusion of lurid scenes of sexual violence in movies and TV shows is often justified on the basis of "historical accuracy."[11] However, the chronicles offer startling little evidence for Viking rape. The *Anglo-Saxon Chronicle* and the writings of Alcuin do not mention rape as a crime committed by the Vikings.[12] Only one Frankish document from the ninth century, written by Adrevald of Fleury, includes an explicit mention of the Vikings committing rape—he writes of "the enslavement of matrons, the ludibria virginium [rape of maidens], and all the monstrous kinds of torment which victors can inflict upon the victims." *Ludibria* is a term that in classical Latin could mean rape, but usually signified mockery. For example, the *Miracula sancti Genulfi* mentions that the Vikings spared "no human being, made no distinction between the divine and the human in their ludibria, destroying holy places, utterly filling everything with burnings and killings." In the Vulgate Bible, Hebrews 11:36 includes *ludibria* as one of the sufferings of the faithful, and it was translated as "mockery." Perhaps the term was simply a way for a prudish religious chronicler to avoid a direct reference to sexual assault, but medieval chroniclers did not hesitate to mention rapes committed by other armies, notably the Franks.[13] Given the context, it is probably more accurate to translate Adrevald's phrase "ludibria virginium" as "abuse of maidens," a phrase that could have a wide range of meanings.[14] The Vikings certainly were involved in raiding, but their current reputation for sexual violence is undeserved.

If problems related to translation and the rhetorical objectives of the authors limit the usefulness of the Christian chronicles, similar issues arise in relation to the sagas and skaldic poetry. The sagas likely originated as oral accounts of heroic deeds that took place in the ninth and tenth centuries, and began to be written down roughly 400 years later. By this point the Viking authors were Christians, but the surviving texts still contain valuable material about earlier times. This includes skaldic poetry, which was often integrated into the sagas. Skalds were hired to recite the deeds of powerful individuals, and gained reputations for their ability to conceal meanings in wordplay, riddles, and alliteration. Given that we encounter skaldic poetry third-hand through Norse saga writers who lived centuries after the events they described, using these sources effectively is a daunting challenge.

These issues manifest themselves in the story of the death of King Ella in Northumbria. According to the *Anglo-Saxon Chronicle*, Ella died defending his kingdom from Viking invaders in 867.[15] Sigvat Thordarson, an Icelandic poet, recounted these events in the eleventh century using the phrase "Ivar [Ragnar's purported son], he who resided in York, caused the eagle to cut Ella's back."[16] The phrase is probably best understood as a literary device used by the original skaldic poet. One way to boast of someone's martial prowess was to say that they fed scavenger birds by killing their enemies. But when the sagas were written centuries later, Icelandic saga authors struggled to translate this line. They began to interpret it as "Ivar, he who resided in York, cut the eagle on Ella's back." While this is grammatically possible, it makes no sense in context. Nonetheless, saga writers went to great imaginative lengths to explain it. First they wrote that Ivar cut an image of an eagle in Ella's back, allegedly because Ella had executed his father (the legendary Ragnar Lodbrok) in a snake pit. This created an exciting story and narrative arc, but it was a literal representation of an abstract verse. In the fourteenth century another saga author stretched this image further by labeling this the "blood-eagle," a form of torture where the shape of an eagle was carved in the victim's back, his ribs severed from his backbone, and then his lungs slowly pulled from his body.[17] While it is common knowledge among academics that the "blood-eagle" is a fiction created by saga authors writing at least 500 years after the events they describe, it remains a staple of pop culture, and was featured in a recent episode of the TV show *The Vikings*.[18]

Another example of supposed Viking ferocity stems from the sagas, and again, problems with translating skaldic verse seem to have been responsible. At issue are the Viking berserkers. In the saga of Ynglings, for example, berserkers form Odin's supernatural army. They are as crazy as dogs or wolves, bite their shields as they go into battle, and go into a frenzy of killing.[19] The Lewis Chessmen, carved in twelfth-century Scotland, depict a berserker. Describing this piece, Neil MacGregor writes that "berserker is an Icelandic word for a soldier wearing a shirt made of bearskin, and the word 'berserk' even today is synonymous with wild, destructive violence. More than any piece on this [chess] board, the berserkers take us to the terrifying world of Norse warfare."[20] On the surface this explanation is compelling, and again contributes to the image of the Vikings as uniquely ferocious warriors.

But only one contemporary source mentions berserkers. All other examples, including the sagas and the Lewis Chessmen, were created hundreds of years later. The original reference is a poem to Harald Finehair which describes the Battle of Hafrsfjord with the phrase "bear-shirts [berserkir] bellowed … wolf-skins howled."[21] The original intent of the skaldic author was likely to find an artful way of stating that Harald's

Figure 9.1 Norse chessman found on the Isle of Lewis, Scotland, *c.* twelfth century CE. The figure in the center biting his shield is a berserker, a ferocious, elite, and possibly mythical type of Viking warrior. Courtesy of Hulton via Getty Images.

warriors wore chain-mail shirts. But to later saga writers, these fierce warriors wearing bear-shirts and wolf-skins were a source of fascination. Perhaps they were unable to fully appreciate the skald's intent, and so they used the term to refer to elite, pagan warriors from Norway's pre-Christian past. This invention captured the imagination of saga readers, and ultimately found its way into the English lexicon despite its dubious factual basis.

So if the Vikings were not the raping berserkers of today's popular culture, then who were they? Starting in the 1960s, many archaeologists argued that the Vikings were far more interested in trade than raids. In 1999, a Viking hoard containing 14,295 coins was found on the island of Gotland. Despite its location in the middle of the Baltic Sea, the vast majority of these coins came from Persia, the oasis cities of Central Asia, and the Abbasid Caliphate. This hoard is only one of many and archaeologists have found over 80,000 Arab dirhams on Gotland alone.[22] The much smaller Vale of York hoard, hidden by a Viking in northern England, also contained numerous coins from these regions.[23] Excavations at the important market town of Hedeby, founded in 811 on the site of the current city of Schleswig in northern Germany, reveal the extent of these trade networks. Merchants from the south would bring valuable trade items like silk, silver, brass, jewelry, amber, and iron, and exchange them for northern products like fur, woven textiles, walrus ivory, Norwegian soapstone, and reindeer antlers.[24] Viking culture was similarly vibrant—beautiful wood carving found in the Oseberg burial attests to their skills as artisans, and the content of the sagas suggests that women exercised a degree of control over their lives "unparalleled in any other European literature."[25] More recently, scholars have pointed out that the Vikings were extremely hygienic, stylish dressers, and skilled craftsmen. The Vikings, they contend, can best be understood as "a settled and remarkably civilized people who integrated into community life and joined the property-owning classes."[26]

This new, "politically correct" Viking has itself generated a scholarly counter-reaction. Much of the archaeological evidence cited above contains eerie echoes of the significance of combat to Viking life. Since coins were generally not used for commercial transactions in the Viking world, it is most likely that they were acquired through looting, or as tribute from foreign rulers terrified of Viking raids.[27] The Vale of York hoard not only contains coins but also a stunning silver cup that was likely looted from a monastery in Europe. Raiding these types of artifacts may well have stimulated the European economy (by bringing inert silver into circulation), but it also reflects the scale of Viking violence.[28]

Figure 9.2 Byzantine and Islamic coins found in Sweden, dating to the eleventh century CE. These coins may have been used in trade, but they also may have been part of diplomatic payments, ransoms, or pay for mercenaries. Courtesy of Werner Forman/UIG via Getty Images.

This combination of trading and raiding is evident throughout the historical record. Another important find at the market of Hedeby was an iron lock, using to bind the fetters of slaves who were another crucial trade good available there. Indeed, the Vikings enslaved so many Slavic-speaking peoples that this became the origin of the word in the English language today.[29] Elite burials like the one that took place on the Oseberg ship almost certainly involved human sacrifices, as described by Ibn Fadlan.[30] And while artifacts like the Inchmarnock Hostage Stone seem to depict Viking men with remarkably stylish haircuts, they are pictured in the process of capturing monks and looting a sacred relic.[31] While it is fair to say that the Vikings were not unusually cruel killers depicted in the chronicles, they were also not gentle traders and craftsmen with elegant hipster beards. As Jonathan Jarrett points out on his popular blog, "they were all of these things!"[32]

Conclusion

Reconstructing the past is extremely difficult, especially when the information we have is extremely partial. With the Vikings, this has enabled the rapid spread of interpretations that are not based on compelling evidence. The Christian chroniclers, despising the "pagan" peoples who looted their religious centers with such ease, demonized them. These crimes grew with the telling, and ultimately fueled an image of the Vikings as a vicious people. The authors of the sagas did little to counter this image, and earlier Christian stereotypes influenced the way these sources were interpreted. The result was that particularly nasty forms of violence represented by the berserkers and the "blood-eagle" entered the popular lexicon despite having a flimsy factual base.

The Second World War made the violent image of the Vikings less tenable. The Nazi takeover of Norway and Denmark revealed that the Vikings had great appeal to white supremacists as exemplars of the Aryan race, and this led to a reevaluation of just who the Vikings were. Conscious that the written sources contained significant biases, archaeologists became convinced that the Vikings were being unjustly maligned, and could be better understood as cosmopolitan traders.[33] Their focus on elements of material culture provided a compelling response to white supremacists' continuing fascination with the Vikings, one linked to the hate crimes of Anders Breivik and Jeremy Christian. However, at times well-meaning academics may have strayed too far in the opposite direction, minimizing Viking involvement in warfare to the point that they ceased to resemble their past selves.

Understanding the past without importing contemporary perceptions is extremely difficult. The chronicles, sagas, and archaeological record are all extremely complex, and there are no simple answers when trying to determine whether the Vikings were a uniquely violent people. But as historians, it is important to be aware of how the types of evidence we use might be shaped by the assumptions of those who compiled them or the repetition of earlier errors. This is the key to historical empathy—assessing the past on its own terms so as to more accurately represent what it means in the present.

Further reading

Brown, Nancy. *The Far Traveler*. New York: Harcourt, 2007. A fascinating reconstruction of the life of Gudrid that is based on the author's collaborations with academic specialists.

Coupland, Simon. "The Vikings on the Continent in Myth and History." *History* 88 (2003): 186–203. This article argues that the Vikings reputation for violence may have been exaggerated by hostile chroniclers.

Grierson, Philip. "Commerce in the Dark Ages." In *Transactions of the Royal Historical Society*, 5th Series, vol. 9 (London: Cambridge University Press, 1959), 123–140. An article, often overlooked by world historians, that suggests the presence of foreign coins and luxury goods in the medieval period is not proof of the existence of long-distance trade.

Sawyer, Peter. *The Age of the Vikings*, 2nd edn. London: Edward Arnold, 1972. An overview of the Vikings from a leader in the field, with excellent sections on their raids and the reasons for them.

Somerville, Angus and R. Andrew McDonald, eds. *The Viking Age: A Reader*. Toronto: University of Toronto Press, 2010. An extraordinary compilation of primary sources from the Viking Age.

Winroth, Anders. *The Age of the Vikings*. Princeton, NJ: Princeton University Press, 2014. A thematic overview of the history of the Vikings, with particular emphasis on their cultural contributions and legacy.

10

This Island Earth

"It took courage to write this book, and it will take courage to read it." So begins Erich von Däniken's classic *Chariots of the Gods? Unsolved Mysteries of the Past*. In this bestselling manifesto, he argues that extraterrestrial space travelers visited the ancient world, mated with the primate inhabitants, and in the process created *homo sapiens*. As evidence he claims that "there is something unusual about our archaeology!" Whether it is the Piri Reis map, the Nazca lines, the pyramids in Egypt, or the rust-proof iron pillar in Delhi, he suggests that they cannot be explained through conventional means. Using his vivid imagination as a guide, he argues that alien relics are buried beneath Earth's ancient monuments, relics which are capable of vastly improving our understanding of space travel.[1]

Needless to say, Däniken's book is a mess. The evidence is entirely subjective, and relies on the reader seeing a 1960s astronaut in a piece of Mayan art, to give one example. But, focused as he is on "unsolved mysteries of the past," Däniken is an excellent guide to the aspects of history that defy easy explanation. And he devotes an entire chapter to Easter Island, also known as Rapa Nui.[2]

Located 2,200 miles from South America and 1,300 miles from the nearest inhabited island, Rapa Nui is one of the most isolated places on earth. Formed by three dormant volcanoes, it sits alone in the middle of the Pacific Ocean, its grassy surface a stark contrast to the lush jungles typical of most Polynesian islands. When Jacob Roggeveen, a Dutch explorer, spotted it on Easter Sunday in 1722, he was shocked to discover that it was already inhabited by a small number of people. Even more shocking was the condition of their canoes, which he described as "bad and frail ... and very leaky." They looked inadequate for a simple fishing trip, let alone the two and a half week sea voyage necessary to reach this place. How had these people settled Rapa Nui?

Figure 10.1 Erich von Däniken presents at Alien-Con 2018 in Baltimore, Maryland. He argued that an alien visit to Rapa Nui led to the creation of the *moai*. His theories are ridiculed by the academic community, but they remain very popular with non-specialists. Courtesy of Riccardo Savi via Getty Images.

This mystery was compounded by the baffling presence of almost 1,000 massive stone statues called *moai*. Roggeveen wrote, "The stone images at first caused us to be struck with astonishment, because we could not comprehend how it was possible that these people, who are devoid of thick heavy timber for making any machines, as well as strong ropes, nevertheless had been able to erect such images, which were fully 30 ft high and thick in proportion."[3] Perhaps if the island supported a large population the number of *moai* would not have been as shocking, but only two thousand people lived there at the time of Roggeveen's visit.

To Däniken, the *moai* could not have been constructed by the indigenous population. Deriding what he calls the "heave-ho" method of construction, he argues the more likely explanation stemmed from an oral tradition that claimed the island was visited by flying men who landed and lit fires. This he connected to the legend of Viracocha, the god of creation in Tiwanaku on the South American mainland. Viracocha and his two assistants were known as the "sons of the gods," and had "instructed mankind in all kinds of arts and then disappeared."[4] Locals perceived them to be gods, but Däniken believes that the three visitors were actually extraterrestrials.

Figure 10.2 A surviving example of a *moai*, located on Rapa Nui (Easter Island). How these massive stone sculptures were carved and erected continues to generate historical debate to this day. Courtesy of Robert Nickelsberg/The LIFE Images Collection via Getty Images.

To recap, Däniken argues that the *moai* of Rapa Nui are so extraordinary that only alien "gods" could have built them. And while Däniken is a terrible archaeologist, he has sold over 70 million books worldwide. Are *moai* this incomprehensible? And what really happened on Rapa Nui? The best explanations involve no aliens, but they offer insight into a crucial skill for any historian; how we assess the question of progress and decline.

Rapa Nui as metaphor

Rapa Nui is a part of most world history narratives, but significant differences exist over basic facts like the first date of human settlement. Some scholars argue that Polynesian sailors reached the island as early as *c.*400 CE, but the earliest incontrovertible archaeological evidence of human beings dates to *c.*1100 CE. This chronological gap is of vital significance when it comes to understanding what we can learn from Rapa Nui's ecological decline. Rapa Nui is usually presented as a cautionary tale, one that reveals the destructive consequences of humanity's thirst for power and glory. The era of *moai* construction, which took place between *c.*1100 and 1500 CE, is described as a golden age, but one that "placed tremendous pressure on the island's resources."[5] One consequence of this was deforestation, which stripped the island of the large palm trees necessary to build *moai* or ocean-going ships.[6] Now completely isolated, the inhabitants then fought a series of destructive wars from 1500 to 1600 CE, wars marked by numerous atrocities, the disintegration of society, and even cannibalism as the food supply collapsed.[7] The message is made crystal clear on the Big History Project website, where Easter Island is discussed in a section on the future entitled "Overconsumption."[8] If we don't change our ways, the argument goes, we could end up like the residents of Easter Island, struggling to survive on a tiny habitable space stripped of its most precious resources.

The narrative is an excellent example of progress and decline. It begins with the stunning exploration and settlement of the island by Polynesian sailors, the establishment of a flourishing society from 1100 to 1500 CE, and then a sharp decline around 1600. This decline continued through the eighteenth and nineteenth centuries due to European conquest and disease. This closely mirrors the specialist literature on the subject, but it is worth looking at certain key areas of disagreement to show how our understanding of Rapa Nui has evolved over time.

The most influential figure in bringing Rapa Nui into the global consciousness was Thor Heyerdahl, a Norwegian archaeologist. He was originally fascinated by animal migrations in Polynesia, but developed an interest in the diffusion of human beings as well. After visiting Rapa Nui, he became convinced that the masonry and artistic styles originated in South America. The delicately shaped sea wall of Ahu Vinapu, in particular, was singled-out for its similarities to Incan masonry.[9] He felt that traces of this Incan visit could be found in oral traditions of a conflict between "Long Ears" and "Short Ears" gathered in the early twentieth century. Heyerdahl believed the light-skinned South American "Long Ears" (so named for an Incan tradition of distending their earlobes) arrived *c.*400 CE and colonized the island. They were responsible for designing and coordinating the construction of the *moai*, although the labor was performed by a group of Polynesian "Short Ears." Heyerdahl suggests these darker-skinned migrants might have been captured, enslaved, and forcibly brought to the island by the "Long Ears." However, the "Short Ears" annihilated the "Long Ears" at Poike in a massive rebellion known as "The AD 1680 Event," and the political institutions and masonry skill of the South Americans disappeared with them. The people Roggeveen met on Rapa Nui in 1722 were the descendants of the "Short Ears"—primitive, struggling to survive, and isolated.[10]

Heyerdahl's thesis garnered attention because of his unorthodox methods. Seeking to demonstrate that a voyage from South America to Polynesia was possible, in 1947 he built a balsawood raft based on technologies available in the early first millennium CE and headed out to sea. He reached the Tuamotus 101 days after leaving Peru, proving that such a voyage would have been possible.[11] He had a film crew accompany him on the voyage, and footage of it was seen by millions of people. When he arrived he noted that the locals believed his ship closely resembled those used by their distant ancestors for ocean voyages.[12]

The academic consensus about Heyerdahl is that he "was never taken seriously by scholars."[13] But he also shaped how countless people understand the history of Rapa Nui. First, the raft was named after the god of creation in the ancient state of Tiwanaku, Kon-Tiki Viracocha.[14] This is the same flying god identified by Däniken as bringing civilization to the residents of Easter Island. And second, the idea that the region experienced a collapse, as expressed in "The AD 1680 Event", became an integral part of the region's historical narrative. Heyerdahl based his account on oral traditions of a battle at Poike trench, confirmed by a single radiocarbon date that roughly corresponded with genealogical research on one of the purported participants.[15]

But Heyerdahl forced researchers to question some of their assumptions about the settlement of Easter Island. The culmination of these studies was John Flenley and Paul Bahn's *The Enigmas of Easter Island*, which was explicitly written to counter Heyerdahl and Däniken.[16] Flenley and Bahn were particularly keen to disprove the persistent notion that Rapa Nui had been settled by South Americans. For example, they were not convinced that "Long Ears" and "Short Ears" were synonymous with South American and Polynesian ancestry. The terms used in Heyerdahl's oral traditions, *Hanau Eepe* and *Hanau Momoko*, were probably better translated as "heavy-set" and "slender," suggesting that the conflict may have been oriented around class rather than race.[17] They also noted that the *Kon-Tiki* voyage might not have been a convincing replica of past migrations. Heyerdahl had to be towed fifty miles out to sea before he started drifting in order to avoid the Peru Coastal Current, which would otherwise make travel west very difficult. Even the presence of a sail was out of character with the coastal ships of pre-colonial South America. To the best of our knowledge, most were small rafts propelled by paddles. The Polynesians, on the other hand, were skilled navigators with a long and well-documented history of open-ocean sailing and exploration. Occam's razor suggested it was far more likely that Rapa Nui was settled by them.[18]

This was an important correction, but Flenley and Bahn also made certain claims that were problematic. Using a combination of glottochronology, genealogy, and radiocarbon dating, they believed that the island was likely settled sometime around 400 CE. This was primarily based on a single radiocarbon date, again found by Heyerdahl, which no other archaeologists could replicate. Even more alarming was that Heyerdahl's sample was a piece of charcoal. Since the rings of a tree are older in the center and younger on the edges, this creates something called an "old wood" problem that renders radiocarbon dates wildly inaccurate. The other methods Flenley and Bahn used to confirm the arrival of humans *c.*400 CE were even more prone to error.[19]

This early date shapes how they understand the relative progress and decline of the island. Flenley and Bahn argue that humans may have arrived *c.*400 CE, but the first evidence of human impact on the environment (possible forest clearance in the Rano Kau crater) begins at least 400 years later. The implication is that this was a golden age of appropriate care for the environment that lasted until deforestation began in 1400, when changing pollen profiles reveal it escalated dramatically. This is the start of Rapa Nui's decline. By 1640, the last forest had been cut. After this point, Catherine Orliac observes that islanders began using twigs or smaller brush for cooking fires.[20] Why were the forests cleared? Firewood was one important use, but Flenley and Bahn also argue that palms were cut to build canoes, rafts, and sledges for transporting the *moai*, most of which were erected between 1250 and 1500 CE.[21] They describe this "building-mania" as "a compulsion that became a little insane," and believe that focusing on this led to a neglect of basic subsistence needs. In the end, "the islanders brought disaster upon themselves."[22]

With its resources exhausted, Flenley and Bahn argue that Rapa Nui was swept by a loss of faith, general famine, warfare, and economic collapse. They then made an important conceptual leap by arguing that Rapa Nui is "a microcosm of our own world."[23] Writing at a time when fears about climate change had reached a feverish pitch, Flenley and Bahn's bleak argument was taken further by the prominent public intellectual Jared Diamond. In *Collapse*, he suggested that building the *moai* and their platforms was the cause of Rapa Nui's environmental crisis. Like Flenley and Bahn, he placed the blame squarely on the Polynesian inhabitants, at one point asking "what did the Easter Islander who cut down the last palm tree say while he was doing it?"[24] To Diamond, the inhabitants of Rapa Nui refused to make the cultural changes needed to save the environment. Instead, they committed ecocide. The parallels to the modern world were "chillingly obvious."

But this narrative has not gone unchallenged, and emphasizing different pieces of evidence yields a very different story. Research by Terry Hunt and Carl Lipo suggests that the inhabitants of the island were excellent stewards of their environment, but found their efforts undone by circumstances beyond their control. A key part of this new narrative is the date when human beings arrived. At Anakena Beach, which according to legend was the original landing point of the Polynesians, Hunt and Lipo identified the oldest layer of human occupation and unearthed numerous small artifacts— small fragments of obsidian, fish and animal bones, and charcoal. But to their surprise, these items dated to roughly 1200 CE, hundreds of years later than the dates cited by Flenley and Bahn. This inspired them to reassess the carbon-dated material that was "proof" of human settlement prior to that date. They excluded charcoal, since varying ages in a single piece can be difficult to accurately date, and marine samples, since aquatic life often absorbs dissolved carbon dioxide that can distort results. The result was no conclusive evidence of humans on Rapa Nui prior to 1200.[25]

This was groundbreaking. Flenley and Bahn argued that humans lived in harmony with the environment for hundreds of years before deforestation began. Hunt and Lipo suggested this golden age never existed. Instead, deforestation began immediately after human beings arrived. Sediment cores reveal that in c.1200 CE the palm forest entered a decline, grasslands began to expand, and soil erosion became a problem on the slopes of Rano Raraku. Daniel Mann's team concluded that human-initiated deforestation was underway by 1250, and was complete by 1650.[26] Catherine Orliac's charcoal analysis confirms this narrative, with grass, ferns, and sweet potato vines replacing forest products in cooking fires by 1650.[27]

Hunt and Lipo were not convinced that deforestation was entirely fueled by human beings. Research on the Hawaiian island of Oahu suggested that palm forests could be destroyed by *rattus exulans*, or the Polynesian rat.[28] These rats were passengers on Polynesian outrigger canoes and may have been brought to the island deliberately as a food source. Upon reaching Rapa Nui, however, they suddenly had access to virtually unlimited food in the form of palm nuts, and aside from humans were not in danger from major predators. Under these conditions they would have been capable of explosive population growth, with their population doubling every forty-seven days. Within two years, Rapa Nui was likely home to millions of Polynesian rats. On Oahu the variety of terrain and microclimates ensured some trees survived. On Rapa Nui, which is much smaller, the limited diversity of plant life ensured the impact of rats was far more dramatic. Gnawing on the palm nuts rendered them sterile, preventing the regeneration of the forest and resulting in its slow but inevitable decline. Flenley and Bahn were given a handful of palm nuts and successfully identified them as *jubaea chilensis*.[29] They also correctly observed that the gnaw marks readily observable on the nuts were created by the Polynesian rat.[30] But in their conclusion, they focused on intentional human activity. Hunt and Lipo, in contrast, argue that the impact of the rat could never have been anticipated. Deforestation had natural causes.

What if our understanding of Rapa Nui is entirely backwards? If humans arrived later and, due to rats, the forests began shrinking almost immediately, how did they eke out a living on the desolate slopes of the island? The same evidence cited above suggests the population peaked in 1350 at about 3,000 inhabitants. Slowing population growth and then a gentle demographic decline in the face of a changing environment makes sense, but it raises a variety of new questions. How did they grow food on the island? Where does "The AD 1680 Event" come from if there was not a critical shortage of resources? And most importantly, how did this small group of people ever raise the almost 1,000 *moai* that still dot the island today?

Unlike most of Polynesia, Rapa Nui does not have a barrier reef, and the Polynesians do not seem to have brought any domesticated animals larger than a chicken. But when Europeans first arrived in the eighteenth century, they observed a variety of crops being grown, including banana, taro, sugarcane, and sweet potato. Given the harsh winds that send tiny droplets of salt water miles inland, keeping these crops alive was extremely difficult. One way islanders sought to protect the plants, especially when they were vulnerable saplings, was by constructing *manavai*. These were small enclosed pens made of stone, and over 2,300 have been identified today, enclosing almost 10 percent of the island's surface area.[31]

Another innovation was lithic mulching. Practiced by many ancient societies situated in arid lands, this involves placing stones on the ground alongside plants as they grow. This makes walking in the fields very difficult, but it has numerous beneficial impacts. First, it generates turbulent airflow over the garden, which helps moderate temperatures. Second, it offers some protection from direct winds. And third, the rocks used for mulching release minerals into the soil.[32] This is critical on Rapa Nui since its soils have always been extremely unproductive.

Of course, if the islanders solved their subsistence crisis through these kinds of innovations, why do we see a spike in conflict around 1680? Here the question needs to be handled with care. Certainly conflict on an island like this existed, and oral traditions recount a battle of the "Short Ears" versus the "Long Ears" at Poike—"The AD 1680 Event." Flenley and Bahn were skeptical that any battle took place at that location due to a lack of physical evidence, in particular the obsidian blades known as *mataa* that became very common just before the arrival of Europeans. They did, however, believe that the increasing use of weapons and the decision of many people to live in caves were indications that violence became a major problem by the seventeenth century.[33] In this way they reproduce Heyerdahl's general narrative even as they disprove key aspects of his theory.

But looking at *mataa*, it is hard to see them as a product of a warlike society. They are crudely-hewn and asymmetrical flakes of obsidian that possess sharp edges. The lack of balance and heavy weight renders them useless as projectiles, and the lack of a sharp point makes them unlikely stabbing weapons. The wear patterns on the "blades" reveal that they were primarily used to cut and scrape plants. In the type of Hobbesian environment described by Heyerdahl, one would expect designers to rapidly identify and then develop efficient weapons. The design of the *mataa* suggests that this never happened on Rapa Nui. A person could certainly use a *mataa* to defend themselves, but they were not efficient weapons of war.[34]

Last but not least, if the population never expanded to 15,000 or even 30,000 as Diamond hypothesizes, then how were the inhabitants ever able to construct so many massive *moai*?[35] We generally assume that ancient works of monumental architecture were a product of hierarchical societies. When the *moai* were discovered, this led to speculation that an ancient monarch had directed their construction, ordering thousands to carve and drag stones across an island in his honor. But again, the evidence for this is extremely weak. The use of large numbers of laborers make sense if the statues were pulled on sleds made of wood, as Jo Anne Van Tilburg suggests, and this fits neatly with the ecocide theory—by constructing massive monuments, they were inadvertently denuding the island of its most valuable resource.[36] The more we learn about the statues, the less sense this makes. Roads designed to move sculptures have been mapped all over the island, and they do not show any sign of being centrally planned. Dragging statues across these roads has been tried on many occasions, including by Heyerdahl in 1955, but it was extremely slow and laborious. More promising was an attempt by a Czech engineer named Pavel Pavel who saw Heyerdahl's films in 1986. He came up with the refrigerator method, a technique that involved two groups of people with ropes, one pulling the statue onto its side edge, and then the other pulling that side forward. It resembled more of a waddle than a walk, but islanders confirmed they had songs for moving statues. Most importantly, Pavel and sixteen other people were able to easily move a twelve ton *moai*.[37]

If Pavel's method is correct, the construction of the *moai* never required a large number of slaves, or the deforestation of the island, or an elusive visit by a flying alien sun-god. Instead, it only required cooperation between neighboring families. Rather than being the product of a spectacular rise and a subsequent fall, it is possible the *moai* were simply the religious symbols of people living in a difficult environment, one impoverished by the depredations of the Polynesian rat. Arguing that these people are a textbook example of "Overconsumption," as the Big History Project does, seems very uncharitable.

Only 155 islanders lived on Rapa Nui by 1882. But this collapse is much easier to explain. After Roggeveen, European sailors became regular visitors to the island, and they brought with them venereal diseases that devastated local women's fertility. The men became targets for blackbirding, a practice that involved kidnapping and enslaving them in order to acquire labor for the guano mines off the coast of Peru. Of the 1,500 men captured this way, only 12 ever returned to Rapa Nui. Hunger, suicide, and tuberculosis struck those who remained, and in the nineteenth century Jean-Baptiste Dutrou-Bornier essentially turned the island into a giant sheep farm. His propensity for kidnapping and raping young women eventually led to his murder, but an English company retained control of the island and its sheep until the mid-twentieth century. They even constructed walls around the main town and forbade the inhabitants from leaving unless they were employees. European missionaries, fearful that their rebellious flock might return to their old gods, seem to have either emphasized or even created stories of cannibalism in Rapa Nui's past.[38] Shifting our focus to the nineteenth and twentieth centuries reveals a story that looks less like ecocide and more like genocide. Such is the importance of accurately identifying the causes of Rapa Nui's decline.

Conclusion

Assessing the moral lessons of the past is tricky, and requires the historian to exercise judgment on what they see. Rapa Nui is fascinating precisely because we may have gotten it so wrong. Flenley and Bahn were aware of virtually all the evidence of human creativity I have described above—the *manavai*, lithic mulching, and the Polynesian rat were all discussed in their conclusions. But to them, Rapa Nui's past was a warning about environmental exploitation leading to collapse. Relying on a timeline that suggested humans lived in harmony with the island for hundreds of years, they could argue that a combination of population growth and monument building triggered a decline. But even small changes to this story, like later human settlement, a reduced population, and a better understanding of how the *moai* were built, force us to dramatically reconsider what we can learn from Rapa Nui.

Progress and decline is a subtle skill. Diamond angrily writes that there is "resistance among both islanders and scholars to acknowledging the reality of self-inflicted environmental damage before Roggeveen's arrival."[39] But this is deeply misleading. Why do we need to force the evidence to imply that the islanders were voracious overconsumers when there is abundant proof, even from the history of Rapa Nui, that people of European descent were far guiltier of this sin? By changing the area of emphasis, historians can shape the lessons we learn from the past.

Further reading

Däniken, Erich von. *Chariots of the Gods?* New York: G.P. Putnam's, 1970. Not recommended for its factual basis, but this book provides a window into the vast popularity of conspiracy theories that historians find themselves debunking.

Diamond, Jared. *Collapse*. New York: Viking, 2005. A bestselling monograph that argues overconsumption has driven numerous societies to damage their environments and commit ecocide.

Flenley, John and Paul Bahn. *The Enigmas of Easter Island*. Oxford: Oxford University Press, 2003. The scholarly basis for Diamond's thesis, this book includes a wide range of archaeological evidence and reaches a similar conclusion.

Hunt, Terry and Carl Lipo. *The Statues That Walked*. Berkeley, CA: Counterpoint, 2012. A vital monograph that challenges the ecocide narrative, preferring to view the inhabitants of Rapa Nui as careful stewards of their environment.

McAnany, Patricia and Norman Yoffee, eds. *Beyond Collapse*. New York: Cambridge University Press, 2009. A compilation of essays by historians, archaeologists, and anthropologists that aim to offer more complex explanations than Diamond as to why societies fail.

11

Supreme Sacrifice

In 2015, a team of archaeologists working in Mexico City made a chilling discovery. Thirty-five human skulls, mortared together on the inside edge of a circle, were unearthed beneath a colonial-era house. The careful placement of the skulls and their location close to the Mexica temple complex known as the *Templo Mayor* suggested that the archaeologists had found a *tzompantli*, or a skull rack. The Spanish conquistador Andrés de Tapia described one in his account of the battle of Tenochtitlan (1521 CE), and claimed that it held over 136,000 human skulls.[1] Raùl Barrera Rodríguez, director of the INAH Urban Archaeological Team, observed that "there are 35 skulls that we can see, but ... as we continue to dig, the number is going to rise a lot."[2] By 2017, 676 skulls had been uncovered but the lower rings of the *tzompantli* still remained hidden.[3] This was by far the most detailed evidence of the scale of the Mexica practice of ritualized human sacrifice.

When conquistadors reached the New World, they often provided lurid descriptions of sacrificial rituals performed by the inhabitants. In a letter to King Charles V, Hernán Cortés wrote the following about the island of Cozumel:

> They have another horrible and abominable custom, worthy of being punished, worse than anything seen elsewhere. When they want to ask for something from their idols, for greater efficacy and to ensure acceptance of their petition, they take many girls and boys, and also older men and women, and in the presence of their idols, they open their chests and take out their hearts and entrails, burning these [organs] and offering the smoke as a sacrifice. A few of us have seen this [ceremony] and say it is the most terrible and horrifying thing that can ever be witnessed.[4]

Speculating about the larger context, Cortés suggested three to four thousand people were sacrificed annually in that region alone. But

Figure 11.1 Anthropologists working with the National Institute of Anthropology and History examine skulls unearthed at the Templo Mayor in 2017. Courtesy of Anadolu Agency via Getty Images.

historians have long been troubled by the context in which Cortés wrote. His letter proposed the region be placed under control of the Spanish Crown in order to facilitate conversion of these "barbarous" peoples. Cortés then asked for titles and money "so that those of us who are here in your service may be favored and benefit [from the endeavor]."[5] Human sacrifice represented a justification for conquest and colonization, one that seemed a little too convenient. After all, first encounters with different cultures lead to misunderstandings even in the best of circumstances. How far could anyone trust these accounts?

The discovery of the *tzompantli* in 2015 was just one of many twists and turns in this debate, a debate oriented around the reliability of sources and how we use evidence. As we will see, numerous interpretations of human sacrifice in the New World have been proposed, from the suggestion that it helped overcome an acute dietary deficiency to the contention that it did not happen at all. This chapter will examine these arguments, and try to show students the different types of evidence historians use to support them.

Meaningful sacrifices?

The encounter between the Old and New Worlds, generally associated with Christopher Columbus and his voyage in 1492, is one of history's most intriguing moments. European explorers were stunned to discover societies flourishing in places unmentioned in the Bible, and Native Americans were similarly fascinated by the bizarre men who arrived from across the sea. All world history textbooks discuss this moment in depth, and as a result the Mexica receive a disproportionate amount of coverage. Human sacrifice, as one of the key justifications for European conquest, is universally discussed. But there are problems that stem from long-standing misconceptions that have wormed their way into the public consciousness. One lies in the term Aztec. According to myth this name was only used until Huitzilopochtli changed it to Mexica in the eleventh century CE.[6] By the time they became a powerful empire hundreds of years later, they were known as the Mexica, were speakers of Nahua languages, and were members of numerous *altepetl*, a term that refers to something akin to a city-state. Another problem lies in the misidentification of Cortés's extremely important translator as Malinche. This was a Nahuatl term of respect at the time, but its meanings have shifted. She is more accurately called Doña Marina or Malintzin, a Nahua effort to pronounce her baptismal name (this language lacked an "r" sound) combined with the honorific *-tzin*.[7] These are not grievous errors, but they reflect the power of earlier misconceptions about the Mexica. This is important to keep in mind in terms of evidence for human sacrifice as well.

During this encounter, it became clear that blood sacrifice was an important aspect of Mexica religious practices. Mexica cosmology posited that the world had been destroyed four times before, and was currently in the midst of a fifth "sun." A powerful noble named Tlacaelel (1398–1480 CE) transformed this cosmology by crediting the god of war, Huitzilopochtli, with keeping the fifth sun in the sky. Humans could aid Huitzilopochtli in this task through blood sacrifice, which Tlacaelel believed contained sacred energy. Only by acquiring numerous captives for sacrifice could the end of the world be averted.[8] While this may seem brutal, an important caveat is that "we can also point to numerous societies in Africa, Asia, and Europe that at one time or another either slaughtered innocents to appease the powers of the universe or performed gruesome public executions on an appalling scale."[9] Indeed, one scholar estimates that the English executed twice as many people as the Mexica did at their peak, in many cases at spectacles attended by thousands.[10]

How should scholars interpret human sacrifice among the Mexica? The key issue lies in the sources and how they are interpreted. This debate originated immediately after the fall of Tenochtitlan in 1521 and continues to this day. Two conquistadors, Hernán Cortés and Bernal Díaz, wrote lengthy accounts of their role in the defeat of the Mexica, and in the process provided us with compelling written evidence of human sacrifice. The following was written by Díaz:

> Again there was sounded the dismal drum of Huichilobos [Huitzilopochtli] … and we all looked towards the lofty Cue where they were being sounded, and saw that our comrades whom they had captured when they defeated Cortes were being carried by force up the steps, and they were taking them to be sacrificed. When they got them up to a small square in front of the oratory, where their accursed idols are kept, we saw them place plumes on the heads of many of them and with things like fans they forced them to dance before Huichilobos, and after they had danced they immediately placed them on their backs on some rather narrow stones which had been prepped as places for sacrifice, and with stone knives they sawed open their chests and drew out their palpitating hearts and offered them to the idols that were there, and they kicked the bodies down the steps, and Indian butchers who were waiting below cut off the arms and feet and flayed the skin off the faces, and prepared it afterwards like glove leather with the beards on, and kept those for festivals when they celebrated drunken orgies, and the flesh they ate in chilmole.[11]

There were reasons to be skeptical of this vivid account. Díaz claimed to have witnessed this event after being driven off the causeways to Tenochtitlan due to fierce Mexica resistance. But this places him on the shores of Lake Texcoco, over three miles from the *Templo Mayor*. Without being in the temple complex itself, it was unlikely he could see or hear anything, and scholars who believe the scale of Mexica human sacrifice has been exaggerated point to this inconsistency.[12] Díaz's account is also part of a text known as a *probanza*. This was a written account that highlighted an individual's service to the Spanish Crown in hopes of receiving lands, titles, or pensions.[13] In this context, men like Díaz had ample reason to emphasize atrocities committed by their enemies without necessarily understanding what they were seeing. As the nineteenth-century American ethnographer Lewis Henry Morgan argued, Mexica society was a mystery to conquistadors, and they "invoked the imagination to supply whatever was necessary to fill out the picture."[14]

One website aiming to challenge cultural myths about ancient Americans suggests that historians read the accounts of Cortés and Díaz at face value, which allows these texts to become the lens through which Mexica culture is understood. The result is circular logic that uses racial stereotypes to reproduce the findings of the conquistadors:

> 1. The Spaniards, along with christianized Natives claimed that human sacrifice existed. 2. Such claims are eagerly accepted without ever questioning the motives of the Spaniards. 3. Archeaologists [*sic*] assume that human sacrifice took place, and whenever they discover human remains, they credit their findings to sacrifice. 4. The works of such archeologists are published, reinforcing the myth of human sacrifice. Such writings are then blindly accepted as fact, based on historical "evidence," such as ... ... 1. The Spaniards, along with christianized Natives claimed that human sacrifice existed ... etc., etc.[15]

Part of the reason for skepticism about human sacrifice is the absence of bodies. If, as one Dominican chronicler claimed, as many as 80,000 people were sacrificed during the consecration of the renovated *Templo Mayor* in 1487, shouldn't there be ample archaeological evidence confirming this massacre?[16] One world history textbook observes that only 126 skeletons have been found at the *Templo Mayor* in Tenochtitlan, which "encourage doubts about the magnitude of human sacrifices in temple ceremonies."[17] Perhaps Mexica sacrifice was simply an invention of Spaniards eager to justify their own atrocities, including the appalling murder of over 20,000 people during the Cholula Massacre.[18]

Historiographically, the accuracy of the primary sources represents a key divide. Although there are reasons to question certain events described by the conquistadors, the majority of scholars would argue that human sacrifice was an extremely significant element of Mesoamerican life prior to the arrival of Europeans. The combination of written records and archaeological evidence is too compelling to discard, and on certain religious issues the latter has been used to confirm the former.[19] This has led to an extraordinary range of explanations for Mexica sacrifices which revolve around the perceived underlying causes as well as the sources used.

Early historians did tend to rely heavily on the conquistador's written accounts, and this often led to harsh assessments of the Mexica. William Prescott, writing in the nineteenth century, claimed that "the influence of these practices on the Aztec character was as disastrous as might have been expected ... bloody rites of sacrifice steeled the heart against human sympathy, and begat a thirst for carnage ... The whole nation, from the peasant to the prince, bowed their necks to the worst kind of tyranny—that of blind fanaticism."[20] Prescott's Mexica were despotic, bloodthirsty, and barbaric, a reflection of how his most important sources, the conquistadors, had portrayed them three centuries earlier.

Many scholars, especially in the 1980s and early 1990s, preferred to rely on instrumental explanations for Mexica sacrifices. They argued that victims were produced in wars, and that warfare was either a cause or consequence of human sacrifice. In this way, the sacrifices were "rational," in the sense that they fit into a larger imperial project. The most striking example of this was a 1977 article by Michael Harner, who argued that a scarcity of animal protein in the New World led to the extraordinary scale of human sacrifice among the Mexica. The lack of large domesticated mammals generated environmental pressures that made it possible to "understand and respect" their religious focus on ritual cannibalism as a response to material conditions. In this way, Harner argued that "the Aztecs were unique among the world's states in having a cannibal empire."[21]

While Harner's aim might have been admirable, his argument was not. Both domesticated turkeys and dogs were common sources of meat, and Harner's reading of Spanish sources like Cortés, Tapia, and Díaz was much too credulous.[22] While the Mexica likely did consume pieces of certain sacrificial victims, as Sahagún indicates, this was only done during specific religious ceremonies and usually involved pieces weighing less than half an ounce. One critic noted that Harner also wrote during the protein diet craze of the 1970s, a time when many nutritionists believed large quantities of meat were essential to good health.[23] As an explanation for human sacrifice, Harner's argument fell short.

Another explanation comes from Geoffrey Conrad and Arthur Demarest. In *Religion and Empire*, they go beyond Harner's cultural determinism to argue that religious ideology was crucial at generating Mexica expansion. Relying heavily on Diego Durán's account of Aztec history, Conrad and Demarest argue that Itzcoatl and Tlacaelel transformed Mexica ideology to emphasize the role of Huitzilopochtli, the god of war who demanded large numbers of human sacrifices in order to stave off the end of the world. This shift in cosmology led to incessant warfare to acquire captives, and thus contributed to Mexica expansion.[24] According to this theory, human sacrifice predated the origins of the Mexica, but the decision to emphasize those rituals was made in order to justify continuous conquest and expansion.[25] Sacrifice provided a rationale for warfare, but it was a widely accepted religious practice as well.

This intermingling of religion and politics was not universally accepted. Ross Hassig, for example, argued that the main goal of Mexica warfare was the acquisition of captives who were sacrificed to intimidate other potential rivals. This stems from his perception, shared by many Americans during the late Cold War, that the ideal way to maintain an empire was through deterrence as opposed to combat. To Hassig, the Mexica used the threat of a horrible death on the *Templo Mayor* as a very public method of minimizing resistance and ensuring the timely delivery of tribute. They were clearly aware of the impact of these ceremonies on potential adversaries. For example, Durán noted that they invited several neighboring monarchs to attend a massive sacrifice of captives acquired during war with the Huaxtecs. These monarchs returned home "filled with astonishment and fright," and the Aztecs believed "they had intimidated the whole world."[26] Hassig argued that "Aztec practices were as rational as those of any other society," with their focus on indirect rule over neighbors sustained by the perception of power.[27] Human sacrifice was crucial to the success of this form of empire-building.

John Ingham takes this one step further. While acknowledging that human sacrifice enabled the Mexica to sustain an empire, he directed attention to the internal workings of society. Arguing that tribute demands against commoners often amounted to everything not necessary for survival, he suggested that sacrifice helped avert resistance and rebellion, including among ordinary Mexica. Ingham cites Mexica mythology as an example, with the defeat of Quetzalcoatl by Tezcatlipoca reflecting the subordination of artisans to the warrior-nobility.[28] The elite warrior-nobles were required to fight with courage in battle, but in exchange their social status was considered divinely ordained. This was reproduced during sacrificial feasts, where the majority of the victims were slaves. To Ingham, "gods and nobles alike consumed the labor, production, and even the bodies of common people."[29]

These instrumental approaches suggested that Mexica society was not so different from our own. Using sacrifice as an imperial ideology, as a form of deterrence, or as a justification for a hierarchical society resonates precisely because we can see parallels with our own world. Even if we do not participate in human sacrifice today, we can readily comprehend how a vicious ideology might legitimate empire. However, these accounts generally relied heavily on Durán, a Dominican friar who likely spent over forty years in the New World and was a fluent Nahuatl speaker. He was an outsider who believed Mexica religion was inspired by the devil, and does not seem to have involved his informants closely in the writing process (unlike

Sahagún). Perhaps in the process of translating these concepts into Spanish, Durán emphasized elements that were most readily comprehensible to him—namely, the instrumental aspects.[30]

It is possible that, by assuming the Mexica viewed the world just like us, we end up misrepresenting the past. More recent scholarship suggests that it might be wiser to privilege the Mexica religious meanings of these sacrifices through the use of more challenging sources. These include pictorial representations, archaeological evidence, and reading with the archival grain in order to capture hints of Mexica sentiment in documents mediated by Spanish or Christian eyes. We can see the way new approaches to evidence shape new interpretations in the writings of Inga Clendinnen, David Carrasco, and Ximena Chávez Balderas.

Inga Clendinnen provides an intriguing example of this approach. She relies primarily on the work of Bernardino de Sahagún, a Franciscan missionary who arrived in New Spain in 1529. He created a team of assistants fluent in Spanish, Latin, and Nahuatl and interviewed surviving Mexica about their pre-colonial cultural life. Thanks to the *Florentine Codex* (discovered in 1979), Clendinnen was able to use Sahagún to uncover how ordinary Mexica understood the elaborate ceremonies described in post-Conquest texts.[31] An example of this comes from the way human flesh was often juxtaposed with maize meal. During the festival of Huey Tozoztli, for example, women made a thick maize meal and presented it to the priests. When warm "it spread shining, it spread scintillating; it was gleaming with heat … and when it had cooled, when it was cold, when it had thickened, when it lay in place, it spread contracting, it spread quivering." Clendinnen argues that this reflected a "parallel transformation" between maize and human flesh, one which the ceremony explored through the application of heat.[32]

Another example is the festival of Panquetzaliztli, which was dedicated to Huitzilopochtli. On some occasions a captive would be required to impersonate this god before being sacrificed, but at this event Huitzilopochtli's representation was made of seed-dough. After "killing" this figure with an arrow, the emperor Moctezuma consumed the pierced "heart" himself. The "bones" were distributed among the warriors, and by eating the seed-dough they became slaves to Huitzilopochtli for the subsequent year. Representations of gods were known as *ixiptlas*, and while some were humans trained as impersonators, many were constructed of dough, stone, or other organic materials. The fact that this material was not human flesh did nothing to diminish the sacredness of the *ixiptlas*, and consuming

Figure 11.2 A page from the Florentine Codex, a bilingual (Spanish and Nahuatl) history of New Spain compiled by Fray Bernardino de Sahagún (1499–1590). Courtesy of De Agostini via Getty Images.

seed-dough *ixiptlas* possessed the eater as powerfully as consuming human flesh.[33] Rather than think of these rituals as a "primitive technology" used to achieve political or economic ends, it might be more accurate to think about their sacred and aesthetic properties.

A similar approach informs David Carrasco, who argues that the Mexica sense of self can be found in its purest essence in the images of the *Codex Mendoza*. This was compiled by Mexica artists in the 1540s at the direction of the Viceroy of New Spain, Don Antonio de Mendoza, and included numerous depictions of historical events, tribute payment, and day-to-day life.[34] One moment depicted in great detail was the New Fire Ceremony. Every fifty-two years, the solar (365 day) and divinatory (260 day) calendars of the Mexica aligned. The five days leading up to this were a time of widespread trepidation as all fires were extinguished, hearthstones thrown away, and houses swept clean. A procession of deity impersonators left Tenochtitlan bound for the Hill of the Star, including Xiuhtlamin, a "well-born" captive dressed to resemble Quetzalcoatl and Tlaloc. After carefully observing the motion of the stars, the priests then killed him and started a fire on his chest. Once the fire had begun, the heart of Xiuhtlamin was cast into the flames, and this new fire was then brought back to the *Templo Mayor*. Runners then distributed the sacred flames across the entire empire, first to the temples in each community, and from there to schools and neighborhoods.[35]

Symbolizing victory over never-ending night, this was an important ritual in cosmological terms. But the redistribution of the sacred fire when it was brought from the *Templo Mayor* to the rest of the empire suggested something else—that it was a performance calculated to reinforce the position of Tenochtitlan as the ritual center of the universe.[36] He cites Paul Wheatley, who argued that ancient urban centers were places where people "strove to bring the human social order into coordination and harmony with the divine society of the gods."[37] The *Templo Mayor*, the center of Mexica religious and political power, represented the apex of this alignment, and the importance of this is emphasized in the images of the *Codex Mendoza*.

Finally, the recently discovered *tzompantli* (described in the introduction to this chapter) enabled scholars to gain new insights into the victims at the *Templo Mayor*. An osteobiographical analysis conducted by Ximena Chávez Balderas reveals that most skeletal remains did not contain evidence of battlefield injuries, suggesting that few of those sacrificed were warrior-captives. The presence of large numbers of women (25 percent of all remains, while a further 19 percent could not be determined) reinforced this point. The large numbers of children buried at the *Templo Mayor*, including forty-two dedicated to Tlaloc, the god of rain, indicate that these ceremonies were often focused on rituals to ensure abundant rainfall for crops.[38] Genetic analysis of the remains has thus far been inconclusive, but it may soon be possible to trace the origins of victims, something which might reveal how many were purchased or captured on the fringes of the Mexica Empire. Regardless, new technologies combined with fresh interpretations enabled scholars to rethink what we know about Mexica sacrifices. The findings of Chávez Balderas, for example, suggest that scholars had exaggerated the importance of warfare as either a cause or a consequence of human sacrifice.

Conclusion

The scale of Mexica human sacrifice has long beggared the imagination. Whether it was the 136,000 skulls on the *tzompantli* described by Tapia or the 80,000 lives Durán claimed were sacrificed to inaugurate the *Templo Mayor*, the descriptions left academics struggling for explanations. Some denied they were accurate, and pointed to the small number of human remains and the obvious flaws with the accounts produced by conquistadors. But the recent uncovering of a major *tzompantli* suggests human sacrifice was an integral part of Mexica society, and took place on an astonishingly large scale. New evidence has once again helped move our understanding of the past forward.

Where do we go from here? Clendinnen, reflecting on the scale of Mexica brutalities, writes that it threatens the vision "of an ultimately common humanity."[39] Is this true? How should we try to make sense of Mexica rituals that led to the death of thousands? One path lies in an instrumentalist approach. This allows scholars to argue that human sacrifices were not a mark of barbarism, but rather a system that enabled the Mexica to justify imperial expansion or acquire tribute in an economical fashion. Another path acknowledges the brutality of Mexica sacrifices while also contextualizing them through comparisons to lynching, public executions, witchcraft trials, or even the gladiatorial combats described in an earlier chapter. As Chávez Balderas points out, the political and religious aspects of human sacrifice went "hand in hand." Thanks to the archaeological evidence being unearthed at the *Templo Mayor*, it is possible to acquire incredibly detailed information about the sacrificial victims.[40] How they died, where they were from, and what was done to them after their deaths are all questions that we are just beginning to answer, and in tandem with the problematic but still valuable eyewitness accounts, better understandings of Mexica society seem to be within our grasp.

Further reading

Balderas, Ximena Chávez. "Sacrifice at the Templo Mayor of Tenochtitlan and Its Role in Regard to Warfare." In *Embattled Bodies, Embattled Places*, edited by Andrew Scherer and John Verano. Washington, DC: Dumbarton Oaks Research Library and Collection, 2014. Part of a lavishly illustrated volume on war in pre-Colombian Mesoamerica, the author presents a detailed account of the human remains at the *Templo Mayor*.

Carrasco, David. *City of Sacrifice*. Boston, MA: Beacon Press, 1999. An investigation into the meanings that human sacrifice held for the Mexica, one that prioritizes the spiritual over the instrumental.

Clendinnen, Inga. *Aztecs*. New York: Cambridge University Press, 1991. A fascinating book that uses Sahagún to better understand how ordinary Mexica understood religious rituals.

Restall, Matthew. *Seven Myths of the Spanish Conquest*. New York: Oxford University Press, 2003. A wonderful synthesis of the major problems with popular understandings of the Spanish conquest of the Americas.

Townsend, Camilla. *Malintzin's Choices: An Indian Woman in the Conquest of Mexico*. Albuquerque: University of New Mexico Press, 2006. A biography of this controversial figure that aims to humanize her despite the limited range of extant sources.

12

Orunmila Saves

In 1959, Fidel Castro's rebels ousted Cuban President Fulgencio Baptista. As Castro drew closer to the Eastern Bloc, many Cuban families fled the country, usually settling around Miami. Numbering in the hundreds of thousands, these refugees transformed southern Florida with their unique cultures, cuisines, and in some cases, religious practices. While the majority of the migrants were Catholic, a significant minority practiced Santería, or "the way of the saints." Throughout the 1960s and '70s, Santería expanded rapidly. *Santeros* and *santeras*, the "priests" of this order, established small shops called *botánicas* to sell devotional items, herbs, and other things necessary for sacrifices. Worshippers created organized orders, like the Church of the Lukumi Babalú-Ayé which was founded in 1973 in the city of Hialeah.

Long persecuted in Cuba, Santería was usually practiced in the shadows. But in 1987, the Church of the Lukumi Babalú-Ayé purchased a property where it was hoped they could openly practice their faith. This alarmed members of Hialeah's city council who held an emergency session and passed a resolution declaring that "certain religions may propose to engage in practices which are inconsistent with public morals, peace or safety."[1] More directly, the chaplain of the Police Department stated at the public meeting "that Santeria was a sin, 'foolishness,' 'an abomination to the Lord,' and the worship of 'demons.'"[2] After the city council passed a series of resolutions making it illegal to sacrifice animals within city limits, the church leader sued the city. This case ultimately made its way to the Supreme Court, which found in favor of the church and established an important precedent protecting forms of religious expression.

The city council's contempt for Santería was not unusual. The Vodou faith of Haiti, which shares much of its cosmology with Santería, has long been dismissed as demon-worship. Speaking on the "700 Club" television show after the devastating 2010 Haitian earthquake claimed at least 100,000 lives, Pat Robertson argued that Vodou was responsible. Referring to the Bois Caïmen ceremony held to coordinate a major slave rebellion in 1791, Robertson stated "they were under the heel of the French. You know, Napoleon III and whatever. And they got together and swore a pact to the devil. They said, 'We will serve you if you will get us free from the French.' True story. And so, the devil said, 'OK, it's a deal.'"[3]

This contempt reflects more widely held prejudices. Some historians still divide religions into two categories; the first includes smaller-scale faiths focused on salvation as a material, worldly issue, and the second comprises the so-called "world religions" that consider salvation only in the here-after. The former, which are commonly polytheistic, tend to be viewed as static and unchanging, doomed to be replaced by more dynamic monotheistic faiths. The result is that religions seem to move naturally through stages from "naturalism" to "polytheism" to "monotheism" in ways that mimic the old Western Civilizations paradigm of "tribes" to "states" to "civilizations." This is a major problem with world history narratives that emphasize "growing complexity" over time. The unfortunate message that students receive is that polytheisms are ancient, unchanging, and doomed to fail. The triumph of a monotheistic God who "cares deeply about his creation and continually uplifts his people in body spirit" over polytheistic spirits who "behave unpredictably and indifferently" seems almost inevitable.[4]

This chapter will argue that this is a tragic mistake. The best example is orisa worship, a polytheistic faith that originated in West Africa and subsequently spread around the world in syncretic forms as Santería in Cuba, Vodou in Haiti, Shango in Trinidad, and Candomblé in Brazil. While some might assume that orisa worship would be doomed by closer contact with world religions, it has moved from strength to strength. By better understanding the specific histories of polytheistic faiths, we can also begin to understand why they are a significant part of world history.

The history of orisa worship

Why is orisa worship worth studying? I would argue that it is significant to world history for three main reasons. The first is the easiest to demonstrate—its global scale. Variants of orisa worship are practiced across the Americas as well as West Africa, and the total number of practitioners may be as high as 75 million people.[5] Even if this is an overestimate, there is no question that the number of orisa worshippers today dwarfs that of other major world religions addressed in most world history classes, including Jainism, Sikhism, Judaism, and Zoroastrianism. If orisa worship has spread around the world, has millions of followers, and continues to be active to this day, why should it be ignored while much more obscure faiths receive extensive coverage?

Second, orisa worship has a dynamic history that can teach us a great deal about religious change more generally. This point is much more complicated than the first, and will require some knowledge of what orisa worship is and how it has been practiced over the years. So what exactly does orisa worship entail? In essence, it involves venerating Olodumare as a distant creator god through approximately 400 lesser divinities known as orisas. According to this creation myth, Olodumare created the orisas and then decided to create the earth. Obatala, the father of all orisas, was initially given this task, but became distracted after he drank palm wine. Odudwa noticed this and finished the act of creation at Ile-Ife, a town that became sacred to the Yoruba. The earliest orisas, including Orunmila, Sango, Esu, and Ogun, were then sent to the earth to prevent the newly created humans from falling into chaos.[6] Since the orisas were believed to play an active role in people's day-to-day life, sacrifices were made to them to ensure specific, material aims. In this way a hunter might have appealed to Ogun to ensure a successful hunt, while a woman seeking a successful pregnancy would have approached Osun, the orisa linked to fertility. Sacrifices to most orisas did not require the expertise of a priest (known as a *babalawo*), just a shrine and appropriate items. *Babalawo* likely played a pragmatic role as healers, and used chants to activate the powers of an extraordinary array of medicinal plants. Many of the earliest *babalawo* were women.[7]

The key characteristic of early orisa worship was its diversity. Different orisas came to be associated with different towns, and since this did not happen simultaneously everywhere it led to considerable overlap in their functions. For example, orisas linked to rivers included Yemoja (in the west of Yorubaland), Osun (in the center-east), and Oya (in the north). Even Sango, whose name was given to this religion in Trinidad, was initially only active in the area around Oyo.[8] J.D.Y. Peel goes so far as to argue that the diversity of the orisas makes it impossible to speak about a unified Yoruba traditional religion prior to the nineteenth century.

The historical origins of orisa worship remain shrouded in mystery. Cornelius Adepegba noted that the worship of Ogun may have begun with the introduction of iron working into the region, and archaeological finds indicate this took place as early as the second century CE.[9] Ogun's connection to hunting dogs and woven palm fronds also seems indicative of a time that predates the widespread adoption of agriculture and cotton cultivation. Certain orisas like Sango, the god of lightning, likely originated much later. The leather wallet and gourd rattle associated with his shrine are all specific to the city of Old Oyo, where an overbearing king named Sango ruled in the sixteenth century CE. It seems likely that he was deified after his death, and worship of Sango subsequently spread across the region.[10] As new orisas appeared and received veneration, a wide range of neighboring peoples adopted them into their own pantheons, including the Edo, Ewe, Akan, Igbo, and Fon.[11]

Sango worship developed at the same time that another major shift in orisa worship was taking place. This was the emergence of Ifa, a system of divination. According to its origin story, Ifa was linked to Orunmila, who was the only orisa to make the appropriate sacrifices to Olodumare before leaving for earth. Orunmila then became the vessel for divine knowledge which was comprised of a corpus of sacred verses (called *odu*), songs, and proverbs. Divination based on this involved a trained priest who tossed the *ikin* (16 palm kernel nuts) on a divination tray. Once the priest connected the pattern to one of the 256 *odus*, they used this to determine the supplicant's destiny.[12] Ifa priests spent years training to memorize and correctly pronounce the various combinations of *odu*. As they traveled around West Africa training new initiates, they brought their language with them.[13]

Brenner dates the genesis of Ifa divination to the fifteenth or sixteenth century, approximately the same time that Islam arrived in the region.[14] The first Muslims were called *imale* in the Yoruba language, presumably after the Islamic state of Mali, and their relations with orisa worshippers seem to have been amicable.[15] The creation of the Ifa divination system likely stems from cross-pollination between orisa worship and an Islamic form of divination called *khatt ar-raml*.[16] Ifa's insistence on Olodumare (the Supreme God) as its source, its base-16 system of divination (common in West Asian religions), and references to Islam in the Ifa corpus all stem from these close links. Sometimes Ifa diviners would even recommend that clients become Muslims.[17] But this interaction was not one-sided. The ritual utterances of Yoruba imams today, such as "Olorun gba," (god receives), echo the words of *babalawo* ("orisa gba," or the deity receives) during a sacrifice.[18] Orisa worship remained a ubiquitous part of Yoruba daily life, and in 1855 one Muslim preacher reportedly said that "Muslims should accommodate some form of Yoruba religious rites."[19] H.O Danmolé goes so far as to claim that Islam was "domesticated" in Yorubaland.[20]

Contact with the Atlantic World was less amiable. Yoruba slaves were sold in vast numbers out of Lagos and Dahomey. And while they would be present in Saint-Domingue during the 1791 slave rebellion, they would arrive in even greater numbers in Cuba in the early to mid-nineteenth century. Enslaved Yorubas brought their religious practices with them, but they lacked sufficient ritual leaders to maintain the diversity of orisa at home. For this reason they joined different forms of orisa worship together in one practice called *La Regla de Ocha*, and associated the names of Catholic saints with the different orisas so they could conceal their religion from slave owners.[21] Afro-Cuban devotion to these "saints" led to the name given to it by outsiders—Santería. During the twentieth century the drumming and chants of Santería would reach the United States in Florida and New York City, where they would find enthusiastic audiences among African Americans seeking authentic African traditions, as well as Cuban migrants to the United States struggling to maintain a distinct identity and sense of culture.[22] Brazil, another destination for Yoruba slaves, developed its own syncretic religious form called Candomblé at roughly the same time. It included ritual chants to the orisas that continue to be sung in archaic forms of Yoruba to this day. Passed down from generation to generation, the general sense of the chants remains known even as fluency in the language has disappeared.[23]

Ironically, the main area where orisa worship is in decline is in Nigeria itself. Pentecostalism has proven extremely popular within the Yoruba Christian community, combining a perceived power to heal with the appeal of extensive global connections. Even the Ooni of Ife, purportedly the reincarnation of Oduduwa, has had to renounce his divinity under pressure from his wife.[24] She has since built a church on the site of his shrine where visitors can watch a nativity play dramatizing the decline and fall of orisa worship.[25] Islam has also become more assertive, with Salafist reformers in the 1970s demanding that Yoruba Muslims avoid even the slightest forms of syncretism in their behavior. A new organization adhering to these principles has attempted to duplicate the extraordinary success of Pentecostalist churches in Yorubaland. Called NASFAT, it offered a sense of community through overnight prayers, business opportunities for members, and healing practices rooted in the Quran. Christian and Muslim leaders now offer the same type of services that the *babalawo* did for generations, and orisa worship is struggling in its ancestral home. Nonetheless, present-

Figure 12.1 A statue of the Virgin of Regla is carried through the streets of Havana in 2018. This Catholic saint is also recognized by Santería worshippers as Yemaya, a female orisa linked to fertility and water. Courtesy of Sven Creutzmann/Mambo Photos via Getty Images.

day communities of orisa worshippers in the United States, Trinidad, Brazil, Cuba, and Haiti remain vibrant.

The final reason for giving orisa worship a larger role in world history is its continuing relevance today. One aspect of this lies in its innovative healing techniques, which were frequently a key part of a *babalawo*'s craft. Using a wide array of leaves, roots, and barks, *babalawo* created numerous treatments for routine illnesses that are still being researched today.[26] This pharmacopeia was often linked to the worship of Orisa-Oko, the god of the natural world, and in many cases the remedies provided by the *babalawo* had to be activated through specific incantations done by the patient at home. These instructions would be discussed between patient and priest, and would invoke past deities, spirits, or ancestors who suffered from a similar malady. The natural remedies often possess remarkable powers, and divination "is a means by which practitioners diagnose past, present, and future issues—physical, mental, spiritual—much as a physician uses questionnaires."[27] An estimated 80 percent of sub-Saharan Africans rely on traditional healers for their primary health care. Accurately assessing what this care involves is a worthy goal in its own right.

Figure 12.2 The new Ooni of Ife attends his coronation at Ile-Ife in 2015. He is considered the spiritual leader of the Yoruba. Courtesy of Pius Utomi Ekpei/AFP via Getty Images.

But perhaps the most fascinating aspect of orisa is its tolerance of other faiths. Passionately arguing this case is Wole Soyinka, who compares the tenets of orisa with the other major religions present in Nigeria:

> Let us bear in mind that Islam—like its elder sibling, Christianity—invaded the black world, subverted its traditions and religions, often violently and contemptuously. It rivaled the earlier aggressor violence for violence, disdain for disdain, enslavement for enslavement. Both of them proven iconoclasts, yet what wisdom does this largely defamed and near-invisible religion of the Orisa prescribe for its own adherents? Tolerance, it enjoins, tolerance! You humiliate the Moslem or indeed any cleric, warns Ifa, and you will die the death of maggots.[28]

Soyinka worries that the major monotheistic religions, by aspiring to be complete ways of life, lead to fanaticism. But he also notes that antireligious figures like Stalin and Hitler merely replaced religion with ideology and that a comparable sense of certainty can lead to similarly tragic outcomes. What we need, he argues, is "an open marketplace of both ideas and faiths."[29] By providing a sense of belonging without encouraging intolerance, orisa worship might be ideally suited to the modern world.

Conclusion

Studying the history of world religions is a major challenge. Limited space forces authors to stick to a well-trodden path that leads to the spread of monotheistic faiths around the globe. An unfortunate consequence is that students read this teleologically. This means that the rise of major world religions seems inevitable, with "pagan" worship squeezed out between the "venerable East on the one hand and the progressive West on the other."[30]

This narrative is guilty of begging the question. The great monotheistic religions rise because they rose, while polytheism fails because it failed. This is unhelpful. The vibrancy of orisa worship reveals that there was nothing inevitable about the triumph of monotheism over polytheism. It also suggests that the latter is perfectly capable of "going global" if placed in a position to do so. Due to the unhappy incidence of the trans-Atlantic slave trade, orisa worshippers found themselves transported to plantations across the Americas. Here they kept the orisas and Ifa divination alive in the linked practices of Candomblé, Shango, Vodou, and Santería. Today the United States, Brazil, and Cuba are at least as important to the future of orisa worship as Yorubaland.

Finally, we should study orisa on its own terms. This means avoiding "the habit of elision" whereby African traditional religions are studied in the aggregate.[31] Specific histories and forms of worship matter, and with regard to orisa help explain why it is so significant to the world today. The pragmatic *babalawo* and enigmatic corpus of Ifa provide comfort, community, and healing to millions. A quick look at the history of orisa worship reveals its capacity for tolerance and adaptation, two traits badly needed today.

Further reading

Brenner, Louis. "Histories of Religion in Africa," *Journal of Religion in Africa* 30, no. 2 (2000): 143–167. A published lecture that argues Islam and African traditional religions can be studied through a single conceptual framework.

Falola, Toyin, and Ann Genova, eds. *Orişa*. Trenton, NJ: Africa World Press, 2005. This collection of essays introduces new ideas about orisa worship from the perspective of the Yoruba diaspora.

Olupona, Jacob, and Terry Rey, eds. *Òrìṣà Devotion as World Religion*. Madison: University of Wisconsin Press, 2008. This book includes contributions from numerous leading scholars who examine the history of orisa worship and its transformation into a world religion.

Peel, J.D.Y. *Christianity, Islam, and Orişa Religion*. Oakland: University of California Press, 2016. A study of the significance of intertwined Yoruba forms of spirituality, including Christianity, Islam, and orisa worship.

Soyinka, Wole. *Of Africa*. New Haven, CT: Yale University Press, 2013. Africa's first Nobel Prize winner in Literature makes a case for Africa to draw on its homegrown resources, including spirituality.

13

Heavy Metals

Primo Levi was a Holocaust survivor, someone who experienced the horrors of the concentration camps. After the Second World War he often toured around the United States, talking to students about these events. Speaking after one such encounter in a grade 5 classroom, he was taken aback by their reactions. In his experience, the daily struggle to avoid the gas chambers was so all-encompassing that resistance was unthinkable, let alone plausible. But these students weren't interested in that. They wanted him to map out the camp so they could craft a Hollywood-style escape. Their understanding of the death camps, based on contemporary films and myths, made it difficult for them to empathize with the situation Levi described.[1]

Similar moments happen to all history teachers, but they tend to be most frequent when dealing with issues that are beyond the immediate experience of students. While grading one exam, I was shocked to see conditions on slave ships described as analogous to riding a city bus! On the one hand, it is wonderful that students are so unfamiliar with things like slave ships and concentration camps that they struggle to comprehend them. On the other, it can lead to disastrously bad history with regard to some of the discipline's most instructive moments.

This chapter is designed to explore the skill of historical empathy and how it can help us better understand one such moment. After conquering the Incas in South America, the Spanish discovered large deposits of silver. To facilitate the production of this valuable metal, they imposed a system of forced labor on indigenous Americans (Andeans) living near the most important mine at Potosí. This system became known as the *mita*, and it involved forcing Andeans to travel to Potosí or Huancavelica, a mine which produced mercury used to refine Potosí's low-grade silver. A combination of indifference to safety conditions, the spread of disease, and the crippling (and well-known, even in the sixteenth century) side-effects of working with mercury meant the *mita* was extremely dangerous.[2] It devastated Andean communities already grappling with Spanish conquest and the impact of European pathogens.

Spanish silver was critical to creating a more closely linked world. Dennis Flynn and Arturo Giráldez go so far as to argue that it was the origin of the global economy.[3] Although significant quantities of silver were mined in what is modern-day Mexico, the majority originated at Potosí beginning in 1545. The royal *quinto*, a 20 percent tax on all silver produced at Potosí, was the single largest source of revenue in the Spanish Americas, and it "powerfully stimulated global trade." A great deal crossed the Atlantic to fund Spain's religious wars, but another important connection was the galleon route across the Pacific to Manila, where silver was exchanged for Chinese silks.[4]

The goal of this chapter is to describe, contextualize, and then explain the moral debates that raged over the *mita* from its origins in the sixteenth century until its eventual end in the early 1800s. What I find fascinating about the *mita* is the large number of primary sources available to historians,

Figure 13.1 A llama caravan carries silver from Potosí. Engraving by Johann Theodor de Bry, 1602. Courtesy of De Agostini via Getty Images.

which were created by Spanish opponents of the *mita*. Why were these early activists unable to ever get the *mita* banned if conditions were so obviously appalling? And why was resistance to the *mita* among Andeans so erratic even though the suffering of the *mitayos* was well known? This chapter focuses on this debate. How did the Spanish justify forced labor at the time? How was it perceived in the affected indigenous communities? And can either of these debates help us understand the persistence of the *mita*, which was never banned by the Spanish?

"All just and reasonable means"

Silver mining was labor intensive. Workers were needed to haul and smelt the ore, and the less they were paid, the more profitable the mine. Forced labor was a crucial part of the silver industry in the Spanish American colonies. This began in the 1530s with the creation of *encomiendas*, which "entrusted" Andeans in an assigned area to Spaniards. In exchange for educating the Andeans on Christianity, the Spaniard received access to their labor, and by the 1540s some of these workers, known as *encomendados*, were sent to Spanish mines. The Andeans referred to this forced labor as *mit'a* after the term used by the Incans for tribute paid as labor.[5] Originally, the majority of workers in Potosí were wage laborers. These Andeans were crucial to the Spanish who had purchased claims in the area because they had invented a unique smelting method that involved *guayras*, small furnaces fueled by the powerful winds on the slopes of the mountain. Without these, the Spanish could not process the extraordinarily rich ores extracted from the mountains.[6] But after a massive boom in production during the 1550s, the most lucrative veins began to dry up. The 1560s were marked by declining output, the departure of many wage laborers, and increasing pressure from the Spanish Crown to reinvigorate production in Potosí.[7]

Viceroy Francisco de Toledo was sent to Peru in 1569 by the Spanish king, Philip II, with instructions to stabilize Spanish control and enhance royal revenues. It was immediately obvious that accomplishing these tasks would require reviving Potosí's silver mines. Here Toledo faced a difficult choice. Wage laborers had left because the profits available to them did not justify the work required. The Spanish mine owners also refused to pay higher wages to attract free labor. But Philip II's instructions to Toledo explicitly forbade the use of forced labor as a solution to this problem:

Given that the mines of Peru cannot be exploited using Spanish laborers, since those who are there will not work in them, and it is said that slaves cannot withstand the work, owing to the nature and coldness of the land, it appears necessary to employ the Indians. Though these are not to be forced or compelled, as has already been ordered, they must be attracted with **all just and reasonable means**, so that there will be the required number of laborers for the mines.[8]

Toledo discussed the matter with an advisory council in 1570, and they decided that it would be lawful for the Crown to force Andeans to work in Potosí's mines so long as they were paid appropriately and conditions were carefully monitored. Toledo subsequently embarked on a five-year tour of Spain's South American colonies. During this time he relocated and reorganized Andean communities to make them easier to administer, encouraged the expansion of a new form of silver refining known as amalgamation (more on this later), and after winning over the local clergy and administrators in 1572, created the forced labor draft called the *mita* to support the mines in Potosí. All Andeans living within roughly 500 miles of the mines were to be counted, relocated to more accessible sites, and required to perform labor if they wished to retain access to their land. This requirement applied to adult men and had to be performed one year of every seven. They would travel to the mines with a *mita* captain (usually the leader of the community who held the title of *curaca*), be assigned to a particular mine or refining mill, and then work for that employer in shifts of one week on, two weeks off. In theory, Spanish officials were required to ensure the Andeans were fairly paid, that labor conditions were acceptable, and that they were released from this obligation after it had been completed.[9]

The miner owners loved the *mita*. In the 1570s and 1580s it brought as many as 13,500 Andeans to Potosí. The work they were given usually involved hauling ore, and their presence quickly depressed wages. Conditions were appalling. One sympathetic Spanish official, writing in the mid-1630s, observed that they worked underground twenty-three weeks a year "without light, 1,200 to 1,800 feet down, dragging themselves along adits and over supports, cutting ore with [crow]bars weighing 30 pounds, at the expense of blood and sweat."[10] Potosí's elevation at 13,000 feet above sea level made these tasks almost impossibly difficult. Cave-ins, torn ladders, or disorientation due to a complete lack of light (mine owners would not pay for candle wax for miners) claimed the lives of thousands, and perhaps even millions, of *mitayos*.

Figure 13.2 Aerial view of the city of Potosí in 2016, with the Cerro Rico silver mine in the background. Courtesy of Arterra via Getty Images.

Longer-term, silicosis from dust in the mines and refining mills (where the ore was crushed by giant water-powered hammers) took a toll that is hard to quantify. The amalgamation process also involved handling and inhaling large quantities of mercury, a neurological poison. Some *mitayos* were required to walk barelegged in mixtures of ore and mercury in order to encourage the silver and mercury to bond. After this combination of mercury and silver was extracted, the mercury had to be boiled off, exposing workers to its extremely toxic vaporized form. No one working in Potosí could avoid exposure to mercury. But unlike the others, the *mitayos* were forced to be there.[11]

The *mitayos* were paid a set rate of 2.5 pesos each week, far below the 9 pesos a week paid to free laborers. And after the boom times created by amalgamation began to fade, the *mitayos* were also used as a valuable source of income. This began with a general population decline in Andean communities. Infectious diseases like smallpox and measles had taken an enormous toll, and Andeans who wished to avoid serving in the *mita* could simply renounce their ancestral claim to land and become *forasteros* who were free to work for wages elsewhere. This made it harder and harder for communities to meet their assessed *mita* obligations. However, mine owners were livid if a *curaca* did not provide enough workers, and legally the Spanish entrepreneurs were in the right. By the start of the seventeenth century, *curacas* and mine owners reached an agreement—instead of trying to reach the impossible labor quotas, the *curacas* would pay a fee for each worker who did not reach Potosí. This fee was equal to the going wages for free laborers so that, at least in theory, the mine owner could hire a replacement. By 1665, with the mines in decline, these fees accounted for almost half of the *mita* and were keeping many silver mines open that otherwise would have closed long ago. This unofficial tax crippled the leaders of Andean communities, much to the consternation of the Spanish administration. But when they sent an official to Potosí to end this practice in the 1660s, he was poisoned and killed by the mine owners.[12]

The morality of the *mita* spurred intense debate among both the Spanish and the Andeans. Spain's discovery and occupation of the New World was believed to be divinely ordained, but there was considerable skepticism of the motives of the Spanish officers involved. Could an empire be moral if it was founded on greed and exploitation? Ordinary Andeans were generally opposed to the *mita*, but this did not mean that all forms of resistance were acceptable. For example, provinces near Cuzco tended to meet their obligations without complaint despite a lack of immediate coercion. How did they perceive the *mita*?

Understanding the sixteenth- and seventeenth-century Spanish debates over the morality of the *mita* begins with two theorists, Aristotle and Thomas Aquinas. In Aristotle's *Metaphysics*, he argues that a master-worker is wiser than a manual laborer because he understands "the causes of the things that are done" (*Met.* 1.1). Aquinas used this analogy in his commentary, arguing that "the shipbuilder is a superior artist compared with the one who prepares the wood; and the navigator, who uses the completed ship, is a superior artist compared to the shipbuilder."[13] To Aquinas, this analogy could apply in the political sphere, with the divinely inspired king playing the role of the helmsman on a ship. But if the Spanish king was the leader of a perfect community, did he have the right to subjugate Native Americans? In what circumstances was this legal?

Spain's empire originated with three papal bulls in 1493. Issued by Pope Alexander VI (who, perhaps not coincidentally, was from Spain), these recognized Spanish claims to any land not held by a Christian king in the New World. As conquistadors began conquering and pillaging across the Americas, however, consternation about their treatment of Native Americans developed. The Dominican order in particular became staunch advocates for limiting the power of Spanish colonists. In their interpretation, the papal bulls merely allowed the Spanish to convert Native Americans, not force them to work. Both the Laws of Burgos (1512) and New Laws (1542) outlined the precise expectations for Spanish settlers in relation to conquered Native Americans. The first made an effort to rein in abuses against Native Americans, and allowed them to serve Spanish colonists as laborers only when sincere efforts to convert them were being made. The New Laws, signed by King Charles V, took these regulations a step further. They made it illegal to enslave any Native American and required the Spanish to allow tribute to be paid in cash rather than as labor. Forcing Native Americans to work in pearl fisheries and mines was banned.[14] These regulations reflected the views of activist clergy like Bartolomé de Las Casas. He argued that Native Americans lived in sovereign communities, and any use of force against members of these societies constituted a violation of natural law, and thus rendered Spanish conquest unjust.[15]

Viceroy Toledo had little sympathy for this perspective. He fought a war in Vilcabamba against the last remnants of the Incan Empire, and he believed that they were tyrants who had come to power by falsely claiming to be children of the sun.[16] Toledo even initiated a historical investigation to confirm that the Incans had seized land without consent from those living there (or their legitimate prior rulers). When respondents began offering ambiguous answers to investigators that suggested the Inca had been relatively benevolent overlords, he changed the questions to focus on issues connected to labor. Did the Inca keep people constantly working? Were Andeans naturally lazy if left to their own devices? And, perhaps most intriguingly, "did they need a strong ruler to make decisions on their own behalf?"[17]

Toledo was impressed by Incan architecture and public works, especially the extensive road network that crisscrossed the Andes Mountains. But he felt the extraordinary demands the Inca made of their subjects' labor were tyrannical because they stifled individual initiative and necessitated close monitoring of people's day-to-day lives. This bizarre mix of respect and disdain can be seen in his writing on Incan forced labor: "When there were no useful things [to do], they made them work in useless things, such as directing rivers in one direction or another, and making very long walls from one place to another along the roads and stone steps, which were not necessary; this they did because it seemed to them very desirable to keep them always occupied." While Toledo believed that Incan rule was demonically inspired, he also argued that the devil had allowed Incan kings to correctly assess the character of ordinary Andeans as weak and servile. Ironically, Toledo argued, the tyranny of the Incas had rendered Andeans akin to children, in need of constant tasks in order to overcome their degraded character. Even though King Philip II had explicitly forbidden the use of forced labor, Toledo wrote back claiming that the king had a responsibility to "prevent Andeans from being idle, which could only be harmful, given their weak nature."[18] Toledo's arguments may have been flimsy, but the vacillating Spanish kings did nothing to limit the *mita* until after 1650.[19]

Other scholars of empire argued that forms of forced labor like the *mita* could be justified if the evangelical enterprise itself was at stake. The following excerpt comes from a work written by the Jesuit scholar José de Acosta in 1588:

> But, on the other hand, we must stand in awe before the providence and benevolence of our Lord, who employs our human condition to bring the gospel to such remote and barbarous nations, copiously planting these lands with gold and silver in order to awaken our greed. As charity was not enough to inspire us, then at least lust for gold would be sufficient stimulus. Just as in other times the disbelief of Israel was the cause for the salvation of the gentiles, now the greed of Christians has become the cause of the Indians' salvation.[20]

He argued that the Spanish Empire was founded on greed, but that this greed was being used by God to ensure the evangelization of the New World. To produce this wealth, Acosta suggested that Native Americans were obligated to contribute for the preservation of the common good. Since Spaniards were unable or unwilling to work the mines, Native Americans must do so. Acosta acknowledged that it was unjust to force anyone to work, even for a wage, but on the other hand he argued that methods must be adapted to local conditions in order to get things done.[21] Toledo's belief that the Andeans were "servile" persisted, but later writers felt this could be overcome by the direction of a new "master."[22] Using this perverse logic, forcing Andeans to work actually liberated them by allowing them to make money, buy property, and overcome their inherent servility.[23] Andeans may have been "free vassals" of the Spanish Crown, but they were not free to refuse such important labor.

This belief persisted despite the widespread knowledge that mining was incredibly dangerous. Opponents of the *mita* pointed out that Roman criminals were "condemned to metal" and considered dead thereafter. By granting mine owners the right to assign Andean labor to the mines, the state was forcing these workers to perform an impossibly hazardous task, something that most Spanish theologians agreed was illegal.[24] Spanish officials were also well aware of the long-term hazards of mine work. Juan de Solórzano Pereira, a Spanish jurist and former supervisor at the mercury mine in Huancavelica (which also received *mita* laborers since it was so essential to silver production), wrote in 1648 that "the fumes from the same quicksilver [mercury] quickly penetrate to the marrow the bodies of those who boil and refine it, weakening all the limbs, causing constant tremors in them; although by fortune some are of a robust temperament, few do not die within four years."[25] The human cost of the *mita* was abundantly clear. But the arguments that emphasized the importance of Potosi to evangelization and the capacity of labor to "free" the *mitayos* won the day. The *mita* would not end until the nineteenth century.

Andean debates on the *mita* were not as well recorded. On the whole, it is clear that the vast majority opposed it across lines of class, ethnicity, and gender. *Curacas* wrote frequent petitions, often with assistance from sympathetic Spanish officials, detailing the ways the *mita* was destroying their communities—the lack of money for travel (which often took 1–2 months on foot each way), the need to sell personal items just to fund the journey, the need to pay tribute for land that went uncultivated, and the variety of ailments that left *mitayos* who returned home shadows of their former selves.[26] Despite these petitions, nothing was done. However, resistance to the *mita* that did not directly threaten the Spanish became a major problem. The most common way to oppose the *mita* was to flee one's home and become a *forastero. Forasteros* was not subject to labor obligations but they also lost their right to land in their ancestral community. Becoming a *forastero* usually meant renting land far from home for subsistence, and paying that rent with wages earned at nearby Spanish workshops. But as more people fled, the *mita* burden rested on fewer and fewer shoulders, and communities did not necessarily sympathize with those who shirked their obligations. *Mitayos* who returned home early from their labor obligations, for example, might find themselves in trouble with other community members unless they had proof their treatment was particularly bad.[27]

While the *mita* was resented, many Andeans believed it entitled them to special rights from the Crown. Jeremy Mumford describes this dynamic between Incan *curacas* and the Spanish Crown as *servicio* and *merced*. By providing the king with a service, the *curacas* expected to receive a reward, usually the preservation of their privileges as well as the community over which they ruled.[28] For most Andeans, the *mita* was perceived to be reciprocal, with service to the Crown guaranteeing the future of the community, particularly through continued access to land.[29]

This relationship was believed to establish a direct connection with the king himself just as it had under the Inca.[30] The result was an ambivalent view of the *mita*; on the one hand it was capable of destroying communities, but on the other it was necessary to sustain them. For this reason most Andean complaints against the *mita* called for the curbing of abuses, not its outright elimination. Rossana Barragán goes so far as to suggest that *mita* workers and their free associates in Potosí were even able to break the monopoly of Spanish mill owners on silver production. By the eighteenth century *k'ajchas*, self-employed workers who were often also *mitayos*, had begun stealing significant amounts of ore from Spanish mines and sending it to Andean-owned refining mills known as *trapiches*. The scale of this industry varied over time, but at certain moments they sold more refined silver to the Crown than the official refiners. For this reason Spanish officials generally tolerated the *k'ajchas* and *trapiches*, and it helps explain why some Andeans would have participated in the *mita*.[31] This channeled outrage in a way that the Spanish could manage, and helps explain the extraordinary longevity of the *mita*.

Conclusion

The Spanish colonial empire has often been portrayed as uniquely cruel. This argument uses Viceroy Toledo and his hated *mita* as proof of Spain's perfidious nature. Conditions in the silver mines of Potosí demonstrate this point effectively. By exposing conscripted labor to silicosis, mercury poisoning, and the more mundane but very real dangers of mining, the Spanish were guilty of tremendous abuses.

However, it is important not to focus too much on how these conditions diverge from our expectations in the present. Today we expect issues like this to be dealt with through extensive documentation of human rights abuses and public dissemination of those findings. This was not necessarily true with regard to the *mita*. Most Spanish debates focused on whether the Inca matched Aristotle's definition of tyranny, or if the benefits of future silver production to Christianity outweighed the abuse to which *mitayos* would surely be exposed. Andeans seem to have also taken the abuses inherent in the *mita* for granted, but questioned whether the reciprocal ties it created to the Crown could be justified. They also tried to earn their own share of the revenues flowing out of Potosí.

Getting an accurate sense of what people in the past valued is a necessary element of historical empathy. In this case, it reveals just how integral theology was to Spanish notions of justice and legitimacy. For Andeans, it reveals how relationships with conquering powers were undergirded by notions of reciprocity that offered grudging compliance in exchange for community survival, a willingness to curb the most egregious abuses, and perhaps the occasional opportunity to benefit.

Further reading

Bakewell, Peter. *Miners of the Red Mountain*. Albuquerque: University of New Mexico Press, 2010. The author argues that the Black Legend has led to a scholarly focus on forced labor and the *mita* at the expense of the free workers at Potosí.

Barragán, Rossana. "Working Silver for the World," *Hispanic American Historical Review* 97, no. 2 (2017): 193–222. A fascinating look at how indigenous residents of Potosí managed to reconstruct the local economy to privilege their needs over those of the Spanish.

Bentancor, Orlando. *The Matter of Empire*. Pittsburgh, PA: Pittsburgh University Press, 2017. A study of the theological and philosophical justifications used by Spanish apologists for empire.

Cole, Jeffrey. *The Potosi Mita*. Palo Alto, CA: Stanford University Press, 1985. A history of the *mita* as an institution from 1573 to 1700.

Mumford, Jeremy. *Vertical Empire*. Durham, NC: Duke University Press, 2012. A look at how the Incans and Spanish officials created a compact involving the exchange of labor for land, one that allowed the "vertical archipelago" to survive.

Robins, Nicholas. *Mercury, Mining, and Empire*. Bloomington, IN: Indiana University Press, 2011. A devastating look at the toxicity of silver mining in Potosí.

Stavig, Ed. *The World of Túpac Amaru*. Lincoln, NE: University of Nebraska Press, 1999. A social history of two provinces in Cuzco that were deeply affected by the *mita* and subsequently offered support to the rebellion of Túpac Amaru.

14

We'll Always Have Paris

Few cities capture the imagination like Paris. The famous budget travel company Lonely Planet begins its city guide with the claim that "the City of Light is the capital of France, and the epitome of romance, culture, and beauty … if you subscribe to even half of the superlatives thrown its way, it is one of the best places to be, full stop."[1] Short clips of the most famous Parisian sites scroll by at a dizzying pace as the narrator gushes on—the Eiffel Tower, the July Column, Notre Dame de Paris, the Louvre, the Arc de Triomphe, and the Champs-Élysées. It is hard not to be impressed.

When did Paris become the city we know? The city guide offers a hint: "The heart of Paris has changed little since the mid-19th century, when its grand boulevards and Art Nouveau apartments were built."[2] They are drawing on a deeper historical argument here. This argument suggests that Paris was transformed by Georges-Eugène Haussmann, better known by his title of Baron. In 1853 he became the prefect of the Seine with a mandate to improve the healthiness and grandeur of the city. This he did in an eminently modern way—by bulldozing old tenements to create massive new boulevards, and constructing blandly uniform apartments along them. The result was the iconic Parisian streetscape we know today: wide roads, large sidewalks, shady trees, and low-rise buildings. In seventeen extremely active years, Haussmann displaced 350,000 people and built almost 20 percent of the roads in Paris. According to this narrative, the 1867 Exposition marked the culmination of the city's transformation, the moment when Paris became "the Queen of Cities."[3]

Haussmann's impact on the city was extraordinary. But sometimes world historical narratives lack precision when assessing key moments of change. Haussmann's reforms overlapped chronologically with the industrialization of France, so it makes intuitive sense to suggest the two were connected. Haussmann's ulterior motive for building the boulevards, to control working-class agitation against Napoleon III, also points in this direction. The problem with this narrative is that Paris's reputation as a modern city long predates the Industrial Revolution. In the seventeenth century it became known as the City of Light due to a combination of its public mail delivery, public transportation, and street lighting.[4] Paris's residents were also lauded across Europe for their stylish dress and romantic escapades, with Paris possessing an enviable reputation as the place "where the standards for style and fashion were now set."[5]

Paris was even the subject of the first modern guidebook. Writing in the seventeenth century when most tourism involved religious pilgrimages or reading Latin inscriptions off classical-era tombstones, Germain Brice suggested that travelers would "take more delight, without doubt, in the description of a Cabinet, a Library, or an Apartment built after the modern way, than in reading the Epitaphs at *Saint Innocents,* or to pick out the meaning of them."[6] Writing at the same time, Nicolas de Blégny provided readers with information about Paris that seems vital today but had never been of interest before; places to get the best Brie, the best brioches, and the best luxury goods.[7] Paris, it seems, was modern long before Haussmann.

This chapter examines the skill of continuity and change through the lens of Paris. When does it become modern? Instead of focusing on the technological and economic changes associated with the Industrial Revolution, this chapter will make the case that being modern is also about more nebulous cultural factors, factors that are much more difficult to quantify but may provide a more accurate sense of life in the past.

The origins of modernity

If modernity predates industrialization, how can we identify it? This question is probably impossible to answer because there is no single absolute definition for what modernity is. But the key characteristic of urban life in seventeenth-century Paris was the creation of new spaces that encouraged people to interact in new ways. Bernard observes that "the problems confronting the urbanists of the age of Louis XIV [r.1643–1710] were miniscule compared with those of today's urban planners. But they were the same kinds of problems—of circulation, physical security, health, pollution of the environment, education, urban aesthetics, and so on."[8] There was no single shift, as many assume took place under Haussmann, but rather numerous smaller shifts that together created something new, and, quite possibly, modern.

It is fascinating to note that Paris's transformation may well have begun with a bridge. Medieval bridges were dark, dangerous, and expensive. London Bridge, constructed in 1209, was an excellent example. Roughly 900 feet long and 26 wide, it was financed by licensing plots of land located on the bridge surface itself. Pedestrians and carriages were left to share a roadway that at times was as little as twelve feet wide. With buildings looming five stories overhead, ambush and robbery were very real fears. Nobles rarely used the bridge, preferring ferries instead. And due to the enclosures, the bridge offered no views of the city. Instead, it was decorated with the ghoulish remains of people executed for treason.[9]

The Pont Neuf, or New Bridge, was different. First conceived in 1578 as a fairly typical medieval bridge, on completion in 1606 it was three times as wide as the London Bridge. These dimensions were highly unusual, and designed to accommodate the growing number of carriages and wagons crossing the Seine. The decision was also made to leave the edges of the bridge devoid of buildings, and broad sidewalks were included instead. This allowed pedestrians to take in the sites of the city along the river's edge. And since it was funded by a tax on wine, there was no toll to cross. Parisians embraced this as an invitation to freely mingle, a freedom that had been sharply curtailed by the religious violence of the sixteenth century.[10] The first Brice Guide to Paris noted that visitors were shocked at "how busy and crowded" the bridge was, as well as how one might "encounter people from every rank and dressed in every possible way." In a c.1700 painting created by Nicolas Guérard, L'embarras de Paris, the Pont Neuf is pulsating with energy, and riders on horseback, carriages, shopkeepers, buskers, and a wayward flock of sheep all compete for space.[11] Even with its elevated sidewalks and unusual width, the Pont Neuf was home to a modern innovation; the traffic jam. The French word embarrass had meant "embarrassment" or "confusion" until the late seventeenth century. After this point it was also used as a reference to an "encounter in a street of several things that block each other's way." Guérard's painting is possibly the first depiction of traffic congestion.[12]

Nevertheless, the Brice Guide ranked the view from the Pont Neuf of the Parisian cityscape as one of the three finest in the world, alongside the harbors in Constantinople and Goa.[13] Modern technologies like an imported water pump, an elaborate clock, and a freestanding bronze statue of Henry IV also attracted visitors, who by the 1660s were buying prints of

Figure 14.1 The Pont Neuf and the Seine River in 2017. Courtesy of Bruno de Hogues/Gammo-Rapho via Getty Images.

the Pont Neuf as souvenirs of their visit.[14] Many artists were struck by the proximity of the rich and poor on the bridge, and Newman argues that this made it possible to imagine "the rights of man" as they were understood during the Enlightenment.[15] The Pont Neuf was certainly a hub of political activism, with placards, posters, and engraved images all posted here. Literate bystanders read aloud for those unable to do so, and in 1648 when a popular member of the Paris *Parlement* was arrested, news spread rapidly at the bridge. Within fifteen minutes a mob had formed, with one observer noting that "the entire city of Paris" had gathered there. After successfully forcing the Crown to release the political prisoner, the opposition became known as "Pont Neuf rebels."[16]

Creating more public spaces within Paris was a top priority under Louis XIV. Despite his fixation on Versailles and distant wars, early in his reign he recognized that a grand city would reflect well on him personally. One project of crucial importance was the destruction of the crumbling city walls and their replacement with tree-lined boulevards. Beginning in 1670, it aimed to "provide promenades for the bourgeois and inhabitants" around the entire circumference of the city.[17] Thirty years later it was possible to travel around the entire Right Bank of the city on the Cours, as it became known.

This was significant because of how it changed the way people interacted with this space. The phrase *sur le boulevard* was created to describe wandering along this green walkway for pleasure. Pedestrians might look at the new houses under construction nearby, listen to singers performing at the Paris Opera, or simply "be seen."[18] Since access to the Cours was limited, the vast majority of people there were upper class. This was not the case in other green-spaces like the Tuileries gardens. After extensive renovations by Louis XIV's architect André le Nôtre, which began in 1662, the Tuileries became the first public gardens in Paris and a model for similar spaces across Europe. With open spaces for large boisterous gatherings and hidden alleyways offering privacy from prying eyes, the Tuileries was one of the most popular sites in Paris. Guidebooks celebrated its charms, and visitors were often taken aback by the casual way people interacted in this space across gender and class lines. Its cafes became the first public places in Paris where the aristocracy ate and drank in public. These green spaces allowed the city to breathe in a way that had not been possible before.[19]

Walking was no longer just functional—it was also an opportunity to display new styles of clothes.[20] And increased demand for fashionable clothes created a culture that revolved around creating, marketing, and buying these items. Paris thus became a forerunner for modern consumer culture, with the city increasingly identified with *la mode*, or style. This transformation can be seen in the Galerie du Palais. Originally just a site for merchants to make deals, the display of goods in shops was not a priority. After a fire destroyed the Galerie du Palais in 1618, its rebuilt arcades included counters for customers to examine goods, sites for the visible display of inventory, and items to catch the eye of wandering shoppers. The large number of shops in the same building (180 by 1700) ensured that shoppers could compare goods before making a decision, and spend time wandering among the displays. Part of the appeal, just like with the Pont Neuf, was the social mixing. While most visitors were affluent, men and women mingled in the shops together, and visitors often commented on the "unusually attractive women" working behind the counter. Shopping was being transformed from an everyday chore into something that would be familiar today.[21]

Louis XIV, in collaboration with his chief minister Jean-Baptiste Colbert, encouraged the growth of the luxury goods industry. He wore French fabrics, had his ministers do the same, and imposed heavy tariffs on foreign textiles. He also inaugurated a new periodical, *Mercure galant*, in 1672. This publication shamelessly promoted Paris as the center of fashion, and was successful at exporting this image abroad. By 1678 it included images of

Figure 14.2 An engraving of the Galerie du Paris, a shopping arcade, from the eighteenth century. Courtesy of Culture Club via Getty Images.

stylish outfits as well as information on the shops at which one could buy them. Louis XIV's support helped, but French fashion also benefited from other aspects of Paris's transformation. In places where fashion was restricted to the nobility and served as a marker of status, it tended to change slowly. In Paris, however, people of more modest means sought out fashionable outfits for their daily excursions into the city. The ability of all to partake in high fashion was an important element in its popularity, and foreign visitors were a crucial market for Parisian designers. La Frénai, perhaps the most famous Parisian textile merchant, created a chain of boutiques in the city and offered to deliver new clothes to other European capitals for a substantial markup. Paris was the indisputable champion of fashion, home of "l'empire de la mode." The impact was extremely significant, "a veritable treasure for France, both immense and enduring."[22]

While fashion had a more lasting impact, in the seventeenth century the most important Parisian fascination was with the carriage, or *carrosse*. The scale of this transformation was dramatic. In the early 1600s most of the wealthiest people in Paris traveled on the back of mules. One observer suggested that only eight carriages could be seen around the city in 1594. A century later Brice estimated that there were 20,000.[23] Better suspension for comfort and lighter glass for windows made French carriages superior to those built elsewhere, and their popularity surged as a result. Among the wealthy, carriage outings (or *promenade à carrosse*) became extremely fashionable. For some, these involved picnic lunches and lovely country scenery. But the advent of new phrases like "marriage of the Bois de Boulogne" (i.e., "marriage" in the forest) suggests that the carriage also transformed Paris's "hook-up" culture, much to the chagrin of the moralizing bourgeoisie.[24]

Elites sought to monopolize access to carriages but this did not last. Rental carriages known as *fiacres* could be arranged by the 1650s through a stablemaster named Sauvage. For the aspiring social climber, the ability to show up at an elite residence in a carriage of any sort was an extraordinary boon. But for those who had to keep costs to an absolute minimum, public transportation became an option in 1662. Known as *carrosses à cinq sous*, these omnibuses traveled along set routes at set times, and were likely the first public transportation system in world history. Testifying to their cultural impact was a hit play in 1662 entitled *L'Intrigue des carrosses à cinq sous (The Intrigue of the Five-Penny Carriages)*. Its plot revolves around two couples, one involving a philandering husband taking advantage of the mobility of the public carriages to flirt with women who do not realize he is married, and the other with a husband addicted to gambling who uses the carriages to travel between private clubs and squander his wealth.[25] Although this form of public transportation collapsed when royal subsidies came to an end in the 1690s, its existence in the seventeenth century is a startling reminder of Paris's status as a trailblazer of urban life.[26]

In 1662, public life ceased at nightfall. Anyone out after dark either had a servant accompany them with a torch, or they were vulnerable to the many thieves who roamed the streets searching for prey. But a new company began offering the services of torch-bearers for rent to any customer, including the owners of the public carriages.[27] Louis XIV recognized that Paris's crime rate was a major hindrance to its businesses and its "grandeur" more generally. The torch-bearers helped, but a more permanent solution was needed. This began in 1665 when Louis XIV had his leading advisor, Jean-Baptiste Colbert, chair a commission to reform urban administration. In 1667 this led to the appointment of La Reynie as lieutenant general of the Parisian police, and he was given the authority to make significant changes.

In less than six months he announced the beginning of a program to introduce the first public street lighting anywhere in the world.[28] The expense was enormous; thousands of large lanterns made of metal and glass had to be built and distributed around the city, and each night they burned through large tallow candles designed to last for a minimum of eight hours. Locked boxes contained the pulleys needed to lift the lantern into place, and keys were given to appropriate homeowners who were also responsible for refilling the candles.[29] The costs were covered by the *taxes des boues et lanterns*, the only direct taxes paid by Parisians at any time during the reign of Louis XIV.[30] Problems with collection predictably dogged this system, but by 1671 the service was so popular that each arrondissement sent a delegation to *parlement* to indicate they were happy to continue paying for it. La Reynie also greatly expanded the night watch, known as the *guet*. With their numbers tripled and their pay doubled, they were ordered to actively patrol the city rather than merely respond to complaints.[31]

Crime rates predictably plummeted in the City of Light. The street lighting was described as a must-see for tourists, and it spread rapidly around Europe. But more important were the social changes street lights enabled. One guidebook observed that "many shops as well as most cafés and eating establishments stay open until ten or eleven P.M.; they keep lots of lights burning in their windows to make the streets even brighter … [as a result there are] almost as many people out and about at night as during the day." Another guidebook included an image of men and women dining together in a café after dark.[32] The accompanying decline in Paris's crime rate was also a subject of wide amusement. The 1669 play *Les Faux Moscovites (The Fake Muscovites)* made light of this situation by noting that times were so hard for thieves that they had to become card-sharks instead.[33] It is remarkable that something as mundane as street lights could have such wide-ranging implications, but they were an essential part of seventeenth-century Paris' reputation as the stylish, fast-paced city of romance. This reputation remains compelling today.

However, this idyllic image conceals a great deal. Seventeenth-century Paris was shaped by inequality in ways that resemble more recent urban centers. The rising cost of warfare led the French Crown to agree to a new type of loan. Usually done to alleviate "extraordinary" expenses that were occasioned by defeat in battle, the king would sign over future tax revenues to a small number of financiers who charged interest rates as high as 25 percent. Beginning in the 1630s, they began to display their fortunes by building some of the most magnificent residences in the city. More loans to fund an escalating Thirty Years War led to unprecedented real estate speculation, with the state turning over plots of land to developers like Louis Le Barbier, who then created new neighborhoods. By the end of the seventeenth century, financiers had become so powerful that they could monopolize the prestigious townhouses at the Place Louie-Le-Grand despite their often modest backgrounds.[34]

Resentment of the financiers was evident across the city. The comedy *Turcaret*, staged in 1709, had a variety of maids, valets, and relatives conspire to strip the title character of his vast fortune. Songs based on current affairs, known as vaudevilles, contained refrains like "let the hangman string them all up." And pamphleteers denounced the "savage and inhuman" methods the financiers used to extract wealth from both the Crown and the poor.[35] This poverty manifested itself in a significant decline in real wages over the course of the seventeenth century. Most skilled jobs required guild membership, and by this time the guilds were top-heavy, conservative, and did not advocate for the interests of any but the small number of masters. For journeymen laborers their wages stagnated at roughly ten to fifteen sous in most professions, a daily wage that rapidly disappeared to cover the rising costs of bread (1–2 sous for a 12-ounce loaf), wine (4 sous for a quart), and butter (7 sous for a pound). Parisian journeymen organized independent organizations known as *compagnonnages* to advocate for their interests, but the church bitterly denounced their initiation rituals. When workers demanded better wages, owners did not hesitate to lock them out.[36] Paris's ancient guilds lived on, but the declining real wages and frustrated work force suggest that by the end of the seventeenth century they "had taken on some strikingly modern traits."[37]

Conclusion

One of the great challenges in world history is identifying moments of transformation. The Industrial Revolution is one such moment. During the early nineteenth century, it is assumed that a combination of technological, economic, and social changes swept across the world. The industrial city "is seen as quantitatively so different from that which preceded it that it amounted to a qualitative difference."[38]

The example of Paris suggests that this narrative assumes too much, an argument that finds support in Jan de Vries's analysis of European urbanization. He contends that urban growth took place on a different scale after 1800, but also notes that it displayed "many elements of continuity with the past." Rather than the Industrial Revolution "creating the modern urbanized society of the advanced nations," De Vries argues that a large urban system was an essential prerequisite for industrialization. The most plausible time-period for the creation of this urban system: the seventeenth century.[39]

Paris experienced a transformation that predated Haussmann and the Industrial Revolution. This transformation did not necessarily involve a new mode of production, but it did involve the creation of public spaces, the development of a vibrant consumer culture, the provisioning of important municipal services, and growing inequality. Precisely because these changes are such an integral part of life today we tend to take them for granted, or assume that they existed since time immemorial. This is simply untrue, and reveals the limits of an approach that prioritizes technological or economic change at the expense of evidence drawn from drama, art, and even promotional videos.

Further reading

Bernard, Leon. *The Emerging City*. Durham, NC: Duke University Press, 1970. A translated monograph that examines Paris's urban development in seventeenth century.

DeJean, Joan. *How Paris Became Paris*. New York: Bloomsbury, 2014. A study of seventeenth-century Paris that argues it displayed modern forms of urban space two centuries earlier than most scholars indicate.

de Vries, Jan. *European Urbanization, 1500–1800*. Cambridge, MA: Harvard University Press, 1984. A statistical study of the city in early modern Europe that suggests urbanization was extensive before the Industrial Revolution.

Henshall, Nicolas. *The Myth of Absolutism*. New York: Longman, 1992. An irreverent look at the limits of absolutism in early modern Europe.

Newman, Karen. *Cultural Capitals*. Princeton, NJ: Princeton University Press, 2007. A comparative study of seventeenth-century London and Paris that uses cultural texts to examine how they became perceived as exemplars of modernity.

15

Germm Warfare

While doing my PhD research in 2005, I spent several months in the western Kenyan town of Makutano. I lived in a small hotel owned by renowned runner Tegla Loroupe, and would spend days speaking to NGO workers, government officials, or athletes living in the area. But every two weeks I would hop on the motorcycle of my research assistant, Andrew Juma, and together we would travel to the base of the Rift Valley to interview cattle raiders, usually young men who worked in gangs to steal livestock. I found it thoroughly unnerving to stick a recorder in their faces and ask them to tell us all about their illegal activities. Not Andrew. To him, the most dangerous part of this work was the frequent travel between ecotones. He told me that the disease environment at the base of the escarpment was very different from that at the top, and by not allowing the body time to adjust one risked attacks of pneumonia or malaria.

He was correct. We rarely had trouble with cattle raiders, but disease was a constant hassle. My worst experience was a case of malaria. I had not been taking my prophylactic pills, and this malaria attack left me completely incapacitated for almost two days. It took several weeks before I was up for any kind of vehicular travel, and almost six months before I felt like myself again. Andrew also got malaria at the same time, but he was able to quickly shake it off. Despite the remarkable accomplishments of modern medicine, I struggled to function in the foreign disease environment of Western Kenya. Andrew, on the other hand, stayed strong.

My experiences in Kenya no doubt affected me when I first read J.R. McNeill's *Mosquito Empires*. In it, he argues that "differential immunity" played a critical role in the history of the Greater Caribbean.[1] He applies this concept to two diseases, malaria and yellow fever. They inspired terror in the region from the early seventeenth century until the beginning of the First World War. Since these diseases conveyed complete immunity (yellow fever) or stronger resistance (malaria) to those who grow up surrounded by them, he contends that they had a major political impact. People born in the Greater Caribbean were far more likely to survive attacks of these diseases, while those arriving from outside (especially soldiers from Europe) had no immunity and might die in extraordinary numbers as a result. McNeill makes the provocative argument that the mosquitos carrying yellow fever and malaria (*aedes aegyptiae* and *anopheles quadrimaculatus*) "ushered in a new era of independent states."[2]

I soon discovered that Elizabeth Fenn had made similar use of the concept in her study of the smallpox epidemic that ravaged the Americas from 1775 to 1782. Complete immunity to smallpox was conveyed by surviving an attack, but the disease occurred much more frequently in Europe than in North America. This created an imbalance between American and British forces, one the latter tried to exploit to their advantage. She writes that "*Variola* was a virus of empire. It made winners and losers, at once serving the conquerors and determining who they would be."[3] Just as the Age of Revolutions reshaped the world, smallpox reshaped the Americas.

However, it is still not unusual for textbooks to say nothing about the role of disease with regard to the American and Haitian Revolutions.[4] Even in more detailed accounts of events, disease is given a peripheral role. *The Americas in the Age of Revolutions*, for example, briefly mentions disease while explaining why Europeans had to recruit local forces in Saint-Domingue, as well as the devastating impact of yellow fever on Leclerc's expeditionary force in 1802.[5] Laurent Dubois's masterful overview of the Haitian Revolution notes that French soldiers were prone to "tropical disease" and quotes one soldier who wrote "we die here like flies."[6] Jerome Greene's account of the Battle of Yorktown observes that Gen. Henry Clinton feared an extended summer campaign in the malarial swamps of coastal Virginia, while Gen. George Washington feared the English were trying to spread smallpox to the Americans "as usual."[7] However, in each of these texts, disease is treated as an aside rather than a focus. Smallpox and yellow fever matter, but only on a micro-level.[8]

So why do historians often overlook the importance of disease? McNeill argues that they dismiss epidemics as random, and assume that their impacts even out over time. This is particularly true of twentieth- and twenty-first-century historians, who live in a world where humans can "bend the rest of the biosphere to their will."[9] But McNeill and Fenn make compelling cases that things were quite different in the late eighteenth century. They argue that military leaders were extremely conscious of the uneven impacts of disease and tried to incorporate this into their planning. This chapter will use historical empathy to explore the importance of yellow fever, malaria, and smallpox to the course of early modern history.

The ecological context

Although it seems like an integral part of studying the past, environmental history has been around for a relatively short time. Pioneers in the field were inspired by the nascent environmental movement during the 1960s,[10] and also by the sweeping narratives of historians like Fernand Braudel. His division of the past into geographical time (*longue durée*), large-scale socioeconomic change (*la vie matérielle*), and more recent events (*histoire événementielle*) gave the environment a key role in long-term historical processes.[11] This model provided an inspiration for large-scale histories of the Columbian Exchange. Crosby's *The Columbian Exchange* took an explicitly ecological approach to the history of European contact with the Americas, and in *Ecological Imperialism* he famously suggested that European expansion was due to "geographical and ecological luck."[12] In the context of Colonial New England, Cronon argued that the land was transformed into a "world of fields and fences" by settlers from Europe, whether human, plant, or microbe.[13] These historians all felt that long-term ecological change played a decisive role in the past. And in the case of the Columbian Exchange, widespread European immunity to Old World diseases like measles and smallpox was a critical factor in their dramatic victories over Native Americans.

The role of disease in the conquest of the Americas was never in doubt. But as Crosby noted, the significance of major epidemics was often forgotten over time, and this seems to have been the case in relation to smallpox and the American Revolution.[14] Fenn's book on the smallpox epidemic that swept across North America from 1775 to 1782 noted that "it remains almost entirely unknown and unacknowledged by scholars and laypeople alike."[15] Smallpox's lengthy and asymptomatic incubation period allowed it to spread rapidly, but to Fenn the most important characteristic of this disease was the differential levels of immunity present in the New World. Those born and raised in English cities almost always encountered the disease as children, and if they survived they gained lifelong immunity. North American cities, which were smaller and more isolated, were different. Here smallpox only occurred infrequently, and this meant that the number of adults vulnerable to the disease was much higher. Inoculation, the process in which people were deliberately infected with smallpox, existed in the eighteenth century and did help adults survive. However, inoculation was far from a scientific process, and was much more common in Pennsylvania and New York than New England or the South. Native Americans, with limited antigen diversity, and African Americans, who lived on isolated rural plantations, were even more vulnerable.[16]

Fenn argues that these patterns of immunity shaped the course of the Revolutionary War. At the start of combat, Washington's army had widely variable levels of immunity to the disease, especially among recruits from New England. But the British forces were virtually all immune. This meant that smallpox conveyed a significant advantage to the latter. When the epidemic appeared in 1775, the British simply identified the few soldiers

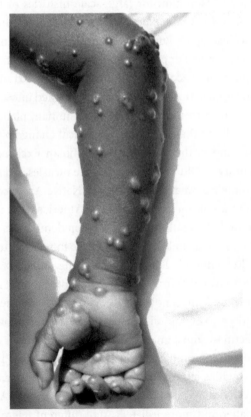

Figure 15.1 Smallpox lesions on the arm of an infant, 1969. Courtesy of Smith Collection/Gado via Getty Images.

in their ranks who had not had the disease and inoculated them. For Washington, this was impossible, since it would cripple the majority of his men for weeks and he risked a major epidemic if those who were inoculated came into contact with vulnerable individuals. For this reason the American army initially banned inoculation of any kind. There was no question that the British knew how to exploit their immunological advantage, however. Gen. Thomas Gage, in charge of the defense of Boston in 1775, had approved reimbursements for various items used "to convey Smallpox to the Indians" earlier in his career. Fears of British plots to convey the disease to the Americans were widespread.[17]

Isolation did not prove possible during the early days of the war. In an effort to seize a major city, an army of American soldiers marched from New England to Quebec in 1775. Smallpox appeared in the American camps as they lay siege to the city. In February Gen. Benedict Arnold wrote in frustration that if smallpox continued to spread it would lead to "the entire ruin of the army."[18] The weakened troops were forced to retreat back to Sorel, Montreal, and eventually Ticonderoga as the disease ran its course. In the process they suffered defeat after defeat. In the early years of the Revolutionary War, it was evident that smallpox "could bring the Continental Army to its knees."[19]

Smallpox was such an issue that in 1777 Washington wrote that "we should have more to dread from it, than from the Sword of the Enemy."[20] On February 5 he decided to take action and require the inoculation of all vulnerable troops. This was an enormous task, and Fenn mentions that in one unit from North Carolina only 23 percent of men had previously had the disease. Those individuals would have to care for the others while they were incapacitated, and the entire event would have to take place in complete secrecy, since the army would temporarily be very weak. The inoculations were successful, and then repeated during the winter of 1778. Ultimately enough soldiers recovered by spring to fight the British to a draw at Monmouth and prevent them from successfully winning in the north.

After Washington's interventions smallpox became a less significant concern in the north, but Clinton's decision to shift the British campaign to the southern colonies provided smallpox with new opportunities. It occasionally crippled rural American militia units, but its most decisive impact was against slaves and Native Americans, both of whom were British allies. Since they lacked immunity to smallpox, they often caught the disease after joining British units. When Gen. Charles Cornwallis squared off against Washington and Rochambeau at Yorktown, it was Cornwallis's black auxiliaries who suffered the most from smallpox. As the siege tightened, Cornwallis forced them out of his camp, even though it left them incapacitated in the forests between the two sides.[21] Washington suspected this was a deliberate attempt by the British to spread the dreaded disease. But by 1781 smallpox could not save Cornwallis's army. Indeed, as Fenn notes, malaria played a more significant role during the Southern campaigns, a disease which McNeill examines in more depth.

McNeill argues that ecological changes in the Carolina Lowcountry helped the malaria vector in the US South, *anopheles quadrimaculatus*. This mosquito preferred stagnant, warm, debris-filled water to breed in, and after 1690 this could be found on the numerous rice plantations located along the coast. *An. quadrimaculatus* also benefited from a growing population of people and cattle, which were its preferred sources of blood.[22] The malaria parasite came in two main forms, recurring vivax and the more lethal falciparum, and the disease was "a routine fact of life and death" in the US South, especially from August to November when mosquitos were most common.[23] People who lived in this disease environment gradually developed resistance to falciparum malaria, making them far more likely to survive the most dangerous attacks. Southerners also developed a number of coping mechanisms that allowed them to avoid malaria during the summer months when *A. quadrimaculatus* was most active. Situating houses on breezy locations like the tops of hills or in peninsular cities like Charleston helped minimize the risks, as did moving inland away from the rice plantations. American southerners enjoyed a significant immunological advantage over the British, which in 1778 drew two-thirds of their new recruits from malaria-free Scotland.[24]

The Southern Strategy was designed by the British to take advantage of presumed Loyalist enthusiasm in the region. These Loyalists, it was hoped, would rally to Cornwallis as he swept American forces out of the region. But the disease environment made this impossible. Cornwallis easily took Charleston in 1780 and won battles at Camden and Guildford Courthourse, but malarial fevers incapacitated his forces during the summer months. This forced British soldiers to abandon the interior lands they had captured to American militias enjoying resistance to malaria. Cornwallis became discouraged by the ravages of disease in April 1781, and after resupplying in Wilmington decided to march north toward Virginia, hoping that the area would be healthier for his troops.[25] But this was not true along the Chesapeake coast where malaria was known to be a major problem.

Clinton demanded that Cornwallis stay along the coast so that he could be evacuated by sea, but the French Admiral de Grasse was able to defeat the Royal Navy and briefly achieve naval supremacy. Washington and Rochambeau then deployed a combined force to besiege Cornwallis at Yorktown beginning in late September. By October 19 it was over. Cornwallis's explanation of his surrender is worth quoting at length:

> I have the mortification to inform your Excellency that I have been forced to give up the post … and surrender the troops under my command. The troops being much weakened by sickness, as well as by the fire of the besiegers; and observing that the enemy had not only secured their flanks but proceeded in every respect with the utmost regularity and caution I could not venture so large sorties as to hope from them any considerable effect … Our force diminished daily by Sickness and other losses, I was reduced, when we offered to capitulate on this side to little more than 3,200 rank & file fit for duty.[26]

Cornwallis could obviously have been exaggerating the impact of disease on his forces, preferring to blame pathogens than his own tactical failings. But the above statement would have been investigated by a military board of inquiry, with execution a possible punishment for "failure to do his utmost." And the figures he gives are shocking. At the start of the siege, Cornwallis commanded 8,700 men, and lost roughly 150–300 dead and 300–600 wounded during combat. When he surrendered, he had 7,660 still at his disposal. If only 3,200 were fit for duty, it meant over half his army was severely ill.[27] Washington and Rochambeau's forces suffered from malaria as well, but they arrived in the region two months later than Cornwallis. On the final day of the siege 1,430 American and French troops were sick, but by then the battle was over. McNeill suggested that malaria prevented Cornwallis from holding Georgia and the Carolinas indefinitely, and ensured that the plantation colonies became part of the United States. In his words, "tiny female *An. quadrimaculatus* stands tall among the founding mothers of the United States."[28]

McNeill also contends that a "full and proper understanding" of the events of the Haitian Revolution cannot be achieved without reference to the ecological context in which it happened. From roughly 1640–1750 sugar cultivation reached the Caribbean islands, and these plantations were ideal habitat for *aedes aegypti*, the mosquito vector for yellow fever. Partially boiled cane juice stored outside in clay jars provided a ready food source, water storage barrels found on ships crisscrossing the region were an ideal site for mosquito eggs, and flourishing port cities exporting sugar ensured a dense host population. The sugar revolution created ideal conditions for *aedes aegypti*.[29] Most importantly, the Atlantic slave trade brought millions of West Africans to the Caribbean plantations where this sugar was grown.

It seems extremely likely that both yellow fever and *aedes aegypti* reached the New World on these slave ships, probably in the early seventeenth century, with the first epidemic reported in the Yucatán Peninsula in 1648.[30] In contrast to malaria, yellow fever had symptoms easily recognized by an unskilled observer; in particular, the black vomit that is the source of the Spanish name for the disease (*vómito negro*).[31] For this reason, we can be fairly certain that yellow fever did not reach the Americas long before 1648.

The disease carried by these mosquitos found the transformed plantation ecologies of the region very welcoming. Three conditions must exist to trigger a yellow fever epidemic: warm weather to ensure *aedes aegypti* eggs hatch, a densely concentrated vector population to ensure the virus is transmitted efficiently, and the presence of a large number of people vulnerable to infection. Since lifelong immunity results if a person survives a single attack, this means the constant arrival of non-immune travelers is essential. The sugar trade, which brought countless European sailors to the region, ensured that yellow fever could find new victims to infect each year.[32]

McNeill argues that "by and large, revolutionary forces enjoyed far greater immunity to these twin killers than did those sent out to quell revolutions, and they learned to exploit that fact."[33] The most dramatic instance of this took place in the French colony of Saint-Domingue. The site of over 8,000 plantations by the 1780s, it was home to 500,000 slaves, 30,000 *gens de couleur* (free people, usually of mixed African and European ancestry), and 40,000 whites. Both malaria and yellow fever were present, as well as abundant mosquito vectors, but yellow fever posed little immediate threat since the vast majority of people living there were immune.[34]

A series of rebellions occasioned by news of the French Revolution created an influx of nonimmune soldiers. *Gens de couleur* seeking legal equality with whites rebelled first in 1790, and in the ensuing chaos a major slave revolt erupted. French soldiers arrived in December 1791 to put down this revolt, but within a few months half were dead. The death of Louis XVI led to war between France and Britain, and the latter sent an expedition to occupy Saint-Domingue that looked certain to succeed. France's official representatives in the colony sought to rally mass support by abolishing slavery, while Britain courted the *gens de couleur* who were often slave owners. The British soldiers managed to occupy one third of the colony, including the vital city of Port-au-Prince, but yellow fever began taking its toll. The British sent approximately 25,000 troops to Saint-Domingue from 1793 until 1798. Despite "trivial" losses in battle, almost 15,000 of those men died there.[35] Needless to say, the British were unable to occupy the island.

The rise of Napoleon transformed the conflict. After coming to power in a *coup d'état*, he sought to re-enslave blacks on Saint-Domingue and restart its lucrative plantation economy. For the task he sent 22,000 soldiers and 20,000 sailors under the command of his brother-in-law, Charles Leclerc. Aware of the shocking mortality caused by fevers during the summer months, they arrived in January 1802.[36] Within a month they had occupied all the key port cities, but faced an enemy adept at scorched earth tactics and unwilling to risk a decisive battle. By betraying Toussaint Louverture, Leclerc was able to arrest his most powerful rival in June 1802, and it briefly appeared that the French had won the war, but as the rainy season began his soldiers started falling ill. Yellow fever was the most important killer. By September 1802 he had 28,000 dead and another 6,000 men unfit for combat. Leclerc tried to win over black leaders who had participated in the slave revolt, and initially enjoyed some success. But news that the French in Guadeloupe had reinstated slavery reached Saint-Domingue around the same time, triggering mass defections to the surviving revolutionary leaders Christophe and Jean-Jacques Dessalines. By 1803 the French position was untenable and their remaining forces abandoned the region, allowing Dessalines to found the modern nation of Haiti. Of the 60,000–65,000 troops France sent to Saint-Domingue, probably 35,000–45,000 died of disease, primarily yellow fever.[37]

The impact of disease on the Haitian Revolution was never in doubt. But the problem lies in the narrative emphasis. If the success or failure of the war was determined by yellow fever, doesn't this diminish the role of the people involved in the revolt? Racist historians in the nineteenth and early twentieth centuries were loath to credit Toussaint or Dessalines with leadership skills or tactical acumen—doesn't the argument that mosquitos won the war lead one to a similar conclusion? McNeill is aware of these dangers, and in a section entitled "The Genius of Toussaint," he issues an important rebuttal. To him, Toussaint and Dessalines were great commanders precisely because they understood the disease environment. McNeill notes that while fighting the British and later Leclerc, Toussaint occupied the mountains and limited the Europeans to the disease-afflicted ports. He argues this was intentional. In an intercepted letter to Dessalines in 1802, Toussaint wrote "do not forget that while waiting for the rainy season, which will rid us of our enemies, we have only destruction and fire as our weapons."[38] It is a slender piece of evidence but crucial nonetheless. Aware of the devastating impact yellow fever had on European armies, Toussaint tried to keep his forces intact until the rainy season laid waste to his enemies. While not as dramatic as a battlefield triumph, it was equally decisive.

Figure 15.2 Charles LeClerc's French expeditionary force lands at Cap-Français (now Cap-Haïten) in 1802. This army was decimated by yellow fever and Haiti won its independence soon after. Courtesy of Roger Viollet Collection via Getty Images.

Conclusion

The argument that disease helped shape the Age of Revolutions is a fascinating one. The evidence that it was an important contemporary concern can be found in the writings of the most important revolutionary leaders. Washington, Cornwallis, Toussaint, and Leclerc were aware of its significance to their actions, although only Washington (through his inoculation campaigns) and Toussaint (through his determination to fight campaigns during the rainy season) were able to exploit this knowledge to the fullest. Using historical empathy allows us to bring these important considerations to light.

But did the environment determine the outcome of these revolutions? That argument is far less convincing. Had France not tried to reintroduce slavery, it is entirely possible that black and *gens de couleur* allies from Saint-Domingue could have won the war for Napoleon. And it is not at all clear that Cornwallis was doomed by malaria. The inexplicable procrastination of Clinton in sending him reinforcements was probably more significant to the course of the Battle of Yorktown. But even with these caveats there is no doubt that the natural environment, and particularly disease, is an important category of analysis.

This chapter illustrates the value of historical empathy. Today we live in a world where the disease is unlikely to determine or even significantly shape the outcome of a major war. But it is important to recognize that generals living in the eighteenth and nineteenth centuries were extremely concerned about the health of their soldiers, and did their best to manage these risks. Smallpox nearly crippled the Continental Army before Washington's inoculation campaigns in 1777–8. Malaria robbed Cornwallis of the men he needed to stave off Washington in 1781. And yellow fever ensured that the slaves of Saint-Domingue were able to fend off armies from Britain and France before gaining their independence in 1804. As William Cronon once wrote, "All human history has a natural context."[39]

Further reading

Braudel, Fernand. *The Mediterranean and the Mediterranean World in the Age of Philip II*, vols. 1, 2. New York: Harper and Row, 1972. A classic in the field that links the slow processes of geological and ecological change to more recent political events.

Crosby, Alfred. *Ecological Imperialism*, 2nd edn. New York: Cambridge University Press, 2004. This famous book links European expansion around the world to the spread of European organisms like pests, plants, and disease.

Dubois, Laurent. *Avengers of the New World*. Cambridge, MA: Belknap Press of Harvard University Press, 2004. An outstanding overview of the Haitian Revolution with particular attention to the significance of racial categories and their role in the conflict.

Fenn, Elizabeth. *Pox Americana*. New York: Hill and Wang, 2001. A history of the smallpox epidemic across North America from 1775 to 1782, an event she feels is desperately underserved by historians.

McNeill, J.R. *Mosquito Empires*. New York: Cambridge University Press, 2010. A classic that uses differential immunity as a way to understand the fate of revolutions in the Greater Caribbean from 1620 to 1914.

16

Tokyo Drift

On July 14, 1853, two powerful nations made contact for the first time. In the Bay of Uraga, near the city of Edo, Commodore Matthew Perry led a squadron of four American ships past a sign reading "Depart immediately and dare not anchor!" His flagship, the *Susquehanna*, was a 2,450-ton steamship that was roughly twenty times larger and significantly faster than any Japanese-built vessel. Astonished fisherman, observing the black smoke emanating from the ships, believed they were on fire. Others recalled the prophetic lyrics of a folk song: "Through a black night of cloud and rain, the Black Ship plies her way, an alien thing of evil mien, across the waters gray … " Japanese representatives could do little more than ask Perry to leave immediately. He declined.[1]

Nonetheless, many Japanese observers looked to the past with hope. In 1281, a divine wind brought by Amaterasu, the goddess from whom the emperor was descended, had prevented a seemingly unstoppable invasion led by the Mongols. Perhaps appeals to this goddess would protect Japan again. But July 15 dawned like any other day, with no indication that a comparable miracle was about to occur. Japan's forced reintegration into the global order had begun.[2]

In the nineteenth century, Westerners considered Japan one of the most isolated locales in the world. This makes it all the more astonishing that the Japanese managed to become "the only country of non-European origin to have achieved modernization."[3] How did this happen? This case study focuses on the issue of continuity and change. Most world historians emphasize the isolation of Tokugawa Japan, the jarring transformation triggered by Perry's arrival, and the subsequent modernization undertaken after the Meiji Restoration beginning in 1868.

However, finding an appropriate balance between continuity and change is an extremely important skill when representing past events. The isolation of Tokugawa Japan was never as complete as many imagine, and reforms to address the challenge posed by the West began long before Perry reached Edo Bay. Similarly, the industrialization that began during the Meiji Restoration was not nearly as rapid as many assume, and continuities to the Tokugawa period remained significant well into the twentieth century. While describing the Japanese encounter with Perry as a turning point in world history seems appropriate on first glance, it is also somewhat misleading.

At the start of the seventeenth century the Tokugawa shogunate was established in Japan. The shogun and his officials (collectively known as the *bakufu*) ruled under the titular authority of a sacred emperor. The emperor had no real power, however, and the shogun's writ rarely held sway outside the major cities. True authority was vested in the *daimyo*, regional lords who ruled over their domains with the assistance of the *samurai*. The *samurai* were best known as warriors, but they also performed a variety of mundane roles for the *daimyo* as administrators, landlords, and tax collectors. Japan did not have a uniform currency or a national army, making central planning dependent on the cooperation of the roughly 250 *daimyo*.[4] This system of politics made unified opposition to the shogun very difficult, but also placed limits on any type of coordinated statewide action. The result was almost three centuries of internal peace.

In order to minimize disruption to this system, the Tokugawa shogunate limited contact with foreigners through a series of exclusion edicts known as *sakoku*. These edicts heavily restricted Westerners access to Japan, forbade Japanese from returning home if they traveled abroad, and outlawed Christianity. The Shimabara Rebellion in 1637, which involved many Japanese Christians, led to draconian repression, and in 1639 the exclusion edicts began to be fully enforced. European contact was restricted to one Dutch ship per year, and its crew was only given access to Deshima Island in Nagasaki harbor.[5] There were numerous exceptions to this isolation, especially for Chinese traders, but it did represent a significant change from earlier policies. The reward was domestic peace, known as the *Pax Togukawa*. But it came at the cost of further decentralization, as the *daimyo* were allowed to reassert control over their realms in exchange for cutting ties with the rest of the world.[6]

The exclusion edicts make the arrival of Commodore Mathew Perry an iconic example of East meeting West. Japanese depictions of the Americans often portray Perry and his second-in-command as hideous goblins, complete with unkempt beards and menacing eyes.[7] Another woodcut called "The Black Ships" shows Perry's ship belching smoke into the sky as a beam of light bursts from its cannons. The anthropomorphized ship seems unnatural and mysterious, with Perry's quarters described as "The Abode of His High and Mighty Mysteriousness."[8] One popular history argues that the impact of this encounter on Japan was comparable to that of extraterrestrials landing on the Earth today.[9]

After the encounter with Perry, the Japanese rapidly modernized along Western lines, particularly during the Meiji Restoration described below. The rapid assimilation of foreign technology and culture make it appear that this was a moment of extraordinary change. The image of the sacred emperor in a Western military uniform and a beard that would have looked stylish in Europe is an excellent example of this. All of this is accurate. But the almost exclusive focus on change neglects important continuities with the past. As we will see, Japan was never as isolated as the exclusion edicts made it appear, and it did not industrialize simply by borrowing Western technologies as quickly as possible.

Figure 16.1 A portrait of the Japanese Emperor Meiji wearing a European military uniform, first published in 1896. Courtesy of De Agostini via Getty Images.

Divine winds of change?

A close look at Japan's history reveals the limits of its isolation. The *bakufu* were well aware of increasing Western imperialism across East Asia, and they were committed to reforming the state to meet these challenges. The first direct evidence of this was a sequence of events involving the Russians. After the Japanese shogun told a Russian ambassador that his ships were not welcome in Japan in 1804, the ambassador went rogue and led a series of retaliatory attacks in the north. This fracas was ultimately smoothed over, but four years later a British ship named the *Phaeton* invaded Nagasaki while hunting for Dutch ships. The eighteen-year-old captain bullied the officials in the harbor, took hostages, and then seized supplies before leaving.[10] He was followed by a number of American ships, including the *Morrison* in 1837, which sought to repatriate Japanese castaways, open trade, and spread Christianity. It was forced to flee after the Japanese opened fire.[11] The *Columbus* and *Vincennes* visited Edo Bay nine years later as part of an official US trade delegation under Commodore Biddle, but he was insulted, physically assaulted, and driven away without meeting anyone of importance.[12] Despite this victory, the Japanese were cautioned by the Dutch that the Americans would return, and in possession of technologies that were as advanced as any in the world. Japan may have been startled by the timing of Perry's visit, but it was hardly out of the blue.[13]

The Opium War also raised alarms among Tokugawa officials. In 1839 the Qing Dynasty and England went to war over repeated efforts by European traders to smuggle opium into the country. Despite the massive resources of the Qing, British steamships dominated China's coastal waterways and ultimately won the war. The humiliating Treaty of Nanjing (1842) forced the Qing to pay an indemnity for a war they did not start, to concede that British nationals would not be subject to Chinese law, and to surrender the island of Hong Kong. Reports from the Dutch kept Tokugawa elites informed of events, and this inspired consternation about Japan's prospects should the West turn its attentions further east.[14]

Tokugawa Japan was not weak. It had excellent infrastructure, especially in terms of the well-maintained roads that crisscrossed the region. This was a direct result of Tokugawa policies that forced *daimyo* to spend one year in the capital of Edo after a year in their domains. Japan also had a massive urban population that included three of the world's largest cities in Edo, Kyoto, and Osaka. The economy was extremely vibrant as a result.

Virtually all goods being sent to the major cities had to be shipped to Osaka first, where wholesalers then arranged distribution in Edo and elsewhere. This concentration of capital led to the rapid growth of the nascent banking sector, with loans readily available to the cash-strapped *daimyos*.[15] With so many people living in close proximity literacy rates were high, and roughly 40–50 percent of men in Tokugawa Japan received at least some formal education.[16]

Mizuno Tadakuni, a powerful *bakufu* leader, responded to the Western threat with dramatic changes. Known as the Tenpō reforms of 1842, he tried to assert direct *bakufu* control over the regions surrounding Niigata, Osaka, and Edo. Traditionally these regions were divided among hundreds of minor lords, each of whom was responsible for mobilizing a small number of troops in the event of an attack. In the older Tokugawa environment, this made sense, since the decentralization of military power limited the possibility of a successful rebellion. But in the event of a Western attack, Japan would struggle to coordinate a response. Ultimately Mizuno's reforms triggered wide resistance among lords stripped of their land as well as commoners fearing expanded military service, but the Tenpō reforms do suggest that Perry's visit was hardly a complete surprise.[17]

This did not mean that Japan was fully prepared. The first unequal treaty opening Japanese ports to Americans was signed in 1854 under the guns of Perry's squadron. By 1858 Japan had signed similar agreements with all the major European powers.[18] This undermined efforts at reform. First, it thoroughly discredited *bakufu* officials. The shogun was supposed to be the "Queller of the Barbarians," but he had authorized them to visit, to trade, and even live in Japan without being subject to local laws. The emperor, on the other hand, remained steadfast in his opposition to the foreigners. This combination of anti-foreign sentiment and reverence of the emperor became the core of the *sōnnō-jōi* movement which sought to expel the Europeans. Primarily comprised of young samurai, this movement rapidly grew in popularity during the 1860s.[19]

Second, the *daimyo* became impossible to control. The *bakufu* needed them to become invested in national defense, but their autonomy and limited resources made this process unwieldy. Some *daimyo* embraced this task wholeheartedly, like in Satsuma and Chōshū, where both samurai and commoners were armed with modern firearms and trained like Western soldiers. This was a mixed blessing for the shogunate because the *daimyo* in those domains were strongly opposed to the treaties Japan had signed with foreigners. In other regions the *daimyo* prevaricated, putting off military reforms in the hopes that the shogunate would pay for them. The *bakufu* modernized their own troops, but they were small in number compared to those of the *daimyo*.[20]

Third, reformers quickly recognized that in order to escape the unequal treaties Japan needed to be respected as a Western nation-state. Tokugawa Japan, with its patchwork of autonomous *daimyo*, a nominal emperor, and a shogun trying to hold it all together, was unlikely to be seen that way by any imperialist nation. In late 1866, Shogun Tokugawa Yoshinobu sought to reinvent Japan along the lines of Napoleonic France, complete with "a European-style cabinet system with nationwide financial and economic authority, economic development informed by the advice of Western technical specialists, the abolition of hereditary status distinctions and obligations, and national conscription for a new, modern army and navy."[21] When the *bakufu* was defeated by the anti-foreign *daimyo* armies from Satsuma and Chōshū, these reforms were put on hold. The new rulers, who claimed to be acting on the behalf of the Meiji emperor, combined a hatred for outside intrusions with veneration for the imperial house. The Meiji Restoration, which began in 1868, made a number of sweeping changes, including stripping the *daimyo* of their domains in 1871 and the samurai of their swords in 1876.[22] This change was justified in the name of protecting an even more ancient tradition, that of imperial authority. Invoking the language of an earlier crisis, they declared that for the emperor to protect Japan and "stand with the nations of the world," it would have to dispense with decentralized rule.[23]

Modernization in order to protect traditions was a common theme across Meiji reforms, but this was a haphazard process that generated considerable resistance. The newly restored emperor was explicitly viewed as comparable to a European monarch. Gone was the ritual seclusion that had been practiced for centuries. In its place was an emperor who happily posed for cameras wearing European clothes. The eventual decision in 1881 to design a Western-style constitution represented the culmination of these changes. The Meiji emperor was becoming a constitutional monarch who reflected Western precedents. This would ensure Japan was treated as an equal on the international stage. But the emperor was still viewed as sacred by many members of the government, and his divine origins were celebrated in rituals around Japan.[24]

The Meiji government also struggled to manage the bellicose anti-foreign sentiment that persisted across Japan. China's defeat at the hands of Western gunboats inspired Japanese scholars to advocate strengthening the nation "economically and militarily in order to avoid indignities from other countries."[25] The fact that a Japanese gunboat forced Korea to sign an unequal treaty with Japan in 1876, only eight years after the Meiji Restoration, reflects the combination of intense nationalism and selective foreign adaptation that would characterize much of Japanese history prior to 1945.[26] The frequently cited images of Japanese people wearing Western clothes are misleading. Although these external markers convey a sense of rapid change, in Japan commitment to key Confucian values like filial piety intensified. The rising economic elite publically spurned Western individualism, and claimed to be motivated by "patriotic devotion and a willingness to sacrifice for the common good."[27] The rejection of a French civil code in favor of revisions that dramatically strengthened the position of the male household head in 1898 reveals the limits of Westernization.[28]

The same was true with regard to industrialization, a subject emphasized in narratives regarding Japan's successful adaptation of Western norms. The construction of railroads and skyscrapers represented important technologies that reached Japan after the treaty ports were opened.[29] But it is important to realize the limits of these changes. In the early 1880s, fifteen years after the Meiji Emperor was restored to power, roughly 98 percent of Japan's labor force worked in agriculture, forestry, or fishing. This was virtually unchanged from the Tokugawa era. Textiles were the main form of manufacturing, and the vast majority of raw silk and cotton yarn was produced by "farmers" at home. This remained true until the First World War. By 1900 factories provided only 8 percent of Japan's net domestic product, and since "factory" was defined as any establishment with more than five employees, this likely included a considerable amount of traditional manufacturing.[30] In 1910, 87 percent of all looms in Japan were hand-powered, and light manufacturing of items like matches depended heavily on labor-intensive putting-out systems that resembled those common in pre-Industrial Europe.[31] Japan was economically vibrant, but only part of this came from new Western technologies. The rest were arguably due to the lengthy internal peace and sophisticated internal trade networks created by the *bakufu*.

A similarly slow-paced transformation took place in Japan's heavy industries. Steel production, for example, could only meet a fraction of domestic demand before the First World War, despite massive government investment. Wars with the Chinese from 1894 to 1895 and Russia from 1904 to 1905 ensured lucrative orders, and tariffs were put in place to protect this vital industry after the unequal treaties were finally canceled in 1911. But two years later only a quarter of Japanese demand for rolled steel was met by

Figure 16.2 Steam engine of the iron railroad at Takanawa. This was painted by Ikkei in 1872, and reveals contemporary fascination with industrial technology in Japan. Courtesy of UIG via Getty Images.

domestic production; all the rest had to be imported. Of equal significance was that only one-quarter of all domestic production was generated by private steel mills—the rest were dependent on constant government support.[32] Despite Japan's first railroad being completed in 1872, no locally supplied equipment operated on their tracks until 1900, and Japan did not produce its first locomotive until 1907.[33] Industrialization in Meiji Japan was a gradual process, not a sudden revolution.

So how did Japan acquire the ships, trains, and steel that enabled it to defeat the Chinese and Russians in the late nineteenth and early twentieth centuries? As Sydney Crawcour observes, "Japan's industrial growth before World War I was largely the growth of traditional industry."[34] The key exports were textiles, usually in the form of either silk or cotton, and rapidly growing sales allowed Japan to acquire the foreign currency needed to purchase advanced technologies. According to Masaki Nakabayashi's study of the silk reeling industry in Suwa district of Nagano prefecture, the opening of the treaty ports created a large export market for Japanese silk, but quality control problems limited its competitiveness. This changed with the establishment of the Kaimeisha cooperative shipping association in 1884, and later the founding of Okaya Silk Reeling Co. Both institutions were committed to standardizing the quality of re-reeled silk to meet the specific demands of the US market, and by 1890 were already receiving orders for specific brands from New York City. Their rigorous quality control and elaborate pay scales based on labor productivity, materials productivity, evenness in linear mass density, and the luster of the final product led to a high-quality and standardized product ideal for American manufacturers. And while the largely female workers regularly put in thirteen to fifteen-hour days, the work culture was very different from that in many Western factories, with far less supervision of labor due to the piece-work pay scale. By 1920, Japanese silk comprised 80 percent of the US market and 60 percent of the world market. This manufacturing success was incredibly lucrative. Japanese silk reeling succeeded not because of the low wages (they were roughly equal to those paid in Italy) or imported technology. Instead, this industry found a pay system that rewarded individual skill, and combined this with a focus on producing a standardized, high-quality product.[35]

Japan's cotton weaving industry also experienced rapid growth in the early twentieth century, increasing in value from 19 million yen in 1903 to 405 million yen in 1919. Jun Sasaki, in a study of the advanced cotton weaving industry in Banshū region in Hyōgo prefecture, notes that Western power

Figure 16.3 Two silk weavers at work in Japan, c.1880. Profits from this lucrative export industry were crucial to fueling the Japanese economy in the late nineteenth and early twentieth centuries. Courtesy of Hulton Archive via Getty Images.

looms helped fuel this boom. But Sasaki also notes that these machines did not rapidly transform the nature of work. The shift records of women working in the Okada power loom weaving factory demonstrate that most women worked less than twenty-four days over a two-month period. The factory was almost a centralized workshop for women who continued to have onerous household obligations. The power looms could be quickly connected or disconnected from the central power source, and women were paid on a piece-work basis according to how much cloth they produced. This was very similar to the putting-out system common during the Tokugawa period, and it allowed female textile workers an opportunity to make extra money around their own schedule.[36]

This was quite different from industrialization in the West. In a famous article, E.P. Thompson argued that English peasants lacked a sense of time suitable to the industrial process. This led to a long and bitter struggle with employers who sought to impose time-discipline in their workers.[37] Thompson believed this process was universal, but Thomas Smith argues that conflict over time was far less fraught in Japan. He uses Tokugawa farm manuals to show that peasant farmers had a keen sense of the value of time. Their fragmented holdings, lack of draft animals, and limited access to hired labor meant that time had to be used efficiently from day-to-day and task-to-task. The proper use of time was coordinated at both the family and village levels, and Smith argues this led to a different labor culture in Japanese factories. Workers were more willing to accept long hours and canceled holidays if there was work to be done, but management was similarly more tolerant of absenteeism or lateness during slow times.[38] Changes certainly took place during Japan's industrialization, but understanding the social and economic continuities is also extremely important. Mimicking the West was not the only path to successful modernization.

Conclusion

It is natural that both students and instructors are drawn to moments of intense change. In the context of nineteenth-century Japan, this has led to a focus on two things; Perry arriving in Edo in 1853, and the Meiji Restoration in 1868. Together, these two events have become emblematic of the ultimately successful industrialization of Japan. That this nation would become a great power in the twentieth century lends added weight to its significance. Understanding what enabled this transformation is crucial.

But emphasizing change to the exclusion of all else can create a misleading image of this historical moment. One problem is that Japan's prior isolation is overstated in ways that make the Japanese appear primitive, backwards, and naïve. Another is that the subsequent transformation is overstated in ways that are politically motivated. Niall Ferguson's paean to Western Civilization is an excellent example. To him, Japan's success stems from their efforts to mimic the West as quickly as possible.[39] This narrative suggests that there is only one way for countries to develop: the Western way. This singular path to modernity minimizes vital aspects of Japan's self-strengthening that had local sources, things like its vibrant textile industry and its unique political history.

The life of Fukuzawa Yukichi reveals the blend of continuity and change that existed across Japan at this time. Fukuzawa was a strident backer of Western reforms, and studied Western philosophy long before it became popular in Japan. His belief that the Meiji Restoration marked an end to feudalism and the origins of a new era of scientific progress reflects his adoption of Western cultural norms. He even wrote that Japan should abandon Asian traditions "to join the camp of the civilized countries of the West."[40] But he was also the first person to use the stridently nationalist phrase "rich nation, strong army," and supported efforts to overturn the unequal treaties that had been imposed on Japan. Toward the end of his life in the 1890s, he wrote in favor of new Civil Laws that embedded Confucian hierarchies in family life, particularly with regard to women.[41] Fukuzawa's writing suggests that his world was marked by far more than just Westernization. Continuities throughout Japan's historical experience, even during the most tumultuous moments of the nineteenth century, remain significant.

Further reading

Ravina, Mark. *To Stand with the Nations of the World*. New York: Oxford University Press, 2017. A global history of the Meiji Restoration that emphasizes the complexity of the Tokugawa legacy and Japanese agency during this period.

Smith, Thomas. *Native Sources of Japanese Industrialization, 1750–1920*. Berkeley: University of California Press, 1988. A collection of essays that challenges universal understandings of the character of industrialization.

Stearns, Peter. *The Industrial Revolution in World History*. 4th edn. New York: Routledge, 2012. A global analysis of the Industrial Revolution, including a helpful chapter on Japan.

Tanimoto, Masayuki, ed. *The Role of Tradition in Japan's Industrialization*. New York: Oxford University Press, 2006. A collection of papers examining the indigenous elements of Japan's industrialization.

Yamamura, Kozo, ed. *The Economic Emergence of Modern Japan*. New York: Cambridge University Press, 1997. Seven influential essays on the industrialization of Japan produced by leaders in the field.

17

Shadows of the Past

In 1893, Java came to America. In celebration of the 400-year anniversary of Christopher Columbus's landing in the New World, Chicago hosted the World's Columbian Exposition. Designed to showcase American accomplishments, the main exhibition area was divided between a "White City" of large, modern buildings and a separate "Bazar of all nations" occupied by a variety of peoples they termed "primitive" or "semi-civilized." In the latter was the extremely popular Java Village. Sponsored by Dutch plantation owners interested in advertising their coffee and tea, the village was built in Java and shipped across the Pacific with 125 villagers. Its most popular feature was a 1,000-seat theater, which was the site of numerous performances. Part of the regular schedule was a Javanese *wayang*.[1]

The *wayang* still exist to this day. They are shadow puppet plays that retell core elements of two ancient Indian epics: the Ramayana and the Mahabharata. The puppets are moved and voiced by the *dhalang*,[2] a puppet master who is the single most important figure in the show. The *dhalang* is usually (but not always) male, and he directs both the *gamelan* musicians and the female singer known as the *pesindhen*.[3] There are numerous and diverse characters who are mostly divided between the Pandawa and Kurawa families. The former include Judistira, the quiet philosopher-king, Bima, the blunt and honest warrior, and Kresna, a brilliant strategist who is an incarnation of the god Wisnu. The Kurawa include Karna, a noble warrior of seemingly humble origins, Durna, a ruthless magician, and Sujudana, a great king doomed by his fate. Comic relief is supplied by Semar, a clown character whose uncontrollable farting and gentle jokes stand in stark contrast to his fierce loyalty and deep wisdom.[4] In Java, these shows often continue for eight or nine hours throughout the night, with audiences watching either shadows on a screen that hides the *dhalang* from view, or from backstage with the *dhalangs* exertions on full display. These fascinating stories of gods and kings probably reached Java with Indian traders in the first century CE, and were performed as shadow puppet plays by at least the ninth century CE.[5] For many Americans, the *wayang* and its accompanying *gamelan* music became synonymous with Java during the 1893 Exposition.[6] To their eyes and ears, Javanese culture seemed idyllic, spiritual, and ancient.

This was wildly misguided, and Java was hardly untouched by the modern world. Dutch planters sponsored Java Village because the island was a Dutch colony, ruled by Europeans who exploited it through a brutal system of forced cultivation called *cultuurstelsel*. But colonization affected far more than just economics. Since colonizing powers often introduced legal codes, new forms of education, and in some places, writing, they also began the process of codifying local traditions. Those traditions they respected enough to write down tended to gain the imprint of antiquity to future scholars, while others that did not fit expectations (or were politically unacceptable to the colonial administration) might remain undocumented and slowly fade

Figure 17.1 A *wayang* puppet, *c*.1900. These puppets are used in all-night performances of the ancient Hindu epics like the Ramayana and Mahabharata. Courtesy of Werner Forman via Getty Images.

from view. Colonization was an extremely significant historical moment not only because of how it shaped the way people thought in the past, but also because of how it shaped the way we think about the past today.

Making sense of colonialism

Colonialism is one of the most important themes in world history. The desire to conquer and rule others contributed to the Colombian Exchange, the intensification of contacts across Afro-Eurasia, and the exploitation of billions of people. Describing and explaining these processes is a key goal for world historians.

But there is no simple way to approach this incredibly complex topic. Today most of us think of colonialism as a form of economic exploitation—the granting of *encomiendas* to conquistadors that entitled them to indigenous labor, the distribution of land to European settlers, and the transformation of tropical economies through the forced production of commodities like sugar and cotton. This was certainly true in Indonesia, where in 1830 Dutch King William I introduced the forced cultivation laws known as *cultuurstelsel*. These labor policies were designed to force indigenous farmers to produce cash crops, including indigo and sugar. While this new approach was lucrative for Dutch administrators, they were forcing peasants to grow these crops instead of rice, and this made these farmers much more vulnerable to droughts and famines. In the 1840s, this led to the deaths of roughly 300,000 people.[7] Trailblazing Marxist historians fleshed out this economic interpretation of colonialism in the 1960s and 1970s, with both Walter Rodney's underdevelopment theory and Immanuel Wallerstein's core–periphery model having a dramatic influence on the field. Understanding how to use sources that illuminated the responses of the colonized to this exploitation became critical to doing history on the colonial period.[8]

The 1980s and 1990s marked a change in emphasis. There was increasing awareness that "colonial regimes were neither monolithic nor omnipotent."[9] These regimes needed local allies, and this entailed certain compromises. Technologies that linked colonies to their core nations also brought new ideas, peoples, and behaviors into close contact with one another, and these encounters often transformed both colony and metropole.[10] Efforts by European administrators to govern through local elites (known as indirect rule) required accommodating local traditions, especially as they related to gender, sexuality, age, and religion.[11] This gave local elites, particularly in the nineteenth and twentieth centuries, considerable agency when it came to shaping how "tradition" was defined at the very moment that it was first being recorded for posterity. This often manifested itself in areas like "customary law," which tended to enshrine the views of certain reactionary local elites (usually older men) who mediated between colonial administrators and indigenous subjects.[12]

Java appears in world history narratives as an ancient religious center, a global trading hub, a victim of colonial exploitation, and a home to pioneers of feminist and nationalist thought. But the history of the *wayang* can still tell us a great deal about Java during the colonial period. Through this form of puppet theater we can see how perceptions of the past were and continue to be shaped by the complex interplay between colonized and colonizer.

Performing authentic pasts

The history of the *wayang* is intertwined with that of Java, and dates back at least 1,000 years. To shed light on the colonial era, however, we need only go back a few hundred years. By the sixteenth century the island of Java was a mélange of trading communities, including the Islamic coastal cities called the *pasisir*. Sultan Agung (1613–46) attempted to crush these cities after inheriting the kingdom of Mataram. He was able to defeat them, but under his son they repeatedly rebelled. In 1677 his grandson Amangkurat II turned to the Dutch East India Company, or VOC, to help bring the *pasisir* to heel. The VOC did this successfully, but Amangkurat II was unable to pay them for their services. The Dutch took control of the *pasisir* instead, and in 1744 this arrangement became permanent.[13] Warfare in the interior ended in 1757, and from that point onward the Dutch could effectively control Java's politics. Formal occupation would eventually follow in the nineteenth century.

It seems likely that the modern shadow puppet tradition emerged in the *pasisir* cities during this tumultuous time, and signs of *wayang's* contact with Islam persist. This can be seen in the sacred amulet called Serat Kalimasada carried by Judistira, the quiet philosopher-king of the Pandawa family. The term was derived from the Islamic profession of faith, *kalimah sahadat*. Another *wayang* tradition that originated during this period was the *wahyu* (from the Arabic *wahy*), which are stories about spiritual boons released by the gods to affirm the legitimacy of rulers.[14] This type of *wayang* is extremely popular today, albeit in a Catholic or Christian form invented by Timotheus Wignyosoebroto in the early 1960s.[15] And last but not least, Sufi mystics are credited with inventing certain genres of the *wayang*. One performance describes how the Sunan Kalijaga, an Islamic saint, actually met Judistira in the sixteenth or seventeenth century, recognized the *kalimah sahadat* on his amulet, and convinced him to convert to Islam. Kalijaga then performed an exorcism through the *wayang* to release Judistira's soul to the heavens. This type of performance became known as Ruwatan.[16]

Most *wayang* performances prior to the colonial era took place in both villages and palaces. Drawing on a mix of Indian *bhakti* worship, Sufi *dikir*, and Javanese exorcisms, *dhalang* and the plays they performed were believed to possess supernatural powers.[17] These works varied from time to time and place to place, with *dhalang* often arriving days before a performance in order to familiarize themselves with local gossip. Scenes were improvised in order to make reference to village issues, and the length of the performance made frequent jokes a necessity. The syncretic *wayang* helped facilitate mutual respect across religions, endowing Java with a unique sense of religious tolerance expressed in the terms *santri*, for committed Muslims, and *abangan*, for nominal Muslims who embraced Javanese religious traditions as well.[18] Powerful rulers were aware of the power of the *wayang*, and some rulers like Sultan Jaka Tingkir gave themselves origin stories that emphasized their connections to the tradition.[19] But performances of these politicized stories were relatively rare, and likely followed a truncated format.[20]

The arrival of the Dutch and the beginning of colonial rule led to dramatic changes in the way the *wayang* were understood. This was linked to two major forces at work on Java. On the one hand, there was a new interest in Javanese culture, especially among Dutch scholars in the mid-nineteenth century. On the other was Orientalism, the framework through which these European scholars understood what they were studying. They believed that the East was ancient, despotic, exotic, and unchanging, and the Dutch came to understand the *wayang* through an Orientalist lens.[21] As they began to write them down, their perspectives had a profound influence on how the *wayang* would be understood in the future. For example, they believed that because the Ramayana and Mahabharata stories had originated in India, the Javanese versions were inferior. They were also contemptuous of the Book of Kings compiled by Ranggawarsita in the mid-nineteenth century. He wrote this text based on performances of the *wayang* in rural Java, but Dutch scholars were not impressed by his efforts to create a chronology based on oral traditions and genealogies known only to village *dhalangs*.[22]

They were far more enthusiastic about an obscure collection of the *wayang* compiled by Prince Kusumadilaga from Surakarta, and first published in 1877. Eventually known as the *Serat Sastramiruda*, it used a question and answer format to define the *wayang* and stipulate "best practices" for performers. These suggested that the *dhalang* should be formal and not use crude humor in their shows. Kusumadilaga also recommended that the *dhalang* familiarize themselves with the texts upon which the plays were based, and to perform only a single version rather than varying it from village to village. This adherence to textual authority neatly fit with Dutch preconceptions of the *wayang*, and Kusumadilaga was warmly applauded by these scholars. The key difference between Ranggawarsita and Kusumadilaga lay in their sources. Ranggawarsita gathered his stories from villages across the island, while Kusumadilaga did his research in a palace. Kusumadilaga's vision of the *wayang* as an elite court tradition was more appealing to the Dutch. He shared their belief that the *wayang* was an ancient tradition from India that had gradually degraded in the hands of the *dhalang*, but if they followed his rules, the *wayang's* old grandeur could be restored.[23] Dutch conquest had stripped Javanese nobles of their main functions in terms of political scheming and fighting wars. This left them with time and resources to commit to "perfecting" the *wayang*, and some nobles embraced this with gusto.[24]

Dutch interest in the *wayang* was never purely academic. During both the Java War of 1825–30 and the Aceh War at the end of the nineteenth century, the Dutch found themselves fighting against forces united under the banner of Islam. As a result, Dutch scholars and administrators began to promote a Hindu-Javanese literary culture that might curtail Islamic influences.[25] They also encouraged Javanese elites to emphasize this element of their history. During the early twentieth century many Javanese children from elite families attended Dutch-language schools and were exposed to Dutch views of the *wayang*. The importance of this is evident in 1921 speech by a man named Soetopo at the Java Institute in Yogyakarta where he decried the "deterioration" of the *wayang*. Speaking in Dutch, he stated that the *dhalang* performed the stories incorrectly because they lacked the education necessary to understand the nuances of the plays. The remedy, he believed, was to found schools that could formally train the puppeteers, and the first opened two years later. These schools standardized musical elements of the *wayang*, relegated female singers to a subsidiary role, and generally made the *wayang* more orderly. Certain scenes, like the *jejer* during the first hour which describes the fictional land in which the story will take place, were given a much more prominent role at court schools than they ever received in the villages. The new styles taught at the schools were not very popular outside the palaces. But the Javanese students taught here "came to believe that the *wayang* tradition needed to be cleaned up, the stories needed to be organized, and correct versions of them needed to be taught."[26] They would transform the *wayang* over the next forty years, even after the Dutch recognized Indonesia's independence in 1949.

These schools influenced village performers in many ways. They became repositories of written texts, especially translations of the Book of Kings and *Serat Sastramiruda*. They also became sites of "upgradings" that were attended by village *dhalang* whose magical powers were feared by elites at court. These classes did not necessarily change the way the *wayang* were performed. In many cases the techniques taught here were unsuccessful in rural villages where loud music, knowledge of local gossip, and bawdy jokes still attracted better crowds. But the classes did succeed in convincing *dhalang* that the most authentic versions of the *wayang* could only be found in the written texts held in palace libraries.[27] And the polished techniques of the courtly *dhalang* from the 1920s to the 1960s became the standard against which subsequent performances were judged. Those that adhered to the standards set at these schools were considered "authentic," while those that diverged were considered deviant.

Nonetheless, innovations to the *wayang* continue to the present day. One example is the Rebo Legi performances. Celebrating the Javanese birthday of the legendary puppeteer Ki Anom Suroto, they are well attended by other *dhalang*, most of who have been formally trained in fine arts academies. But the performances defy convention in fascinating ways. The viewing screen is usually set against a wall, so one can only see the show from the side of the puppeteer. Puppets are thrown across the stage in violent or undignified ways, and the courtly emphasis on dignified mannerisms has been replaced with sexualized jokes and bantering with the crowd. The classical style of the courtly *dhalang* is mocked as old-fashioned and out of touch. In a way, the Rabo Legi performances resemble the resistance of village performers to courtly etiquette during the colonial era.[28]

Figure 17.2 Wayang puppets as they appear on screen. This image was taken at a 1996 performance in Yogakarta, Indonesia. Courtesy of Ben Davies/LightRocket via Getty Images.

The *wayang padat* (meaning compressed *wayang*) offer a modern twist on the shadow puppet play. Developed at the Academy in Solo, they are one and a half hours long rather than the usual nine, follow a written script, and use multiple people to play the roles occupied in the past by a single *dhalang*. This means multiple puppeteers, a scriptwriter, and a director, which reflects the influence of Western theatrical performances. But the *wayang padat* are only performed for other Academy members or international audiences. They lack the humor of the Rebo Legi, or the mysticism of the much earlier Ruwatan, but innovations here have spread across Indonesia. Famous performers like Manteb, for example, borrowed the colored lights, noisy music, and dramatic puppet movements from the *wayang padat* and added them to performances whose content more closely resembles that of the Rebo Legi.[29]

These modern innovations suggest that the *wayang* remains a dynamic part of Javanese culture right to the present day. Globalization has brought international recognition, and in 2003 the *wayang* were cited by UNESCO as a "Masterpiece of the Oral and Intangible Heritage of Humanity."[30] But the context is fascinating. The application to be added to this list was made by the Indonesian government, now an independent state free of Dutch control. It argued that the *wayang* were an ancient tradition facing an existential crisis because of the *dhalang* who now focused on jokes and clowning at the expense of the religious and educational elements of the *wayang*.[31] To these government officials, the "real" *wayang* was threatened by pop culture, and needed to be saved.

If you feel a bit of déjà vu, think back to the colonial era. Dutch scholars and Javanese elites essentially created the courtly style in the 1920s, insisting that *dhalang* should avoid the kind of earthy humor and gossipy banter that village audiences loved in favor of more tightly scripted performances, technical expertise, and dignified behavior. In the twenty-first century, these same issues remain contentious long after political independence from the Dutch. In this way, the *wayang* exemplifies the importance of the colonial moment. Even though only a handful of Dutch scholars and officials ever wrote about the *wayang*, they and their early Javanese collaborators were able to establish the norms against which every subsequent form of the *wayang* was judged. This was not the same kind of power that colonial states used to force people off their land, but it was no less real.

Conclusion

One of the most famous *dhalang* today is Ki Enthus Susmono, known as the "crazy dalang" in Indonesia. His performances employ Western theatrical techniques like flashbacks and autobiographical asides, use synthesizers as part of the *gamelan* music, and incorporate Arabic language chants known as Qasidah. He uses colloquial language, banters with the audience, and will occasionally fight a puppet on stage. His extensive collection of puppets includes personal designs representing international figures like George W. Bush and the Teletubbies.[32] At a 2009 museum exhibition dedicated to his career, the press release noted how unorthodox his performances were: "Rough language, sexual allusions, a puppet that drinks beer. Until recently such brutalities were unthinkable in an Indonesia puppet play, the wayang … his performances are innovative and keep the wayang theatre alive."[33]

The *wayang*, like all other cultural traditions, has a history. It responds to contact with outside influences, which in Java have included things like the arrival of Islam, Dutch conquest, Indonesian independence, and global pop culture. Today the *wayang* are recorded, televised, and illustrated in comic books. One scholar even created a *wayang*-based skin for gamers playing Street Fighter IV![34] These are not degenerate versions of a pure original, but part of an ongoing process of creation and destruction.

Today many of us have an intuitive sense of what authentic cultural traditions look like, and it is quite similar to that held by the Americans visiting the Java Village in 1893. These traditions predate the arrival of global religions like Christianity or Islam, are connected to ancient forms of spirituality, and are dignified events, performed by solemn men who possess deep insights into the past. With regard to the *wayang*, this is most closely approximated by shadow plays that mimic the courtly etiquette prescribed by Prince Kusumadilaga and other Dutch scholars. But did these scholars really uncover an ancient tradition unchanged for over a thousand years? Or did they merely encourage the Javanese to embrace what the Dutch thought the *wayang* should look like, bringing into being a courtly tradition that was only one of many in the history of this genre?

Understanding historical significance is tricky. Sometimes it seems self-evident. Colonialism, marked by the conquest of much of the world by Europeans, is a good example. Many students are familiar with the litany of crimes committed by colonizers, and understand that they matter. But significance is not just a matter of military strength. After all, the colonizers were thrown out decades ago. And yet colonization was such a transformative event that it continues to shape the way we think about the past. For world historians, this may well be colonization's most enduring legacy.

Further reading

Anderson, Benedict. *Mythology and the Tolerance of the Javanese*. Ithaca, NY: Cornell University Press, 1996. A study of Java's cultural tolerance by a prominent scholar through the lens of *wayang*.

Brandon, James, ed. *On Thrones of Gold*. Cambridge, MA: Harvard University Press, 1970. A comprehensive study of three *wayang kuilt* plays, including their history, numerous images of the puppets, and narrative details.

Moertono, Soemarsaid. *State and Statecraft in Old Java*. Ithaca, NY: Cornell University Press, 1968. A classic survey of politics on Java from the sixteenth to nineteenth century, one that emphasizes the divine nature of kingship on the island.

Sears, Laurie. *Shadows of Empire*. Durham, NC: Duke University Press, 1996. A detailed examination of how Javanese shadow theater represented a nexus point between colonial power on the one hand and indigenous traditions on the other.

Stoler, Ann Laura, and Frederick Cooper, eds. *Tensions of Empire*. Berkeley: University of California Press, 1997. An essential work on the nature of colonialism, one that includes several essays on its contradictions, conflicts, and impact on the metropole.

18

Open Wounds

On July 10, 1941, a terrible massacre took place in Jedwabne, a small town in eastern Poland. The horrifying crime took place less than three weeks after the German Army swept through the town. The new mayor ordered the Polish residents to round up their Jewish neighbors, humiliate them publicly, and then kill them. Jerzy Laudański, a Polish policeman, was one of many who answered the call, and he was seen chasing Jews around town and bludgeoning them to death. But it soon became apparent that this form of killing was too labor intensive. Instead, the town's Jews were marched into a barn, hundreds of bodies packed into a tight space. It was then doused in kerosene and set alight. No Germans were present. The Poles heard the screams as the barn went up in flames, smelled the bodies as they burned, and clawed through the rotting corpses for jewelry as dogs gnawed on the bones. Prior to the massacre two-thirds of Jedwabne's population was Jewish, roughly 1,600 people. Only seven survived.

One survivor, Szmul Wasersztajn, recorded a detailed account of the massacre in 1945. This information was passed on to the postwar Polish government, and four years later fifteen Poles were convicted of involvement. Case closed on another sad chapter of the Holocaust. Or so it might seem. But of the fifteen Poles convicted, none served more than eight years in prison before being released. When a monument was erected to commemorate the killings, its inscription subtly altered the narrative of events: "The site of the murder of the Jewish population. On 10 July 1941, the Gestapo and German military police burned 1,600 people alive."[1] Neither Wasersztajn nor the witnesses in the 1949 trial mentioned a significant presence of Germans at the massacre.[2] How did they become part of this story? And why were the killers released after only short spells in prison? What follows is the story of a killing that reveals how evidence can be manipulated to support a particular agenda, and how perceptions of the reliability of the available evidence shape how historians reconstruct the past.

The *Neighbors*

The key figure in the debate over Jedwabne is Jan Gross. A Polish American sociologist and historian, he stumbled upon Wasersztajn's eyewitness account in the Jewish Historical Institute's archives in the mid-1990s. Written in sparse prose and unflinching in assigning guilt, it took Gross almost four years to come to terms with its contents.[3] During that time he tried to locate every possible source on Jedwabne during the Second World War. The famously comprehensive German archives yielded nothing, but the records of the 1949 trial in postwar Poland contained considerable testimony from the perpetrators. A memorial book for Jedwabne's Jews, compiled by Rabbi Baker in 1980, and interviews by Polish filmmaker Agnieszka Arnold in 1998 (conducted for a documentary on the Holocaust entitled *Where Is My Older Brother Cain?*) completed his data set. The result was *Neighbors*, a book about the tragic moment when "half of the population of a small Eastern European town murdered the other half."[4] Gross places responsibility for the crime squarely on the shoulders of the Polish residents, and notes the massacre was part of a long history of anti-Jewish violence in the region.[5] Published in Polish in 2000 and then English in 2001, it was shortlisted for several important literary prizes and was generally well-received by Holocaust scholars.

But *Neighbors* did not receive universal acclaim. In Poland it triggered a nasty debate over the depth of Polish anti-Semitism and the extent of collaboration with the Nazis. Certain researchers and politicians defended Gross and his findings, but in Jedwabne itself the community closed ranks around the killers, defending them with such vehemence that it made accurately memorializing the massacre even more difficult than it had been in the past. Most historians believe that knowing history prevents us from repeating prior errors. Jedwabne reveals this may not be the case.

Gross's book was painstakingly researched, and his account was primarily based on eyewitness accounts recorded in the immediate aftermath of the Second World War. There were problems with these sources, but these were addressed explicitly in the text. To those who questioned the accuracy of Wasersztajn's account, Gross suggested that survivor's testimony should be treated as fact "until we find persuasive arguments to the contrary."[6] Given that 98 percent of the Jews in Poland were killed during the Second World War (as opposed to 5–7 percent of the ethnic Polish population), there were rarely multiple Jewish eyewitnesses.[7] Gross also acknowledged that the

Figure 18.1 The monument to the Jewish victims of the Jedwabne massacre. It was found vandalized with Nazi graffiti on September 1, 2011. Courtesy of Artur Reszko/AFP via Getty Images.

testimony gathered for the 1949 trial likely involved the use of torture by the Polish Security Office. But Gross felt that the perfunctory nature of the depositions and the lack of an obvious political motive for the investigators suggested that the testimony itself was generally accurate.[8]

Those seeking to minimize Polish responsibility attacked Gross's account on three main points. The first was that he ignored evidence of German involvement. Gross acknowledged that he was not able to examine the entirety of the German archives, but general inquiries did not reveal any units in the area at the time.[9] Given the way the Germans scrupulously documented participation in many terrible atrocities, Gross felt it was unlikely they would have gone to any special effort to conceal the massacre at Jedwabne. Gross noted the presence of a unit of eleven gendarmes responsible for keeping order in Jedwabne, and a carful of "Gestapo men" which appeared in town on either the 9th or the 10th of July.[10] However, he felt they were mostly guilty of failing to prevent the massacre rather than organizing it. Indeed, they appeared to have let the mayor and town council take the lead in coordinating the killings. In conclusion, Gross wrote that the German role was "limited, pretty much, to their taking pictures."[11]

However, Polish historians argued Gross ignored evidence that German special units had perpetrated the massacre. Bogdan Musiał, citing a 1960s investigation of German war crimes, suggested that Hermann Schafer, the leader of an *Einsatzgruppen* unit, coordinated the killing.[12] Schafer was present in nearby Radziłów prior to the pogrom there on July 7. But German records indicated Schafer and his men left the region before the killings in Radziłów began, and Schafer was never seen by anyone in Jedwabne.[13] Another narrative emphasizing the role of the Germans comes from Tomasz Szarota, who blamed a German unit under the command of Wolfgang Birkner. There was no surviving archival information confirming this, but a Polish prosecutor named Waldemar Monkiewicz claimed to have uncovered Birkner's involvement during a war crimes investigation from 1969 to 1974.[14] Szarota presented this evidence at a colloquium in Warsaw, claiming "I doubt that the prosecutor plucked those 232 Germans out of the air, or the truck for that matter, or the figure of Wolfgang Birkner. In any case it can't be right that the name Birkner isn't mentioned once in Gross' book."[15] But the German archives indicated that Birkner's unit was in Bialystok on July 10, far to the east, and no witnesses reported its presence in Jedwabne.

The second critique of Gross implied that the Jews of Jedwabne so antagonized their neighbors during the Soviet occupation from 1939 to 1941 that Polish involvement in the killing was understandable. Prior to the publication of Gross's book, Polish studies of the Second World War generally downplayed the suffering of Poland's Jews, and focused instead on crimes committed against ethnic Poles. This narrative of victimhood was fueled by opponents of the Communist government that ruled Poland until 1989. The most passionate opponent was Solidarity, a powerful labor union created in 1980 that had over ten million members at its peak. It combined Polish nationalism and Catholicism into a potent anti-Communist mix, and in 1990 the founder of Solidarity, Lech Wałşea, became Poland's President.

Most Polish historians supported the aims of Solidarity, and this was evident in their work. They generally emphasized the heroic moments of Second World War from the perspective of nationalist partisans, especially the Home Army which led the Warsaw Uprising. Not coincidentally, the area around Jedwabne was a hotbed of nationalist resistance to both the Nazis and the Soviets during the Second World War. A narrative of Polish victimhood followed by patriotic heroism was deeply embedded in Polish historiography, and men like Jerzy Laudański were generally treated as exemplars of the latter—after all, he had fought for Poland against both the Soviets and the Nazis. But Gross complicated this narrative by noting that Laudański had also been a leading participant in the Jedwabne massacre. The backlash was tremendous. In a major article on the subject, a historian and Solidarity politician asked "Is the hubbub surrounding Jedwabne intended to eclipse the responsibility of Jews for communism and the Soviet occupation of Poland?"[16]

Tomasz Strzembosz, a well-respected historian of the Polish partisans near Jedwabne, published a response to Gross in January 2001 that made a similar argument. Despite stating that "murders carried out on any group of civilians cannot be justified," he proceeded to make the case that Jewish collaboration with the hated Soviets led their Polish neighbors to retaliate after the Germans arrived.[17] Strzembosz concluded "even if the Jews didn't see Poland as their fatherland, they didn't have to treat it like the occupying forces did and work with Poland's mortal enemy [i.e., the Soviet Union] to kill Polish soldiers and murder Polish civilians fleeing eastward. Nor did they have to take part in selecting their neighbors for deportation, those terrible acts of collective responsibility."[18] Strzembosz's work was widely cited, and in 2001 he was named Person of the Year by *Solidarity Weekly* for "seeking the truth" about Poland.[19]

Strzembosz's argument seems to miss the point, but his evidence is even more problematic. He includes a lot of material recorded during the war that is now held at the Hoover Institution. These testimonies involved Poles deported to the USSR before the Jedwabne massacre. Thus the informants did not know anything about the killing, but could contextualize the occupation period of 1939–41. And they make a litany of accusations against the Jews. The most frequent were that the Jews welcomed the Soviets, and that they joined the NKVD to help the authorities capture Polish partisans.[20]

This reveals the main problem with this testimony. It proves that a lot of people from the area believed that Jews collaborated with the Soviets. But this could be easily explained by the anti-Semitism of the informants. When they make general accusations, the Jews are often the target. But when discussing specific events, Jews were rarely responsible. Thanks to the survival of Soviet archives in the area, Krzysztof Jasiewicz was able to determine the backgrounds of the 181 careerist collaborators with the NKVD in Jedwabne region. They included 126 Poles (70 percent), 45 Jews (25 percent), and ten others.[21] Strzembosz's reliance on the Hoover archive, based as it is on broad prejudices, is a major weakness.

Last but not least, Gross's opponents resorted to *ad hominem* attacks that revealed an ugly streak of anti-Semitism. Richard Lukas, a professor of history at Tennessee Technological University, described Jan Gross as "a Jew who emigrated to the West from Poland in 1968," and attacked him for ignoring Jewish guilt over collaboration with Poland's enemies. Lukas argued that Gross's "obviously flawed" book was only published because it was part of the "'Holocaust industry.'"[22] This theme was repeated by many prominent Polish historians. Andrezj Szczesniak, the author of most of Poland's history textbooks in the 1980s and 1990s, wrote that "they are trying to take that martyrology away from us. It's a theft of suffering. The hysteria around Jedwabne is aimed at shocking Poles and extracting sixty-five million dollars from our people in the framework of the 'Holocaust business.'"[23] That certain Polish academics were validating this dangerously anti-Semitic narrative filtered back to Jedwabne, where residents cited it as proof they were being smeared in order to line Jewish pockets.[24]

Gross focused heavily on testimony written in the immediate aftermath of the killing. His opponents, however, often relied on much more recent testimony. For example, Strzembosz included interviews with five people speaking fifty years later.[25] This was a serious problem for a number of reasons. Informants might forget crucial details, or reshape their story to align it with accounts that emerged later. And all these accounts were shaped by the context in which they were gathered. This brings us to the debate over the extent of anti-Semitism in Jedwabne, both past and present, and how it may have influenced accounts of the massacre.

Although Poles and Jews lived alongside one another for centuries, their relations were not always cordial. Poland's Jewish community dates to the ninth century CE, and from the 1300s to 1500s they enjoyed considerable rights and freedoms. Abraham Brumberg argued that the arrival of the Jesuits during the Counter-reformation led to heightened suspicion of religious tolerance, and Polish-ness came to be linked with Catholicism. By the end of the nineteenth century this had coalesced into a virulent anti-Semitism. The National Democratic Party (*Endecja*), co-founded by Roman Dmowski in 1897, went so far as to advocate for the expulsion of all Jews. One Polish poet wrote in the 1930s that anti-Semitism became so entrenched that it "reached the level of a psychosis and eventually total insanity."[26] *Endecja* organized violent boycotts of Jewish businesses in the Jedwabne region, including a pogrom in Radzilow in 1933 which resulted in deaths of four people.[27] While the Polish government tried to suppress this type of behavior, *Endecja* defended the violence as "anti-Communist." On the four year anniversary of the pogrom, supporters of *Endecja* laid a wreath on the grave of a nationalist shot by the police during the rioting. Over 1,000 people attended.[28]

Part of *Endecja*'s support derived from its close ties to the Catholic Church. In the 1930s these two institutions agreed that Jews were to blame for Poland's problems. They could safely ignore Jewish political opinion since the electoral system was heavily gerrymandered to prevent them from ever representing a majority.[29] Sermons at church often focused on Jewish responsibility for the suffering of Christ, and one Jewish woman was killed in Jedwabne during Easter violence in 1934 after an inflammatory prayer service. When children disappeared, priests accused Jews of baking Christian blood into Passover matzo.[30]

The church closely collaborated with *Endecja*. In 1936 the largest church paper in the area, *The Catholic Cause*, reported that a service was directly followed by an *Endecja* rally that attracted 1,500 people. During this procession participants shouted "Long live the Polish nation," "Long live Polish national trade," and "Down with Jewish Communism." Father Cyprian Łozowski then had his church choir sign a song titled "Lord, Rid Poland of the Jews."[31] In 1937, the same paper happily noted that "the mood of excitement has turned into a systematic campaign in which the whole county population takes part. Farmers refuse to sell food to Jews, and entering villages, one sees signs that say 'No Jews.' Jewish shops are empty, water mills and windmills stand still, for no one gives them grain to grind."[32] In 1939 at the Eucharistic procession participants sang "Ah, beloved Poland,/you've people in the millions/and on top of all that/you're filled up with Jews./Rise up, white eagle,/smite Jews with your claws,/so that they will never/play the master over us."[33] The Church and *Endecja* were united in their desire to keep Polish Jews powerless long before the Nazis entered Poland.

When Soviet troops marched into Poland in late 1939, everyone in the occupied zone was affected. Polish Jews bitterly resented the atheism of the Communist Party, and because many were small business owners they bore the brunt of Stalinist redistribution. They also were targets for resettlement. The wave of deportations in June 1940, organized by the NKVD, explicitly targeted Polish Jews, and they comprised 80 percent of those who were forcibly relocated.[34] But Anna Bikont argues Polish anger at their Jewish neighbors stemmed from changes implemented by the Soviets. The new rulers did not tolerate the kind of overt discrimination against Polish Jews that had been common in the 1930s. For example, prior to the occupation Polish nationalists like Czesław Laudański (father of Jerzy) organized boycotts of classes taught by Jewish teachers.[35] But after the Soviets arrived one informant remembered that Polish Jews could sit wherever they wanted in public school classrooms, rather than be forced to the back. Another informant recalled that "Jews felt good, very free. They could walk down any street, even where they had formerly been pelted with stones. You didn't hear anyone say 'dirty Jew.'" Much later, one resident recalled "if the Jews had kept quiet under the Soviets like they did before the war, things wouldn't have ended the way they did."[36] For many Poles the occupation left them feeling helpless, and they came to believe that their Jewish neighbors were benefiting from the new order. This was not true, but when the Germans arrived in June 1941, these Poles saw a chance to level the score.

Occasional violence against Jews in the region rapidly escalated into a series of pogroms. The first took place at Wąsosz, where on July 5 the police and other residents took up the "sacred task" of slaughtering all Jewish men, women, and children. Hundreds died. Then on July 7 a similar massacre took place in the town of Radziłów. Three days later the violence came to Jedwabne. Numerous eyewitness accounts survive from the Soviet trial in 1949, and together they place ninety-nine Polish men at the scene. Jerzy Laudański was one of the individuals named. His father Czesław was an *Endecja* activist and an important member of the church, and had been arrested by the Soviets. Jerzy had ample motive to seek revenge on the people he believed responsible, the Jewish Communists, and he may well have looted money, jewelry, and even a fur coat from the victims.[37] On July 10 Jerzy was the head policeman in Jedwabne, and eyewitnesses described him beating multiple people on the day of the massacre.[38] He did not try to deny participating during his legal troubles. When he petitioned for an early release from his prison sentence in 1956, he told the Communist government "Since I was raised in an area of intense struggles against the Jews, and during the war Germans mass-murdered Jews over there ... why should I be the only one treated with the full severity of the law?" As Gross notes, he had a point. He was convicted by the postwar government for collaborating with Germans, but in Jerzy's mind he had never done so—if anything, he was "a regular guy, a good patriot acting in collaboration, at most, with his own neighbors."[39]

Sadly the alliance between Polish nationalists and the Catholic Church did not end with the Second World War. When two Jewish survivors of the pogrom in Radziłów surfaced in 1945, they were immediately killed by nationalist partisans.[40] Violence against the small number of surviving Polish Jews escalated in 1946 with the Kielce pogrom, when a group of Polish soldiers and police officers murdered forty-two Jews.[41] Surviving Polish Jews fled the country. By the time Gross's book was published, there was only a single Jewish woman living in Jedwabne, and she was terrified to speak to anyone. Her savior, Antonina Wyrszykowska, had been attacked by Home Army partisans in 1945 for saving the seven Jedwabne Jews from the killers. The anti-Semitic ravings by both politicians and priests continued. In 2001, when Anna Bikont interviewed residents of Jedwabne, she encountered a pamphlet with the following poem: "The Germans did it, learned Mister Gross/It's time you kissed us Poles upon the nose./It was the Jews who helped, you pseudo-Neighbor,/Deport Poles Eastward to do hard labor./By that time the Jews had already forgot/how Judas was with silver bought./So if there's a fashion for apology,/Let the Jews apologize for Calvary."[42]

The Catholic Church in Poland continued to struggle with anti-Semitism. In 2001 Cardinal Józef Glemp told the Catholic Information Services, "we wonder whether the Jews should not acknowledge that they have a burden of responsibility towards the Poles, in particular for the period of close cooperation with the Bolsheviks." In a revealing moment he claimed that anti-Semitism did not exist in Poland, despite the fact that the Pope had previously apologized to Poland's Jews for it.[43] Paintings depicting stereotypical Jews luring children and draining their blood were displayed at Sandomierz cathedral until 2006.[44]

Efforts to more accurately represent the killings on the Jedwabne monument were hamstrung by disagreements over the text; ultimately a compromise was reached that said nothing about culpability for the massacre.[45] Even an effort to rename a Jedwabne school after the Wyrzykowskis was stymied by vehement community opposition.[46] In an atmosphere like this, it is easy to understand why Gross's book would receive such a negative reception. But it is disappointing that certain historians would serve as accomplices to the anti-Semitic backlash. By minimizing important aspects of Gross's evidence, privileging interviews that took place decades after the massacre, and ignoring important contextual factors, they created a potent counternarrative that became popular with those hoping to conceal this painful chapter of Poland's history.

Conclusion

Gross's book inspired many historians. Omer Bartov, among others, used Gross's approach to shed new light on the Holocaust elsewhere in Eastern Europe.[47] Gross's book also inspired many Poles. President Kaśniewski, at great political cost, made a moving apology on the sixtieth anniversary of the killings in Jedwabne.[48] So did the mayor of Jedwabne. But it is no coincidence that both were immediately voted out of office, replaced by opponents who argued that Gross was viciously smearing Poland's good name. Their nationalism has subsequently grown in significance.

In February 2018, Poland's ruling Law and Justice Party passed a bill criminalizing the intentional attribution of the crimes of Nazi Germany to Poland. The reason, states Samuel Kassow, is that "the Law and Justice Party … has a base that is very nationalistic and that is very angry at what it sees as people ignoring Polish suffering during the war." The very first case filed under the new legislation was against an Argentine newspaper, *Pagina/12*, that had published a story about Jedwabne based on Jan Gross's research.[49] Israel reacted with outrage, recalling its ambassador and stating "no law will change the facts."[50] But to this day the law remains on the books.

When the president attended the ceremony for the sixtieth anniversary of the massacre, the residents of Jedwabne played their radios at the highest possible volume in order to drown it out.[51] This is an apt metaphor for the conflict between memory and history. The noisy dominance of comforting narratives makes it easy for historians to misrepresent the unpalatable moments of the past. By ignoring certain types of evidence in favor of others, historians can be complicit in this enterprise. But by amplifying those voices that might otherwise be silenced, historians can also force a moment of reckoning. Gross's book certainly did this.

Figure 18.2 Polish President Aleksander Kwasmiewski lays a wreath at the Jedwabne monument, July 10, 2001. Courtesy of Wojtek Laski/Hulton via Getty Images.

Further reading

Bartov, Omer. *Anatomy of a Genocide*. New York: Simon and Schuster, 2018. A leading Holocaust scholar investigates a related massacre in his home town of Buczacz. His approach was shaped by the work of Jan Gross.

Bikont, Anna. *The Crime and the Silence*. New York: Farrar, Straus and Giroux, 2015. A gripping account of the Polish response to *Neighbors* that delves into the Jedwabne Massacre and the efforts to cover it up.

Brand, William, ed. *Thou Shalt Not Kill*. Warsaw: Więź, 2001. An anthology of Polish language sources addressing the controversy created by Gross's book. None were available in English at the time.

Gross, Jan. *Neighbors*. Princeton, NJ: Princeton University Press, 2001. The trailblazing monograph that triggered a Polish debate over the massacre in Jedwabne.

Polonsky, Antony, and Joanna Michlic, eds. *The Neighbors Respond*. Princeton, NJ: Princeton University Press, 2004. A collection of numerous articles written after the publication of *Neighbors*.

19

Global Goals

From 1948 to 1994, South Africa was ruled according to the system of institutionalized white supremacy known as apartheid. Competition between black and white athletes was forbidden, and this eventually led to international sanctions against South African sports teams. The release of Nelson Mandela in 1990 and his victory in free and fair elections four years later represented a turning point. The sanctions ended, and in 1995 South Africa hosted the Rugby World Cup. Their subsequent victory was so dramatic that it became the subject of the feature film *Invictus*. Nine years later, soccer's governing body FIFA (*Fédération Internationale de Football Association*) chose South Africa to host the 2010 World Cup.

The World Cup is the most important soccer competition in the world. Each country can field a team comprised of their best players, and during periodic breaks in club competition they compete in qualifying matches. If a nation is one of the thirty-two qualifiers, they are then invited to the World Cup. Qualifying positions are assigned to regional associations, ensuring that teams from all over the world attend. Held every four years, it takes place over one month, with games happening across the host nation. Massive audiences from around the world watch on television, with the 2006 final between Italy and France attracting roughly 715 million viewers. FIFA rakes in enormous sums of money by selling TV rights and exclusive advertising deals to its corporate partners. For the host nation, a successful World Cup can lead to a surge in tourism and offers an opportunity to showcase the nation to a global audience.

When South Africa won the right to host the 2010 World Cup, many pundits worried that it would be a disaster. Some of their fears were sensationalistic, but lingering income inequality from the apartheid era, a tragically widespread HIV/AIDS epidemic, and dangerous levels of violence in many parts of the country were real concerns. I happened to be in Kenya during the World Cup, and I flew down to see a game between Algeria and the United States. It was a gripping spectacle, with Landon Donovan scoring a stoppage time winner to ensure the United States moved on. After the game, both sets of fans mingled around the pitch, singing arm in arm despite the tensions that existed between the two nations. I then walked the mile back to my host family's house without ever feeling in danger. On that day, it was easy to believe that soccer was a global force capable of overcoming national, religious, or ethnic divisions. Ultimately the 2010 World Cup was deemed a success, and the once-skeptical pundits lauded South Africa for its impeccable performance as host.

But there were also whispers that the 2010 World Cup might not have been such a wonderful accomplishment. The bidding process was marred by allegations of corruption, and the $3.5 billion spent on new stadiums and supporting infrastructure seemed problematic given the large number of South Africans who continued to live in poverty.[1] Was successfully hosting what is effectively a party for the global elite really worth such a massive price tag? This chapter examines globalization through the lens of progress and decline, and asks how historians should assess it. Is globalization a force for good? Or do the costs outweigh the benefits?

World historians (and many other academics!) have a lot to say about globalization, defined as the recent tightening of long-distance connections around the world and the subsequent creation of a global culture. Modern globalization represents an unprecedented level of economic and cultural integration, with corporate capitalism and migration chipping away at previous sacrosanct boundaries. Without the advantage of hindsight, this is always going to be more difficult to assess than the distant past. Historians generally draw on two main theories to explain globalization as an example of progress or decline, one created by Francis Fukuyama, and the other by Benjamin Barber.

Fukuyama's theory stems from an essay he wrote in 1989. Fukuyama argued that the West, represented by liberal democracies with successful consumer cultures, had triumphed over its two main ideological rivals: fascism and communism. Since there was no obvious alternative remaining, this would lead to "the universalization of Western liberal democracy as the final form of human government."[2] While he was careful to state that this would happen "in the long run" rather than in the immediate future, his argument was clear. The end of the Cold War, and with it the end of communism as a rival to liberal democracies, entailed "the end of history." The future would no longer involve conflict on a grand scale, and instead focus on mundane "economic calculation, the endless solving of technical problems, environmental concerns, and the satisfaction of sophisticated consumer demands."[3] Milton Friedman expanded on these insights, arguing that information technology and globalization are leveling the global economic playing field. In this new, "flat" world, a person's place of birth mattered less than their work ethic and skills.[4] This perspective suggested that globalization is a positive change.

Not all analysts were as optimistic as Fukuyama and Friedman. Benjamin Barber, in a famous 1992 article, argued that the future of the world would be shaped by two "axial forces" of tribalism and globalism. The first, which he labeled "Jihad," encompassed violence in the name of religion, nationalism, or ethnicity. The forces of Jihad would emerge in opposition to the homogeneous global consumer culture based on "fast music, fast computers, and fast food." To Barber, this alternative future was "McWorld."[5]

What makes Barber's theory interesting is that he argues that both Jihad and McWorld are threats to democracy. When it comes to Jihad, this challenge is an explicit rejection of liberal and democratic values. But the corporate globalists, he contends, pose a similar challenge. Obsessed with efficiency and productivity even at the expense of people's right to self-government, the technocrats of McWorld are guided more by laissez-faire economics than civic participation. Naomi Klein argues that this happened in South Africa during its famous elections that ended apartheid in 1994. Despite a clear popular mandate under the Freedom Charter to redistribute land and undermine white control, the ANC ultimately embraced a form of neoliberal economics that made these goals impossible and worsened inequality. Despite the overwhelming opposition of South African voters, the ANC was told "the world has changed; none of that left[ist] stuff means anything anymore. This is the only game in town."[6] To Barber and Klein, globalization is not the victory of liberal democracy, but a new threat to it.

World historians struggle to reconcile these divergent views of the post–Cold War world. They recount with breathless enthusiasm the new global village being created as old national boundaries become obsolete.[7] Economic prosperity, universal human rights, and a widening of cultural influences around the world also have real appeal to world historians. Fukuyama's narrative of democracy triumphing over fascism and communism, for example, deeply influences narratives of the twentieth century.[8] However, world historians acknowledge the significant negative impacts of globalization, like the persistence of extreme poverty around the world and the threat that the globalization of consumer culture poses to the environment.[9]

So is globalization a force for good or a problem to be solved? One way of rendering these disputes visible is by zooming in on a specific aspect of this overwhelming phenomenon. This is where soccer fits in. Fun, cheap, and easy to learn, this sport has become popular around the world. In sub-Saharan Africa, it arrived during the colonial era. European administrators, missionaries, and workers all introduced soccer to Africans, who in turn set up their own leagues and adapted the game to suit local cultures.[10] When African nations gained independence in the 1960s and 1970s, they often built large stadiums and directed significant resources to their teams as a matter of national pride.[11] But African soccer remained on the margins of the global game until the end of the Cold War. Its integration into that space thus offers a lens into the impacts, both positive and negative, of globalization.

Africa, soccer, and the global era

Following Fukuyama and Friedman, the argument that globalization is a force for good generally is connected to a belief that free markets can solve social or political problems. One example of this approach comes from Simon Kuper and Stefan Szymanski. In a chapter from *Soccernomics*, they use a regression analysis to uncover whether players of color were underpaid relative to their team's success. They found that in the 1980s "black players were systematically better value for money than whites," likely because certain clubs refused to employ black players even though they were more talented than some of their white teammates. However, by the late 1990s this changed drastically, and Kuper and Syzmanski could no longer find any evidence that black players were undervalued. They argued that "the economic forces of competition drove white men to ditch their prejudices."[12] They attribute this to the transparency of the market. In a sport like soccer, the skill of the best players is quite evident in relation to their peers. If you want to field the best team, it needs to include the best players, regardless of race, ethnicity, or religion. And they believe it was no coincidence that teams became more interested in signing the best possible players in the 1990s, when television revenues for major European leagues skyrocketed and the monetary rewards for winning championships increased accordingly.

This was also the moment when international boundaries became more porous for players based in sub-Saharan Africa. Prior to the early 1980s they rarely joined clubs in Europe. Visa rules, nationality restrictions in Europe, and the racism mentioned above ensured most African players stayed in African domestic leagues. The enormous sums paid by Sky Sports for the TV rights to the English Premier League in 1992 (£304 million over four years) transformed the situation. Clubs in Europe now had far more revenue than clubs based in Africa, and could pay far higher salaries. The Bosman ruling of 1995 further enhanced player mobility by releasing them at the end of their contracts, allowing elite athletes to enter free agency.[13] This unsurprisingly benefited the very best African soccer players. Steven Pienaar, born in the impoverished townships of Johannesburg, is a good example. After showing excellent form as a youngster, he was signed by one of the top clubs in South Africa, Ajax Cape Town, in 1999. They won the prestigious Rothman's Cup while he was there, but the team paid players poorly. One exposé revealed that some of their starters received wages of ZAR 2,500 per month, roughly $350.[14] Once he left to play abroad, however, Pienaar was able to earn far more, including the roughly £3.05 million per year he made at Tottenham in the English Premier League.[15] As a high-profile South African player in a top European league, Pienaar even joined global megastar Lionel Messi as part of a major Adidas advertising campaign in the run-up to the 2010 World Cup.[16] From the perspective of top African players, globalization offered new and unparalleled opportunities. European leagues paid the best wages in order to attract the best players and compete with other top teams. It is no surprise that the most talented African stars ended up playing there.

The arrival of soccer migrants even reshaped European national identities, often in a more inclusive way. Laurent Dubois used the 2014 World Cup qualification campaign of the French national soccer team to illustrate these changes. Dubois observed that many young families from Francophone African countries moved to France to escape poverty or conflict in their homelands. Their children often loved soccer, and as French citizens were eligible to play for the national team. Several did, including Mamadou Sakho (born in Paris to Senegalese parents) and Paul Pogba (born just outside Paris to Guinean parents).

This team eventually had to win a two-legged playoff against Ukraine to qualify. Following a 2–0 loss in the first leg, right-wing politician Marine Le Pen blamed the defeat on "ultraliberalism" in the sport. To her, "there is a real rupture [with] the French people. A team can't be pushed forward only by the desire for monetary gain or individual egos. It has to be carried by the entire people."[17] Her father (and political mentor) told the press that French coaches had "exaggerated the number of players of color on the team," and that as a result the French people no longer felt represented by them.[18] To

Le Pen, players of color were not really French, and should not represent the nation even if they were French citizens.

While some may have shared her sentiments at the time, France managed to win the return match 3–0 in front of a home crowd, and qualified for the World Cup. Sakho, who scored two of the three goals, said the following after the match:

> I just want to say that the players in the squad represent everyone in France, the multicultural society of France. When we represent France we know we are playing for the multicultural French nation. We love France and everything that is France. I want the supporters to know that we really fight for that shirt. The cultural mix of France is represented in that squad and we are determined to win the hearts of the fans by fighting really hard for the shirt. It is not a qualification just for 24 footballers in a squad but for the whole nation … France is made up of Arab culture, black African culture, black West Indian culture and white culture and we, a squad that reflects that multiculturalism, are all fighting in the same way and are united behind France qualifying for the World Cup.[19]

Figure 19.1 Mamadou Sakho celebrates scoring a goal in the second leg of the World Cup qualifying playoff between France and Ukraine, November 19, 2013. Courtesy of Franck Fife/AFP via Getty Images.

It is hard not to get swept up in this type of infectious multiculturalism. Borders are breaking down, identities being reshaped, and everyone seems to benefit. But of course this is not the whole story. Mamadou Sakho could just as easily have been playing for the Senegalese national team. The fact he is not reveals a key problem with global markets—in many cases, the rich get richer.

No soccer-playing nation embodies the contradictions of globalization better than Senegal. A French colony until 1960, historic ties ensured many Senegalese players played their club football in France, lived in France, and then would fly "home" to Senegal during international breaks to play for the Senegalese national team. Thanks to the elite level of competition in France's top league, the quality of Senegal's team improved dramatically at the end of the twentieth century, and in 2002 they qualified for their first-ever trip to the World Cup. The team was promoted with the slogan "*Le Senegal qui gagne*," meaning "the Senegal that wins." The team captain, El-Hadji Diouf, said he felt like "the leader of a country," and when Senegal beat France 1–0 in their first World Cup match, fans again poured into the streets. One Senegalese supporter said it was "a victory for black people everywhere."[20]

The contradictions of globalization were embodied in players like Khalilou Fadiga. He left Senegal at the age of six, grew up in France, and told reporters, "I know the streets of Paris better than the streets of Dakar." Fadiga's loyalties ultimately rested with his ancestral land, and he noted that "When I was home, everybody would speak our language and we listened to Senegalese radio and music ... I share both [French and Senegalese] cultures but I have a lot of family over in Senegal and my color is Senegalese."[21] A profound irony lay in the fact that "*le Senegal qui gagne*" was primarily composed of people who had left Senegal. In a globalized world, the elite representatives of a nation might not spend much time there. Devesh Kapur and John McHale wrote an extensive study of brain drains in the global economy, and included a brief section on soccer and Africa. They argued that the migration of Africa's best players to Europe has greatly improved the quality of African national teams, but they also noted that this denuded African domestic leagues of talent since they offer competitive wages to quality players. This has led to smaller crowds, lower revenues, and even more out-migration by top players. Globalization offers no easy solution to this dilemma, and it appears that African club football will remain a poor substitute to the European version for the foreseeable future.[22]

The talent drain created by globalization affected more than just elite players. Rafaelle Poli, in a study dating to the 2002–03 season, found that

African players were overrepresented in Europe's less prestigious leagues. These European clubs offered African players low salaries, lower than those considered minimally acceptable to Europeans. The clubs knew they could get away with this since the African players were desperate to avoid being sent home to even worse conditions. Poli concludes that "the transnational networks set up for the training, recruitment, and transfer of African players are almost always controlled from 'above' and serve the needs of the European football economy more than the African one."[23] These less prominent players were vulnerable to all kinds of exploitation. In 2011, seven Zambian players were convicted of accepting bribes to fix matches while playing north of the Arctic Circle for Rovaniemi, a team in the Finnish League. Thanks to their relatively poor wages and the expansion of global gambling markets in Asia, they were ideal targets for match-fixers who made roughly 470,000 euros from this league alone before getting caught. The remaining black players in Rovaniemi then faced racial abuse in this tiny community.[24]

As a final example of the hazards of globalization, it is worth returning to the 2010 World Cup. Today it is generally seen as a success, with South Africa's Deputy Sports Minister Gert Oosthuizen claiming "we built stadiums and infrastructure. We were way ahead of schedule, everything went perfectly, everything was in place ... But it was much more than that. More important was the nation-building and the social cohesion that we achieved. We felt proudly South African—and simply African." More tourists visited South Africa during the World Cup than during the entire previous year. The final game was watched on television by 909 million people, and at least 60,000 jobs were created in construction alone.[25] Many Americans, especially those willing to travel abroad, gained a much more positive view of South Africa as a result of the World Cup.[26]

But this was hardly the full story. Later investigations revealed that South Africa had won the right to host the World Cup in part because they paid a $10 million bribe to FIFA Vice President Jack Warner.[27] The construction companies tasked with building the new stadiums often received extraordinarily lucrative contracts, so much so that they were investigated by competition authorities. Powerful South African politicians like Tokyo Sexwale held shares in these construction firms, and it created suspicion that the rich and well connected were using the public funds set aside for the World Cup to make massive personal profits.[28] In contrast, most ordinary South Africans were unable to attend any games because of steep ticket prices.[29]

The power of FIFA infused every aspect of the World Cup. One example was Cape Town's iconic stadium. Originally the municipal government wanted to build it in Athlone on the Cape Flats. This was a poorer neighborhood, but also where most of Cape Town's soccer fans lived. The hope was a stadium at that site would be sustainable after the World Cup spectators left because the fans could easily attend the matches of their local clubs. But FIFA insisted that the ZAR 4.5 billion (USD $600 million) stadium be constructed in the city center. Thanks to the byzantine Host Country Agreement signed by South Africa, FIFA enjoyed almost complete legal authority over all aspects of the World Cup, even if the elected government happened to object. Ultimately the stadium was built in the swish Green Point neighborhood, ideal for affluent international visitors but far from the homes of Cape Town's local soccer fans.[30] Unsurprisingly it became a white elephant costing the municipality ZAR 436 million (EUR 45 million) annually to maintain, money that would be better spent on crippling water shortages and limited infrastructure in the Cape Flats. Many residents simply want to tear it down.[31]

FIFA also used its power to ensure its corporate partners were kept happy. South Africa's informal street merchants, so important to the local economy, were banned from operating close to the World Cup sites. Only Budweiser was served at the stadiums, despite the company lacking sufficient capacity in the region to keep up with demand. The atmosphere

Figure 19.2 A picture of Greenpoint Stadium in Cape Town taken in 2009. A key venue for the 2010 World Cup, it quickly became a costly white elephant for the city. Courtesy of Dan Kitwood via Getty Images.

was so corporate that two observers felt South Africa had transitioned from "the Rainbow Nation to Rainbow Nation, Inc." Even the *vuvuzela*, the most distinctive symbol of the 2010 World Cup, was given an invented African history and used to brand the event.[32] With most of the participants coming from abroad, there was little distinctively South African about the World Cup.

The leaders of South Africa embraced the World Cup for a variety of reasons. In part, they wanted to show that South Africa had become one of the world's leading nations. They also wanted to use the games to encourage national unity despite lingering tensions from the apartheid era. Sadly, the World Cup revealed the persistent inequality between South African whites and people of color. After almost £308 million was spent renovating the nearby FNB Stadium, residents of the nearby black township of Riverlea organized a series of violent protests. Touching on a major problem in post-apartheid South Africa, they observed that if the government was able to find money to pay for the World Cup, "why are they not pouring money into housing?"[33] Poor South Africans rarely received any direct benefits from the event, but the authorities did make sure they stayed out of sight. One shameful example of this took place in Cape Town, where the urban poor were taken to a newly constructed "tin-can" camp called Blikkiesdorf on the edge of the city, far from tourists' prying eyes.[34]

Desperate poverty led to the scapegoating of South Africa's immigrant population, and rumors spread that after the World Cup they would be forcibly deported. Attacks in 2008 had left 62 migrants dead and 100,000 displaced, so many lived in fear throughout the event. Ultimately the rumored violence did not occur, but the tense atmosphere led one commentator to write the following:

> Yet one cannot help but wonder what the impact on xenophobic resentments and ultimately on the violence itself might have been if even a small percentage of the forty billion rand spent on World Cup stadiums, new and upgraded airports, roads, and fan parks had instead been used to improve basic services such as schools, hospitals, and housing and to create sustainable jobs for the country's poorest. It might have meant a slightly less comfortable stay for our flyby football guests but would also certainly have ensured a better situation for our most vulnerable African nationals as well as for the poor South African majority who have turned such nationals into scapegoats for their socioeconomic discontent.[35]

This is an excellent summary not only of the consequences of the 2010 World Cup, but also of integrating into the global economy as well. On the one hand, South Africa earned plaudits from around the world for successfully hosting the event, and elite South Africans could look back on this as a moment when the nation came together to welcome the world. On the other, it came at an immense cost, especially to the most vulnerable. Not only were resources diverted away from projects that might have alleviated South Africa's immense income gap between white and black, but municipalities continue to bear responsibility for maintaining these immense stadiums that will never turn a profit.

Conclusion

In this chapter we have looked at several starkly different interpretations of globalization, all through the lens of soccer. What do they tell us about how historians interpret this critical historical event? First, those who believe in the power of the free market tend to argue that if it is unleashed by globalization it will reshape society in more "rational" ways. Historians are usually more skeptical. Immanuel Wallerstein's world-systems theory, in particular, suggests that core economies use their power to exploit peripheries, a process that can be seen in the labor politics of globalized soccer.[36] One can even see aspects of Barber's theory at play during the 2010 World Cup, where the elected officials in Cape Town were overruled by an elaborate legal agreement concocted by FIFA, an international organization. Globalization is not solely a force for good.

But it is important to observe that not all impacts of globalization are negative. Some scholars acknowledge that exploitive connections are created by the global economy, but are also careful to note that people exercise a degree of agency over the choices they make. Peter Alegi, for example, argues that while Africa's position in the global economy left it open to exploitation, African "athletes were not passive victims." They sought out the best possible situations for themselves and made major contributions to the sport on the best teams in the world.[37] The arrival of African migrants has even complicated the identity of European national teams, which have become symbols of diversity as a path to success. Assessing globalization is difficult because it is a contemporary issue and historians do not enjoy the full benefit of hindsight. But by examining it through the lens of progress or decline, we can begin to make better sense of this critical force.

Further reading

Alegi, Peter. *African Soccerscapes*. Athens: Ohio University Press, 2010.
A history of soccer in Africa with particular interest in migration,
nationalism, and globalization.

Alegi, Peter, and Chris Bolsmann, eds. *Africa's World Cup*. Ann Arbor:
University of Michigan Press, 2013. A collection of papers that both
critiques and lauds the South African hosts of the 2010 World Cup.

Dubois, Laurent. "Afro-Europe in the World Cup," February 20, 2014, available
at http://roadsandkingdoms.com/2014/afro-europe-in-the-world-cup/. A
look at how the changing racial makeup of the French and Belgian national
soccer teams has contributed to changing concepts of national identity.

20

Poor Numbers

To many, the year 2000 represented a chance at renewal, a chance at a fresh start. The Millennium Development Goals were a product of this enthusiasm. They proposed to measure and then address the most alarming manifestations of global inequality by 2015. It did not take long for the idealism to disappear under a wave of "War on Terror" realpolitik, and by 2007 scholars were upset about the slow progress toward these goals. In *The End of Poverty*, Jeffrey Sachs argued for a renewed commitment to aid to help save the world's poor. But his views were bitterly opposed by scholars like William Easterly, who felt that aid money was most likely to end up in a despot's bank account. Into this debate stepped Paul Collier, a professor of economics and public policy at Oxford University. His approach was neatly summarized in the preface to *The Bottom Billion*:

> Our notions about the problems of the poorest countries are saturated with … images; not just of noble rebels but of starving children, heartless businesses, crooked politicians. You are held prisoner by these images. While you are held prisoner, so are our politicians, because they do what you want. I am going to take you beyond images. Sometimes I am going to smash them. *And my image smasher is statistical evidence.* [emphasis added][1]

Deeply aware of the numerous stereotypes that influence many peoples' image of Africa, he suggests we turn to statistical data for answers. This data, he argues, offers a more representative, accurate, and politically neutral picture of why people are poor and what can be done about it. The answer? To Collier, it is economic growth. If we increase the Gross Domestic Product (GDP) per capita of the "bottom billion," their lives will improve.[2]

This type of statistical argument represents a challenge for historians. Most of us lack formal training in this area, and as a result are instinctively deferent to scholars who can point to "hard numbers." But as the old adage goes, "there are three kinds of lies; lies, damned lies, and statistics." Which image is true? Are statistics truly able to "smash" our preconceived notions by revealing underlying truths? Or are they less authoritative than scholars like Collier might want to believe? Is it possible they are as susceptible to manipulation as any other source?

A combination of expanded data and enhanced computing power has transformed world history, and it has been used to illuminate historical events as diverse as global climate change and the Trans-Atlantic slave trade. The *World History Dataverse* and the *Journal of World Historical Information* are two recently created sites that collect and disseminate this type of information. But when Tamara Shreiner and David Zwart argue, "the increasing availability of big data has made fluency with data and data visualizations a necessary skill in all historical fields, but particularly world history,"[3] this involves not only understanding how to read data, but also how certain methodologies privilege specific world views. Statistical data will be crucial to the future of world history, and this chapter aims to demystify how this type of evidence is produced and presented.

The focus will be on a statistic of crucial importance to global narratives; GDP, GDP per capita, and its direct corollary, GDP per capita growth. As a formula it began life as follows:

$$\text{GNP} = \text{consumption} + \text{investment} + \text{government spending}^4 + \text{exports} - \text{imports}^5$$

Created by Simon Kuznets, GNP first went into use in the United States in 1934. It measured all economic production by residents of a country, and included corporate profits in the region where the company was based. In 1978 the first set of global estimates of GNP per capita were published by Kravis, Heston, and Summers.[6] This statistic was adapted to the post–Cold War world in 1991 when it changed from GNP to GDP, which measured all domestic profits in the area they were created, regardless as to whether those profits were staying there or, as was often the case in a global economy, they were going to be sent to a corporate headquarters located abroad. National income, GNP, and GDP (which I will use as my term of reference going forward) became easy-to-comprehend statistics that are now used to represent the relative prosperity of nations and their inhabitants in a single number.[7]

Angus Maddison even started a project that uses GDP to measure economic performance back in time. The subsequent Maddison Project at the University of Groningen continues this work today, and has made their data available to the public.[8] One of their most important contributions is a sustained comparison between European and Asian economies during the "great divergence" from the sixteenth to the nineteenth century. While this can help observers understand the roots of European affluence, one reviewer notes that it also requires considerable "imagination" to fit our historical knowledge of Asian, African, and Latin American economies into what is essentially a modern statistic.[9]

GDP data is extremely powerful, but it also has its own history. The rest of this chapter will examine this history as well as significant problems with the underlying data. These issues reveal that what we choose to measure can reshape the world, and that compressing the welfare of an entire nation into a single metric silences certain voices and empowers others.

Culture of growth

GDP was created in the immediate aftermath of the Great Depression. President Herbert Hoover believed that the economy would turn-around primarily of its own volition, and policy decisions were made on extremely limited data. When President Franklin D. Roosevelt took over, he faced a persistent crisis and similarly anecdotal evidence about the economy. Kuznets's innovation was to provide systemic information on all economic production by individuals, corporations, and governments. Expressed as a single number, GDP should rise when times are good and fall when the economy is in decline. As a result, it provides vital data on whether government policies are having a desirable impact on the national economy as a whole.[10]

The full value of this information became apparent during the Second World War. One challenge that all major powers faced was how to optimize their economy for war. This generally meant taking over civilian production and repurposing it for war, but doing so too quickly could cripple consumption in ways that would cause lasting economic damage. Kuznets's GDP statistic was used by the War Production Board to gradually strengthen the military without seizing control of civilian industries or damaging long-term growth. Success in this area was so significant that at least one historian has argued it ensured the eventual US victory in 1945.[11]

With Europe in shambles after the war, the United States provided large grants and loans to help in the rebuilding process. This program became known as the Marshall Plan, and American planners decided to use GDP measurements to confirm that this money was being used appropriately. In order for a country to continue receiving aid, it had to show annual GDP growth. Since one of the easiest ways to do this was by increasing government spending, the public sector expanded rapidly as a result. The Marshall Plan was the moment when American economic power helped spread GDP to the rest of the world. National prosperity and GDP growth began to be seen as one and the same.[12]

GDP's ability to measure prosperity also enabled global comparisons of wealth in ways that had not been possible before. The first statistical analysis of poverty around the world took place in 1940, and in the postwar era international organizations began to use GDP as a way to quantify this issue. For example, in 1949 the UN observed that per capita income in the United States was $1,453, while that of Indonesia was only $25.[13] When the World Bank set about quantifying poverty around the world, they defined it as anyone living in a country with an annual per capita income of under $100. Suddenly two-thirds of the world's population was impoverished, even though this metric did not assess whether people had reliable access to food, clean water, or health care.[14] The result was development economics, a field that initially aimed to end poverty by increasing GDP growth. Unsurprisingly, approaches that led to GDP growth were prioritized even if it was obvious that only a small number of people were directly benefiting. Other strategies that might have been more meaningful to impoverished people received little attention.

GDP's blind spots seem obvious in retrospect, and had major consequences when economic plans to alleviate poverty were being created. In 1949, a World Bank mission to Colombia categorized the rural population as follows:

> If we exclude housewives, domestic servants, and indefinite categories from the 3,300,000 rural people classified in the 1938 census, there were in that year about 1,767,000 economically active persons on the 700,000 farms in villages under 1,500.[15]

Women's work was dismissed because, in the American context where GDP was created, it was not considered productive. This was hotly debated in the United States, and was even more inappropriate in contexts where subsistence farming was common, like Colombia. These farms were (and remain) major collective enterprises and they relied on contributions from all family members. The result was that women were typically included in development projects only as mothers primarily responsible for feeding babies and procuring water. Their invisibility meant that development interventions tended to prioritize male needs, and they often made the position of women in the rural economy worse, both in an absolute sense and in relation to men.[16]

Beginning in the 1960s, GDP growth came to be seen as the key to solving another social problem: unemployment. According to "Okun's law," 3 percent annual GDP growth would generate a 1 percent increase in employment. This had wide-ranging implications for public policy, and ensured that generating GDP growth was seen as essential to the overall health of the national economy. The collapse of the Russian economy after the Cold War, when its GDP halved under Boris Yeltsin, reinforced this perception among the public at large. Across the Western world, GDP growth became an overriding political concern.[17]

Despite this shift in the public sphere, GDP and growth were considered problematic by many economists. In 1966 Keith Boulding noted that the nature of GDP encouraged the "reckless, exploitative, romantic, and violent behavior" of a cowboy.[18] This anti-growth position enjoyed considerable political support, including from Robert F. Kennedy's presidential campaign. Speaking only a few weeks before his assassination, Kennedy made the following remarks:

> Our Gross National Product, now, is over $800 billion dollars a year, but that Gross National Product—if we judge the United States of America by that—that Gross National Product counts air pollution and cigarette advertising … it counts the destruction of the redwoods and the loss of our natural wonder in chaotic sprawl. It counts napalm and counts nuclear warheads and armored cars for the police to fight the riots in our cities … Yet the gross national product does not allow for the health of our children, the quality of their education, or the joy of their play.[19]

Environmentalists were prominent critics of GDP growth. Robert Kennedy's critique stemmed in part from the writing of Rachel Carson. Her 1962 book, *Silent Spring*, challenged the perception that unfettered industrial growth was beneficial to humankind. In particular, she observed that long-term damage to the environment might outweigh the short-term economic benefits.[20] This argument was expanded by Aurelio Peccei and the members of the Club of Rome a decade later. They wrote that if present trends continued the Earth would reach "the limits to growth" within a century. In uncomfortably dry language, they noted that this would be marked by "a rather sudden and uncontrollable decline in both population and industrial capacity."[21] Another problem was Easterlin's Paradox, whereby GDP growth fails to improve individual happiness after certain basic needs are met.[22] And last but not least, periods of extended growth in the so-called Third World often did little to improve conditions for the majority of inhabitants. Mahbub ul Haq, a Pakistani economist, observed that 7 percent GDP growth in Brazil achieved little due to "mal-distribution of income." Despite being told that prioritizing GDP growth would reduce unemployment and poverty, there was little evidence of this on the ground.[23] Haq argued that growth was being monopolized by a tiny elite (the "twenty-two families") that benefited from aid money and political support without reinvesting their wealth in the economy. These greedy oligarchs prevented GDP growth from boosting incomes or creating jobs more broadly.[24] Many people recognized that GDP was a flawed statistic, but at the same time sustained GDP growth had become a political necessity. This conflict would continue throughout the late twentieth and twenty-first centuries.

Debates over how to calculate GDP were of vital strategic interest in the Western world, but there was little disagreement that industrial economies *could* be measured. This was not true in states where subsistence agriculture

Figure 20.1 Environmentalists were key critics of GDP. *Silent Spring* by Rachel Carson (pictured above), published in 1962, argued that economic growth did irreparable (and unmeasured) ecological harm. Courtesy of Alfred Eisenstaedt/The LIFE Picture Collection via Getty Images.

predominated. These economies were uniquely challenging to assess due to climate-induced variability and limited data on which crops were being grown in any given year. Problems became obvious during the 1950s. Colonial administrators in sub-Saharan Africa were under pressure to justify colonialism through development, and politicians in Europe believed success could be shown through GDP growth. But how could GDP be calculated if the vast majority of the economy was rural subsistence farming? The results were seemingly meaningful numbers backed by meaningless data. The value of rural agriculture across sub-Saharan Africa was calculated by simply assuming that it increased at a 1:1 ratio to rural population growth.[25] Others tracked certain crop prices and used that to alter their annual estimates, even if they had no idea how much of any given crop was being grown each year. Douglas Rimmer, an economics professor in the British colony of Gold Coast, described the efforts of the Government Statistics Office to calculate national accounts as "rough and ready ... Much was guesswork. Much was also omitted, though not until later did I fully realize the significance of the parallel, unenumerated economy."[26] The size of the informal economy was another major challenge to GDP statistics, especially in oppressive or war-torn states where people have obvious incentives to avoid formal markets. Any economic activity that is not measured is technically never produced, and thus not included in incomes, but of course money earned through smuggling, drug-dealing, prostitution, or corruption is still flowing back into the formal markets.[27] Measuring the informal economy essentially boils down to educated guesswork. Pius Okigbo's GDP estimates for Nigeria from 1950 to 1957 noted "it is impossible to overstate the arbitrariness of the process of 'quantification.'"[28]

When African nations gained independence, they inherited the colonial development state. Most sought to centralize economic planning, and needed better data upon which to base their plans. This proved possible in the 1960s and early 1970s, when national statistics offices used their resources to survey rural production and track changes from year to year. But these improvements dwindled after the OPEC crisis, which devastated African economies. With many nations teetering on bankruptcy, they turned to the major international financial institutions for help. The World Bank and International Monetary Fund (IMF) were only willing to help if African leaders made dramatic macroeconomic reforms. There were enormous human costs to these reforms, particularly due to the elimination of food subsidies that were believed to "distort" the market. But for measuring GDP there were two crucial consequences: first, cuts to government salaries forced many people to join the informal economy to recoup their losses, and second, government statistical offices tasked with measuring growth were slashed to the bone.

Why does this matter? It matters because what we think we know about African economies is often based on extremely bad data. And in many cases this produces large variances in GDP per capita. One example comes from Uganda. This country experienced the terrifyingly incompetent rule of Idi Amin in the 1970s, and then a series of civil wars in the 1980s. The formal economy utterly collapsed, and many people responded by selling their cash crops (especially coffee) to *magendo* traders, who then illegally crossed borders into Kenya and Rwanda to resell it for hard currency.[29] But this crucial source of income never entered the official statistics. Indeed, the only external trade statistics for Uganda prior to 2008 were duties collected on goods passing through the Kenyan port of Mombasa. When data began to be collected on all cross-border trade, including the Democratic Republic of Congo, Sudan, Rwanda, Tanzania, and Kenya, the Ugandan Bureau of Statistics observed that "the informal cross border trade is significant, and contributes immensely to household welfare and the country's economic growth."[30] Poor numbers created an image of the Ugandan economy in sharp decline the 1980s even though a significant part of that decline was merely people moving from formal to informal trade.

Underestimating the informal sector is not the only issue related to the quality of GDP data for Africa. Another problem lies in the limited resources available to the national statistical offices across the continent. It is their responsibility to gather data on population, production, and prices and then compile an overall annual estimate. Ideally, once every decade they should also conduct a comprehensive review of the economy, surveying every key industry, and creating a breakdown of their relative contributions. This becomes the base year, and all future annual estimates depend on its accuracy. But what if they lack the funds to do this job? Morten Jerven visited Zambia's Central Statistical Office in 2010 and discovered that the entire task of compiling national accounts was being done by one person. "What happens if I disappear?" he asked.[31]

Sadly, the answer is GDP will be automatically generated, albeit as increasingly inaccurate estimates. The policy of the World Bank is to complete any missing data, even if the statistical office never collected it. Once this process has happened, it becomes part of the larger World Bank data set of GDPs around the world as though every number is entirely comparable.[32] Scrubbed away is the more prosaic reality, like a Zambian report of their national accounts that distinguished between a "guestimate" and a "guestimate with a weak basis."[33]

It is also important to note that outdated base years can make the World Bank data extremely misleading. An excellent example of this is Ghana. When its base year was 1993, the communications sector included land line phones and the receipts of the national telecommunications company. This remained the basis for every subsequent GDP estimate for Ghana until 2011, when a new base year was completed. Since cellphones had become ubiquitous across Ghana by the mid-2000s, this was a major omission. It even had important political implications. President John Atta Mills had promised to make Ghana a middle-income country in 2008. Once the base year was completed, this promise had been fulfilled by redefining what was measured in the national accounts rather than through rapid economic growth.[34]

So GDP was and is a useful tool for states, but it may not measure what it should, and its comparability between nations is questionable. To make these issues more obvious to students, world historians need to bring qualitative methods to the study of quantitative data. What we choose to measure is a political decision, and this is a story worth examining in depth. One fascinating example is the ill-fated decision by China to introduce "green" GDP in 2004. This would have incorporated environmental damage and resource consumption into resource calculations. The findings were first published in 2006, and revealed that the ecological costs amounted to 3.05 percent of the national economy ($66.3 billion total). Even the National Statistics Bureau agreed that "it is unreasonable to purely seek economic growth while ignoring the importance of the resources and environment."[35] But the Chinese regions that produced the most pollution, like Ningxia, Hebei, Shanzi, and Inner Mongolia, pushed back against this revision. In the past, local authorities were promoted or demoted based on economic growth, and these regions chose to resist the collection of environmental data. Ultimately they were successful, and the National Statistics Bureau pulled out of the project.[36] Similar resistance stymied an American effort to incorporate environmental factors into its national accounts. As one congressman from West Virginia indicated, if air pollution and resource depletion were included, "somebody is going to say ... that the coal industry isn't contributing anything to the country."[37] As Crystal Biruk so effectively demonstrates in the context of statistics on HIV prevalence, better data does not always win policy debates.[38]

Conclusion

Statistical data can illuminate the past like never before. Its power is intoxicating. The ability to map out the relative wealth of every nation on earth offers valuable insights, and so long as that data is available, it will appear in every conceivable format. GDP is perhaps the most frequently cited statistic in world history, and as such it deserves close scrutiny. Its history reveals that it was originally created as a way to measure the overall health of a national economy, and it continues to serve well in this regard. But it is far from flawless. It struggles to account for informal economic activity. It can provide only a guesstimate at the value of subsistence agriculture. And it tends to "reward" relentless exploitation of non-renewable resources by not including the economic damage done to the environment.

Different approaches are available. In 1971, Jigme Singye Wangchuck became king of Bhutan, a small mountain nation nestled between India and China. And in a speech one year later to mark the occasion of Bhutan joining the UN, he argued that "Gross National Happiness [GNH] is more important than Gross National Product."[39] Despite a per capita income of roughly $50 per year, he chose to prioritize better health care and education instead of rapid economic growth. GNH became an official test for any economic policy, and required government ministries to consider whether proposed changes would negatively affect work–life balance, psychological well-being, general health, education, and the physical environment. If this was a possibility, the policy had to be rethought.

The results were striking. Infant and maternal mortality fell, vaccination rates increased, and cases of malaria plummeted. Economic growth was modest but steady. In particular, its spectacular mountain setting could have supported a vastly expanded number of tourists, but a $200/day tax on visitors discouraged all but a handful of Westerners. Bhutan's political leaders recognized that this tax impeded growth in this valuable industry, but on the other hand tried to balance the benefits of jobs and foreign income with ecological damage. If they had been measuring GDP, the path forward was obvious. Bhutan's use of GNH made this question far more complex.[40]

In a world where "what we measure affects what we do," historians need to be aware not only of how data is produced, but also how our understandings of the world are produced by data. This is why the frequent references to GDP in world history are problematic. This statistic is so flawed that even Joseph Stiglitz, a former chief economist of the World Bank, declared it a "swindle."[41]

Figure 20.2 A view of Thimpu, the capital city of Bhutan, in 2018. Beginning in 1971, Bhutan used Gross National Happiness rather than GDP to guide their development strategies. Courtesy of Joanna Slater/Washington Post via Getty Images.

It creates a world in which untrammeled economic growth is lauded even as it does irreparable harm to our planet, harm that we struggle to quantify but nonetheless realize is of vital significance. Statistics can enable us to better understand our world, but thinking critically about these metrics and the underlying data is essential to avoiding a messianic faith in the "hard numbers."

Further reading

Biruk, Crystal. *Cooking Data*. Durham, NC: Duke University Press, 2018. This book analyzes the myriad of ways that statistical information is shaped by those who gather and use it.

Collier, Paul. *The Bottom Billion*. New York: Oxford University Press, 2007. Collier offers an impassioned plea for a seemingly rational strategy to benefit the world's poorest, a renewed focus on economic growth.

Escobar, Arturo. *Encountering Development*. Princeton, NJ: Princeton University Press, 2012. The author argues that development neglected local realities and functioned as a form of neo-colonialism in Colombia during the Cold War era.

Fioramonti, Lorenzo. *Gross Domestic Problem*. New York: Zed Books, 2013. A look at the history of GDP as well as its increasingly apparent problems as a proxy for general well-being.

Jerven, Morten. *Poor Numbers*. Ithaca, NY: Cornell University Press, 2013. This book looks at the way low-quality data gathered in Africa is laundered by groups like the IMF and World Bank, creating an illusion that we know more about these countries than we do.

Haq, Mahbub ul. *The Poverty Curtain*. New York: Columbia University Press, 1976. An important but uneven criticism of growth without development written by a leading Pakistani economist.

Notes

Introduction

1. Peter Seixas, "Foreword," in *Thinking Historically*, ed. Stéphane Lévesque (Toronto: University of Toronto Press, 2008), viii.
2. Sam Wineburg, *Why Learn History (When It's Already on Your Phone)* (Chicago: University of Chicago Press, 2018).
3. Julia Brookins, "Enrollment Declines Continue," *AHA Perspectives on History*, February 12, 2018, available at https://www.historians.org/publications-and-directories/perspectives-on-history/february-2018/enrollment-declines-continue-aha-survey-again-shows-fewer-undergraduates-in-history-courses.
4. Sarah McGrew, Joel Breakstone, Teresa Ortega, Mark Smith, and Sam Wineburg, "Can Students Evaluate Online Sources?" *Theory & Research in Social Education* 46, no. 2 (2018): 165–193.
5. Stéphane Lévesque, *Thinking Historically* (Toronto: University of Toronto Press, 2008), 20.
6. The AP World History program changed their world historical thinking skills several times over the course of writing this book!
7. Lévesque, *Thinking Historically*, 27.
8. Lévesque, *Thinking Historically*, 168.
9. Lévesque, *Thinking Historically*, 130.
10. Keith Barton and Linda Levstik, "'It Wasn't a Good Part of History': National Identity and Students' Explanations of Historical Significance," *Teachers College Record* 99, no. 3 (1998): 484–485.
11. Lévesque, *Thinking Historically*, 15.
12. Gilbert Allardyce, "Toward World History," *Journal of World History* 1, no. 1 (1990): 40.
13. I borrow the categorization "Western Civ Plus" from Robert Bain and Tamara Shreiner, "The Dilemmas of a National Assessment in World History: World Historians and the 12th Grade NAEP," *World History Connected* 3, no. 3 (2015), available at http://worldhistoryconnected.press.illinois.edu/3.3/bain.html.
14. Lendol Calder, "Uncoverage: Toward a Signature Pedagogy for the History Survey," *Journal of American History* 92, no. 4 (2006): 1358–1359.

15. Sam Wineburg, "Probing the Depths of Students' Historical Knowledge," *AHA Perspectives*, March 1, 1992, available at https://www.historians. org/publications-and-directories/perspectives-on-history/march-1992/ probing-the-depths-of-students-historical-knowledge.

16. Jerry Bentley, Herbert Ziegler, and Heather Streets-Salter, *Traditions and Encounters: A Brief Global History*, 4th edn (New York: McGraw-Hill, 2016), 501; Peter von Sivers, Charles Desnoyers, and George Stow, *Patterns of World History*, 2nd edn (New York: Oxford University Press, 2015), 811; Robert Tignor et al., *Worlds Together Worlds Apart*, 5th edn (New York: W.W. Norton, 2018), 642; Robert Strayer and Eric Nelson, *Ways of the World*, 3rd edn (New York: Bedford St. Martin's, 2016), 531–532.

17. Strayer and Nelson, *Ways of the World*, 547.

18. Jared Diamond, *Guns, Germs, and Steel*, 1st edn (New York: W.W. Norton, 1998), 92.

19. von Sivers et al., *Patterns of World History*, 49.

20. Bentley et al., *Traditions and Encounters*, 21; Tignor et al., *Worlds Together Worlds Apart*, 28; David Christian, Cynthia Stokes Brown, and Craig Benjamin, *Big History: Between Nothing and Everything* (New York: McGraw-Hill, 2014), 129.

21. Ross Dunn and Laura Mitchell, *Panorama: A World History* (New York: McGraw-Hill, 2015), xix.

22. Strayer and Nelson, *Ways of the World*, 254–255.

23. von Sivers et al., *Patterns of World History*, 59.

24. Tignor et al., *Worlds Together Worlds Apart*, 546; von Sivers et al., *Patterns of World History*, 590–591; Bentley et al., *Traditions and Encounters*, 426.

25. Wole Soyinka, *Of Africa* (New Haven, CT: Yale University Press, 2013).

26. AP Exam Volume Changes, 2007–2017, available at https://secure-media. collegeboard.org/digitalServices/pdf/research/2017/2017-Exam-Volume-Change.pdf (accessed September 3, 2018).

Chapter 1

1. Timothy Egan, "Tribe Stops Study of Bones," *New York Times* September 30, 1996.

2. James Chatters, "The Recovery and First Analysis of an Early Holocene Human Skeleton from Kennewick, Washington," *American Antiquity* 65, no. 2 (2000): 291–316.

3. There is debate over whether mtDNA is always passed clonally, or if it occasionally undergoes recombination due to paternal leakage. The

consensus is that it can undergo recombination, but only very rarely. See Adam Eyre-Walker, "Do Mitochondria Recombine in Humans?" *Philosophical Transactions of the Royal Society of London* 355 (2000): 1573–1580.

4. Peter Jones and Darby Stapp, "An Anthropological Perspective," in *Kennewick Man*, ed. Heather Burke and Claire Smith (New York: Routledge, 2008), 52–53.

5. Darby Stapp and Peter Jones, "Addendum: The 9th Circuit Courts Decision," in *Kennewick Man*, ed. Heather Burke and Claire Smith (New York: Routledge, 2008), 69.

6. Meghan Howey, *Mound Builders and Monument Makers of the Northern Great Lakes, 1200–1600* (Norman: University of Oklahoma Press, 2012), 6.

7. Joel Gilman, "Kennewick Man," in *Kennewick Man*, ed. Heather Burke and Claire Smith (New York: Routledge, 2008), 85; "New Brand of Racist Odinist Religion," *Southern Poverty Law Center: The Intelligence Report*, Winter 1998, available at https://www.splcenter.org/fighting-hate/intelligence-report/1998/new-brand-racist-odinist-religion-march.

8. David Hurst Thomas, *Skull Wars* (New York: Basic Books, 2001), 59.

9. Cited in Larry Fruhling, "Culture Collides with Archaeology over Ancestors Graves," *The Santa Fe New Mexican*, April 23, 1989.

10. Quoted in Thomas, *Skull Wars*, 200.

11. Thomas, *Skull Wars*, 212.

12. Charles Mann, *1491* (New York: Vintage, 2006), 171–172.

13. C. Vance Haynes Jr., "Fluted Projectile Points: Their Age and Dispersion," *Science* 145 (1964): 1408–1413.

14. Paul Martin, "Prehistoric Overkill," in *Pleistocene Extinctions*, ed. Paul Martin and H. E. Wright (New Haven, CT: Yale University Press, 1967), 75–120.

15. Donald Grayson and David Melzer, "A Requiem for North American Overkill," *Journal of Archaeological Science* 30 (2003): 585–593.

16. Vine Deloria, *Red Earth, White Lies* (Golden, CO: Fulcrum Publishing, 1997), 113.

17. Thomas Dillehay, *The Settlement of the Americas* (New York: Basic Books, 2000).

18. Rex Dalton, "Rule Poses Threat to Museum Bones," *Nature* 464, no. 662 (2010), available at http://www.nature.com/news/2010/100331/full/464662a.html; Gilman, "Kennewick Man," 83–87.

19. Morten Rasmussen et al., "The Ancestry and Affiliations of Kennewick Man," *Nature* 523 (2015): 455–458.

20. Jones and Stapp, "An Anthropological Perspective," 48.

21. J. Shendure and H. Ji, "Next-Generation DNA Sequencing," *Nature Biotechnology* 26, no. 10 (2008): 1135–1145.

22. Rasmussen et al., "The Ancestry," 455–458.
23. Joel Connelly, "Bones of 'Kennewick Man' Returning Home for Burial," September 28, 2016, available at http://www.seattlepi.com/local/politics/article/Bones-of-Kennewick-Man-the-Ancient-One-9395924.php.
24. Rasmussen et al., "The Ancestry," 458.
25. Thomas, *Skull Wars*, 268–276.

Chapter 2

1. David Anthony, *The Horse, the Wheel, and Language* (Princeton, NJ: Princeton University Press, 2007), 6.
2. Asya Pereltsvaig and Martin Lewis, *The Indo-European Controversy* (New York: Cambridge University Press, 2015), 24.
3. Anthony, *The Horse*, 9–10.
4. Colin Renfrew, *Archaeology & Language* (New York: Cambridge University Press, 1992), 266.
5. Anthony, *The Horse*, 91.
6. Anthony, *The Horse*, 34–35.
7. Remco Bouckaert et al., "Mapping the Origins and Expansion of the Indo-European Language Family," *Science* 327 (2012): 957–960 makes the case that PIE is significantly older by using a Bayesian approach that models linguistic change on that of a mutating virus. Because of the numerous problems with this article described in Pereltsvaig and Lewis, *The Indo-European Controversy*, I rely on Anthony's approach.
8. Elena Kuzmina, "Mythological Treatment of the Horse in Indo-European Culture," in *Horses and Humans: The Evolution of Human-Equine Relationships*, ed. Sandra Olsen, Susan Grant, Alice Choyke, and László Bartosiewicz (Oxford: Archaeopress, 2006), 263.
9. Kuzmina, "Mythological Treatment," 264.
10. Sandra L. Olsen, "Early Horse Domestication: Weighing the Evidence," in *Horses and Humans: The Evolution of Human-Equine Relationships*, ed. Sandra Olsen, Susan Grant, Alice Choyke, and László Bartosiewicz (Oxford: Archaeopress, 2006), 81–82.
11. Alessandro Achilli et al., "Mitochondrial Genomes from Modern Horses," *PNAS* 109, no. 7 (2012): 2451.
12. Arne Ludwig et al., "Coat Color Variation at the Beginning of Horse Domestication," *Science* 324 (2009): 485, available at https://www.ncbi.nlm.nih.gov/pmc/articles/PMC5102060/.
13. Olsen, "Early Horse Domestication," 84–85.

14. Joris Peters et al., "Early Animal Husbandry in the Northern Levant," *Paléorient* 25, no. 2 (1999): 30.
15. Norbert Benecke and Angela von den Dreisch, "Horse Exploitation in the Kazakh Steppes during the Eneolithic and Bronze Age," in *Prehistoric Steppe Adaptation and the Horse*, ed. Marsha Levine, Colin Renfrew, and Katie Boyle (New York: Cambridge University Press, 2004), 69–82.
16. Anthony, *The Horse*, 202–204.
17. Marsha Levine, "Botai and the Origins of Horse Domestication," *Journal of Anthropological Archaeology* 18 (1999): 54–57.
18. Anthony, *The Horse, 204–205.*
19. V.I. Bibikova, "On the History of Horse Domestication in Southeast Europe," in *Dereivka: A Settlement and Cemetery of Copper Age Horse Keepers on the Middle Dneiper*, ed. Dmitriy Telegin (Oxford: Archaeopress, 1986), 163–182.
20. Olsen, "Early Horse Domestication," 89.
21. Alan Outram et al., "Horses for the Dead," *Antiquity* 85 (2011): 118.
22. Olsen, "Early Horse Domestication," 104.
23. Olsen, "Early Horse Domestication," 94–95.
24. Olsen, "Early Horse Domestication," 102.
25. Olsen, "Early Horse Domestication," 99.
26. Pita Kelekna, *The Horse in Human History* (New York: Cambridge University Press, 2009), 37–39.
27. Anthony, *The Horse*, 206.
28. Anthony, *The Horse*, 193–224.
29. Anthony, *The Horse*, 214–215.
30. Anthony, *The Horse*, 216–220.
31. Alan Outram et al., "The Earliest Horse Harnessing and Milking," *Science* 323 (2009): 1332–1335.
32. Renfrew, *Archaeology*, 146.
33. Anthony, *The Horse*, 76.
34. Anthony, *The Horse*, 81.
35. Genetic evidence is more equivocal, although it is extremely difficult to interpret. It is important to realize that both herders and farmers were willing and able to migrate depending on conditions; see Roni Jacobsen, "New Evidence Fuels Debate over Origin of Modern Languages," *Scientific American*, 2018, available at https://www.scientificamerican.com/article/new-evidence-fuels-debate-over-the-origin-of-modern-languages/.
36. Anthony, *The Horse*, 388–405. It is possible that genetic evidence will be able to shed more light on ancient migration pattern in the future; see Anna Juras et al., "Diverse Origins of Mitochondrial Lineages in Iron Age Scythians," *Scientific Reports* 7 (2017), available at https://www.nature.com/articles/srep43950.

37. Quoted in "New Research Shows How Indo-European Languages Spread across Asia," *ScienceDaily*, 2018, available at https://www.sciencedaily.com/releases/2018/05/180509185446.htm.

38. Pereltsvaig and Lewis, *The Indo-European Controversy*, 50.

Chapter 3

1. Martin Bernal, "Was Cleopatra Black?" *Newsweek*, September 23, 1991.

2. George James, *Stolen Legacy* (New York: Philosophical Library, 1954) was an earlier example.

3. *Black Athena Revisited*, ed. Mary Lefkowitz and Guy Rogers (Chapel Hill: University of North Carolina Press, 1996).

4. Berlinerblau, *Heresy in the University*, 1.

5. Allan Bloom, *The Closing of the American Mind* (New York: Simon and Schuster, 1987).

6. Jacques Berlinerblau, *Heresy in the University* (New Brunswick, NJ: Rutgers University Press, 1999), 5.

7. Martin Bernal, *Black Athena*, vol. 1 (New Brunswick, NJ: Rutgers University Press, 1987), 51; Berlinerblau, *Heresy in the University*, 68.

8. Martin Bernal, *Black Athena*, vol. 2 (New Brunswick, NJ: Rutgers University Press, 1991), 525–526.

9. Berlinerblau, *Heresy in the University*, 63.

10. Modern scholars are more charitable, writing that "if we will not find him unfailingly honest and objective, is still, in the way he displays evidence, more honest and objective than most." See Rosaria Munson, *Telling Wonders* (Ann Arbor: University of Michigan Press, 2001), 18.

11. Berlinerblau argues that these ideas, even if not explicitly endorsed by scholars in the eighteenth and nineteenth centuries, formed what he calls a *doxa*. Following Wacquant, he defines this as "the realm of implicit and unstated beliefs." Significantly, those who rally to the defense of these unstated beliefs tend be viewed as "orthodox," while those who challenge them are more readily dismissed. See Berlinerblau, *Heresy in the University*, 107–109.

12. Frank Yurco, "*Black Athena*: An Egyptological Review," in *Black Athena Revisited*, ed. Mary Lefkowitz and Guy Rogers (Chapel Hill: University of North Carolina Press, 1996), 91.

13. Yurco, "Black Athena," 83.

14. Jay Jasanoff and Alan Nussbaum, "Word Games: The Linguistic Evidence in Black Athena," in *Black Athena Revisited*, ed. Mary Lefkowitz and Guy Rogers (Chapel Hill: University of North Carolina Press, 1996), 193–194.

15. Bernal, *Black Athena*, vol. 1, 52–53.

16. Frank Snowden Jr., "Bernal's 'Blacks' and the Afrocentrists," in *Black Athena Revisited*, ed. Mary Lefkowitz and Guy Rogers (Chapel Hill: University of North Carolina Press, 1996), 116.

17. Cited in Berlinerblau, *Heresy in the University*, 124.

18. Robert Palter, "Eighteenth-Century Historiography in *Black Athena*," in *Black Athena Revisited*, ed. Mary Lefkowitz and Guy Rogers (Chapel Hill: University of North Carolina Press, 1996), 379.

19. Eric Cline, *1177 BC: The Year Civilization Collapsed* (Princeton, NJ: Princeton University Press, 2014), 33.

20. Berlinerblau, *Heresy in the University*, 125.

21. Martin Bernal, *Black Athena Writes Back* (Durham, NC: Duke University Press, 2001), 184.

22. Yurco, "*Black Athena*," 92.

23. Mary Lefkowitz, *Not Out of Africa* (New York: Basic Books, 1997), 126cf. 168.

24. David Konstan, "Inventing Ancient Greece," *History and Theory* 36, no. 2 (1997): 261–269.

25. J.-F. Nardelli, "Black Athena III," *The Classical Review* 63, no. 1 (2013): 142–144.

Chapter 4

1. Paul Vitello, "Hindu Group Stirs a Debate over Yoga's Soul," *New York Times*, November 27, 2010.

2. Albert Mohler, "The Subtle Body," September 20, 2010, available at http://www.albertmohler.com/2010/09/20/the-subtle-body-should-christians-practice-yoga/.

3. Andrea Jain, *Selling Yoga* (New York: Oxford University Press, 2015), 141.

4. Geoffrey Samuel, *The Origins of Yoga and Tantra* (New York: Cambridge University Press, 2008), 3.

5. David Gordon White, "Yoga, Brief History of an Idea," in *Yoga in Practice*, ed. David Gordon White (Princeton, NJ: Princeton University Press, 2012), 2.

6. Cited in Jain, *Selling Yoga*, 8.

7. Jain, *Selling Yoga*, 10.

8. David Gordon White, *The Yoga Sutra of Patanjali: A Biography* (Princeton, NJ: Princeton University Press, 2014), 13–14.

9. Andrew J. Nicholson, "Is Yoga Hindu?" *Common Knowledge* 19, no. 3 (2013): 494–498.

10. Jain, *Selling Yoga*, 14–15.
11. David Gordon White, *Sinister Yogis* (Chicago, IL: University of Chicago Press, 2011), xi–xii.
12. Carl W. Ernst, "Traces of Sattari Sufism and Yoga in North Africa," *Oriente Moderno* 92, no. 2 (2012): 366–367.
13. James Mallinson, "The Yogi's Latest Trick," *Journal of the Royal Asiatic Society* 24, no. 1 (2014): 173–174.
14. Philip Goldberg, *American Veda* (New York: Harmony, 2014), 77.
15. Jain, *Selling Yoga*, 33.
16. B.K.S. Iyengar, *Astadala Yogamālā* (New Delhi: Allied Publishers, 2000), 60.
17. Mark Singleton, *Yoga Body* (New York: Oxford University Press, 2010), 86.
18. Joseph Alter, *Yoga in Modern India* (Princeton, NJ: Princeton University Press, 2004).
19. Singleton, *Yoga Body*, 124.
20. Singleton, *Yoga Body*, 178–179.
21. Singleton, *Yoga Body*, 187.
22. Singleton, *Yoga Body*, 196.
23. Singleton, *Yoga Body*, 203.
24. Singleton, *Yoga Body*, 206.
25. Mark Singleton, "Globalized Modern Yoga," in *Yoga: The Art of Transformation*, ed. Debra Diamond (Washington, DC: Smithsonian Institution, 2013), 98.
26. Bethany MacLean, "Whose Yoga Is It, Anyway?" *Vanity Fair*, April 2012, available at https://www.vanityfair.com/news/business/2012/04/krishna-pattanbhi-trophy-wife-ashtanga-yoga.
27. Julia Henderson, "Bikram," *30 for 30 Podcasts*, available at https://30for30podcasts.com/episodes/bikram-part-1-arrival/#transcript; Chavie Lieber, "Lululemon Employees Report a Toxic 'Boy's Club' Culture," 2018, available at https://www.racked.com/2018/2/14/17007924/lululemon-work-culture-ceo-laurent-potdevin.
28. Singleton, *Yoga Body*, 197.
29. White, *The Yoga Sutras*, 214.
30. Singleton, *Yoga Body*, 186.

Chapter 5

1. Tom Phillips, "The Cultural Revolution," *The Guardian*, May 10, 2016, available at https://www.theguardian.com/world/2016/may/11/the-cultural-revolution-50-years-on-all-you-need-to-know-about-chinas-political-convulsion.

2. Gabrielle Jaffe, "China's Enthusiastic Re-embrace of Confucius," *The Atlantic*, October 7, 2013, available at https://www.theatlantic.com/china/archive/2013/10/chinas-enthusiastic-re-embrace-of-confucius/280326/.

3. Jaffe, "China's Enthusiastic."

4. Norman Ho, "Unlikely Bedfellows," *Harvard International Review* 31, no. 2 (2009).

5. Samuel Huntington, "The Clash of Civilizations," *Foreign Affairs* 72, no. 3 (1993): 25.

6. von Sivers et al., *Patterns of World History*, 246–247.

7. Anna Sun, *Confucianism as a World Religion* (Princeton, NJ: Princeton University Press, 2013), 28.

8. Quoted in Yonghua Liu, *Confucian Rituals and Chinese Villagers* (Leiden: Brill, 2013), 5.

9. Strayer and Nelson, *Ways of the World*, 150–156.

10. Tignor et al., *Worlds Together Worlds Apart*, 336.

11. For adaptations from Buddhism, see von Sivers et al., *Patterns of World History*, 366.

12. Lionel Jensen, *Manufacturing Confucianism* (Durham, NC: Duke University Press, 1998), 43.

13. Jensen, *Manufacturing*, 45.

14. Jensen, *Manufacturing*, 49.

15. Jensen, *Manufacturing*, 51.

16. Han Yu, "Memorial on the Bone of the Buddha," in *Worlds Together Worlds Apart: A Companion Reader*, vol. 1, ed. Elizabeth Pollard and Clifford Rosenberg (New York: W.W. Norton, 2016): 226–227. Originally published in 819.

17. Julia Murray, "'Idols' in the Temple," *Journal of Asian Studies* 68, no. 2 (2009): 383.

18. Sun, *Confucianism*, 131.

19. Jensen, *Manufacturing*, 58–61.

20. Sun, *Confucianism*, 33.

21. Thomas Wilson, *Genealogy of the Way* (Palo Alto, CA: Stanford University Press, 1995), 30–31.

22. Wilson, *Genealogy*, 39.

23. Murray, "'Idols' in the Temple," 377.

24. John Kieschnick, *The Impact of Buddhism on Chinese Material Culture* (Princeton, NJ: Princeton University Press, 2003), 62–63.

25. Sun, *Confucianism*, 162–163.

26. Liu, *Confucian Rituals*, 56.

27. Liu, *Confucian Rituals*, 264.

28. Liu, *Confucian Rituals*, 100.

29. Liu, *Confucian Rituals*, 102.

30. Liu, *Confucian Rituals*, 233.
31. Liu, *Confucian Rituals*, 238.
32. Tim Barrett, "Confucius: The Key to Understanding China," in *Demystifying China*, ed. Naomi Standen (New York: Rowman and Littlefield, 2012), 41.
33. Liu, *Confucian Rituals*, 263.
34. Cited in Chow Tse-Tung, *The May Fourth Movement* (Cambridge, MA: Harvard University Press, 1960), 310.

Chapter 6

1. This was originally part of a lecture series on "The Rise of Christian Europe" televised by the BBC. It was reprinted in the magazine *The Listener* as part of their November 28, 1964 issue.
2. Ebere Nwaubani, "Kenneth Onwuka Dike, *Trade and Politics*, and the Restoration of the African in History," *History in Africa* 27 (2000): 229.
3. Cornevin cited in Jan Vansina, *Paths in the Rainforest* (Madison: University of Wisconsin Press, 1990), 303 fn 1.
4. Kairn Klieman, *"The Pygmies Were Our Compass": Bantu and Batwa in the History of West Central Africa, Early Times to c. 1900 C.E.* (Portsmouth, NH: Heinemann, 2003), 21.
5. Diamond, *Guns, Germs, and Steel*, 103.
6. Harry Johnston, *A Survey of the Ethnography of Africa* (London: Royal Anthropological Institute of Great Britain and Ireland, 1913), 390.
7. Johnston, *A Survey*, 413.
8. Harry Johnston, *The Backwards Peoples and Our Relations with Them* (Oxford: Oxford University Press, 1920), 45.
9. Malcolm Guthrie, "Some Developments in the Prehistory of Bantu Languages," *Journal of African History* 3, no. 2 (1962): 273–282; Joseph H. Greenberg, "Studies in African Linguistic Classification: III. The Position of Bantu," *Southwestern Journal of Anthropology* 5, no. 4 (1949): 316.
10. Roland Oliver, "The Problem of the Bantu Expansion," *Journal of African History* 7, no. 3 (1966): 362.
11. Oliver, "The Problem," 362.
12. Vansina, *Paths*, 55–65.
13. Vansina, *Paths*, 96.
14. Jan Vansina, "New Linguistic Evidence and 'the Bantu Expansion,'" *Journal of African History* 36, no. 2 (1995): 190.
15. Vansina, "New Linguistic Evidence," 192.

16. Vansina, "New Linguistic Evidence," 191 indicates that he feels a single migration and no migration at all (language spread solely by language shift) are two extremes that are equally unlikely.

17. John Robertson and Rebecca Bradley, "A New Paradigm," *History in Africa* 27 (2000): 314.

18. James Webb Jr., *Humanity's Burden* (New York: Cambridge University Press, 2009), 32.

19. Robertson and Bradley, "A New Paradigm," 308.

20. Robertson and Bradley, "A New Paradigm," 296.

21. Klieman, *The Pygmies Were Our Compass,* 88–89.

22. Klieman, *The Pygmies Were Our Compass,* 58–59.

23. Klieman asserts that proto-Grasslands, proto-Coastlands, proto-Nyong-Lomami, proto-Sangha-Kwa, proto-Nzadi, and proto-Nzebi tongues all were formed during this time across the central African rainforests. Klieman, *The Pygmies Were Our Compass,* 45.

24. Alfred Ngomanda et al., "Seasonality Change," *Quaternary Research* 71 (2009): 312.

25. Katharina Neumann et al., "First Farmers in the Central African Rainforest," *Quaternary International* 249 (2012): 53–62.

26. Thembi Russell et al., "Modelling the Spread of Farming in the Bantu-Speaking Regions of Africa," *PLoS One* 9, no. 1 (2014): 8; see also Ngomanda et al., "Seasonality," 313 which argues that the lack of grass pollen in the archaeological record suggests this "corridor" never became true savanna.

27. Ngomanda et al., "Seasonality," 315.

28. Rebecca Grollemund et al., "Bantu Migration Shows," *PNAS* 112, no. 43 (2015): 13296.

29. Christopher Ehret, "Bantu History," *PNAS* 112, no. 44 (2015): 13428.

30. Oliver, "The Problem," 368.

31. Christophe Mbida et al., "Evidence for Banana Cultivation," *Journal of Archaeological Science* 27 (2000): 157–158; Klieman, *The Pygmies Were Our Compass,* 125 fn 10 provides details on how this date was acquired.

32. Klieman, *The Pygmies Were Our Compass,* 98.

33. Roger Blench, "Bananas and Plantains in Africa," *Ethnobotany Research and Applications* 7 (2009): 376.

34. Klieman, *The Pygmies Were Our Compass,* 102.

35. Klieman, *The Pygmies Were Our Compass,* 107.

36. Christopher Ehret, *The Civilizations of Africa,* 1st edn (Charlottesville: University of Virginia Press, 2002), 159.

37. Vansina, *Paths,* 253.

38. Donald Wright, "What Do You Mean There Weren't Any Tribes in Africa?" *History of Africa* 26 (1999): 410.

39. Diamond, *Guns, Germs, and Steel,* 396.

Chapter 7

1. Note that she mentioned that the Capitol in particular is loaded with Roman references, and that Panem is a reference to Juvenal's *Satires*. See http://www.scholastic.com/thehungergames/media/suzanne_collins_q_and_a.pdf.

2. Govindini Murty, "Decoding the Influences in 'The Hunger Games,'" *The Atlantic*, March 26, 2012, available at https://www.theatlantic.com/entertainment/archive/2012/03/decoding-the-influences-in-hunger-games-from-spartacus-to-survivor/255043/.

3. Edward Luttwak, *The Grand Strategy of the Roman Empire* (Baltimore, MD: Johns Hopkins University Press, 1979); Howard Fast, *Spartacus* (New York: Routledge, 1996).

4. Mary Beard, *The Roman Triumph* (Cambridge, MA: Belknap Press at Harvard University Press, 2007) 5.

5. Michael Crawford, *The Roman Republic*, 2nd edn (London: Fontana Press, 1992), 104.

6. Strayer and Nelson, *Ways of the World*, 206.

7. This is starkly demonstrated in the tag worn by a slave promising a reward in gold to anyone who returns the bearer to the owner. Dunn and Mitchell, *Panorama*, 196.

8. Strayer and Nelson, *Ways of the World*, 209.

9. Dunn and Mitchell, *Panorama*, 199.

10. Peter Heather, *The Fall of the Roman Empire* (London: Macmillan, 2005), 439–440.

11. Tignor et al., *Worlds Together Worlds Apart*, 264–265.

12. This type of evidence can certainly be helpful if used with care, as Jerry Toner does in *The Day Commodus Killed a Rhino* (Baltimore, MD: Johns Hopkins University Press, 2014).

13. Roger Dunkle, *Gladiators* (New York: Pearson Longman, 2008), 68–69.

14. Garrett Fagan, *The Lure of the Arena* (New York: Cambridge University Press, 2011), 32.

15. Dunkle, *Gladiators*, 175.

16. Dunkle, *Gladiators*, 75.

17. Dunkle, *Gladiators*, 69.

18. Dunkle, *Gladiators*, 97.

19. Dunkle, *Gladiators*, 76–78.

20. Dunkle, *Gladiators*, 66. He is quoting the architect Vitruvius.

21. Katherine Welch, *The Roman Amphitheatre* (New York: Cambridge University Press, 2007), 46.

22. Toner, *The Day Commodus Killed a Rhino*, 68.

23. Dunkle, *Gladiators*, 274.
24. Fagan, *The Lure of the Arena*, 143.
25. Dunkle, *Gladiators*, 80.
26. Dunkle, *Gladiators*, 87.
27. Dunkle, *Gladiators*, 92.
28. John Granger Cook, "Crucifixion as Spectacle in Roman Campania," *Novum Testamentum* 54 (2012): 70.
29. Dunkle, *Gladiators*, 129.
30. Thomas Dyer, *Pompeii* (New York: Scribner, Welford and Co., 1870), 235–237.
31. Dunkle, *Gladiators*, 132.
32. Florus, *A Detailed Synopsis of the Spartacus War*, quoted in Brent Shaw, *Spartacus and the Slave Wars* (New York: Bedford St Martin's, 2018), 147.
33. Keith Hopkins and Mary Beard, *The Colosseum* (Cambridge, MA: Harvard University, 2011), 93.
34. Dunkle, *Gladiators*, 141.
35. Ludwig Friedländer, *Roman Life under the Early Empire* (London: Routledge and Kegan Paul, 1908), 16–17.
36. Michael Grant, *Gladiators* (New York: Delacorte Press, 1967), 104.
37. Keith Hopkins, *Death and Renewal* (New York: Cambridge University Press, 1983), 14.
38. Toner, *The Day Commodus Killed a Rhino*, 32.
39. Alison Futrell, *Blood in the Arena* (Austin: University of Texas Press, 2001), 205–210.
40. Fagan, *The Lure of the Arena*, 285.
41. Fagan, *The Lure of the Arena*, 36.
42. Fagan, *The Lure of the Arena*, 79.
43. Welch, *The Roman Amphitheatre*, 4.
44. Toner, *The Day Commodus Killed a Rhino*, 88.

Chapter 8

1. Soodabeh Javadi, "Iran's Women on the Frontline," *BBC*, February 10, 2009, available at http://news.bbc.co.uk/2/hi/middle_east/7879639.stm.
2. Guity Nashat, "Women in the Islamic Republic of Iran," *Iranian Studies* 13, no. 1 (1980): 174.
3. Ziba Mir-Hosseini, "Women and Politics in Post-Khomeini Iran," in *Women and Politics in the Third World*, ed. Haleh Afshar (New York: Routledge, 1996), 153.
4. Nashat, "Women," 174.

5. Tignor et al., *Worlds Together Worlds Apart*, 132.

6. Sahar Amer, *What Is Veiling?* (Chapel Hill: University of North Carolina Press, 2014), 10–16.

7. Ashraf Zahedi, "Concealing and Revealing Female Hair," in *The Veil*, ed. Jennifer Heath (Berkeley: University of California Press, 2008), 252.

8. Leila Ahmed, *Women and Gender in Islam* (New Haven, CT: Yale University Press, 1992), 14–15.

9. Amer, *What Is Veiling*, 7.

10. Désirée G. Koslin, "He Hath Couered My Soule Inwarde," in *The Veil*, ed. Jennifer Heath (Berkeley: University of California Press, 2008), 160; Ahmed, *Women and Gender*, 28.

11. Ahmed, *Women and Gender*, 26, 35.

12. Ahmed, *Women and Gender*, 18.

13. Christian et al., *Big History*, 189.

14. Quran 24: 30–31, cited in Amer, *What Is Veiling*, 27.

15. Amer, *What Is Veiling*, 33.

16. Fatima Mernissi, *The Veil and the Male Elite* (New York: Basic Books, 1991), 98.

17. Quran 33:59, translation cited by Amer, *What Is Veiling*, 44.

18. Amer, *What Is Veiling*, 45.

19. Ahmed, *Women and Gender*, 118.

20. Carole Naggar, "Women Unveiled: Marc Garanger's Contested Portraits of 1960s Algeria," *Time*, April 23, 2013, available at http://time.com/69351/women-unveiled-marc-garangers-contested-portraits-of-1960s-algeria/.

21. Ahmed, *Women and Gender*, 153.

22. Frantz Fanon, *A Dying Colonialism* (New York: Grove Press, 1965), 35–67.

23. Ahmed, *Women and Gender*, 160.

24. Ahmed, *Women and Gender*, 163.

25. Ahmed, *Women and Gender*, 159.

26. Amer, *What Is Veiling*, 135.

27. Ahmed, *Women and Gender*, 176.

28. Amer, *What Is Veiling*, 139.

29. Strayer and Nelson, *Ways of the World*, 1007.

30. Hooman Majd, *The Ayatollah Begs to Differ* (New York: Anchor, 2009), 12–13.

31. Nashat, "Women," 165–194.

32. Mohja Kahf, "From Her Royal Body the Robe Was Removed," in *The Veil*, ed. Jennifer Heath (Berkeley: University of California Press, 2008), 34–35.

33. Fadwa El Guindi, *Veil: Modesty, Privacy and Resistance* (New York: Berg, 1999), 131–140.

34. Mernissi, *The Veil*, 97.

35. Timothy Mitchell, *Carbon Democracy* (New York: Verso, 2013), 214.

36. Kahf, "From Her Royal Body," 35.
37. Mona Eltahawy, "Why Do They Hate Us?" *Foreign Policy* 193 (2012): 64–70.
38. Ayaan Hirsi Ali, *Infidel* (New York: Free Press, 2007), 349–350.
39. Ali, *Infidel*, 128.
40. Ziba Mir-Hosseini, "Out of This Dead-End," *Critical Muslims*, 2008, available at https://criticalmuslim.com/issues/08-men-islam/out-dead-end-ziba-mir-hosseini.
41. Amer, *What Is Veiling*, 153.
42. Kahf, "From Her Royal Body," 35–36.
43. Amer, *What Is Veiling*, 146.
44. Amer, *What Is Veiling*, 99.
45. Amer, *What Is Veiling*, 109.
46. Nassim Hatam, "Iranian Women Threw Off the Hijab—What Happened Next?" *BBC News*, May 19, 2018, available at https://www.bbc.com/news/world-middle-east-44040236.

Chapter 9

1. Doug Brown, "Suspect in Portland Hate Crime Murders Is a Known White Supremacist," *Portland Mercury*, May 27, 2017, available at http://www.portlandmercury.com/blogtown/2017/05/27/19041594/suspect-in-portland-hate-crime-murders-is-a-known-white-supremacist.
2. Andrew Higgins, "Norway again Embraces the Vikings, Minus the Violence," *New York Times*, September 17, 2015, available at https://www.nytimes.com/2015/09/18/world/europe/norway-again-embraces-the-vikings-minus-the-violence.html?_r=0.
3. David Perry, "White Supremacists Love the Vikings. But They've Got History All Wrong," *Washington Post*, May 31, 2017, available at https://www.washingtonpost.com/posteverything/wp/2017/05/31/white-supremacists-love-vikings-but-theyve-got-history-all-wrong/?utm_term=.01cf4f73c64d.
4. Peter Sawyer, *The Age of the Vikings*, 2nd edn (London: Edward Arnold, 1972), 202–203.
5. Wilhelm Holmqvist, *Swedish Vikings on Helgö and Birka* (Stockholm: Swedish Booksellers Association, 1979), 70.
6. "Viking Raids on England," in *The Viking Age: A Reader*, ed. Angus Somerville and R. Andrew McDonald (Toronto: University of Toronto Press, 2010), 230.

7. "Franks and Vikings," in *The Viking Age: A Reader*, ed. Angus Somerville and R. Andrew McDonald (Toronto: University of Toronto Press, 2010), 245.
8. "The Annals of St-Vast," in *The Viking Age: A Reader*, ed. Angus Somerville and R. Andrew McDonald (Toronto: University of Toronto Press, 2010), 262.
9. Anna Jones, "Pitying the Desolation of Such a Place," *Viator* 37, no. 1 (2006): 93.
10. Jones, "Pitying," 98.
11. Erika Sigurdson, "Violence and Historical Authenticity," *Scandinavian Studies* 86, no. 3 (2014): 250.
12. Sigurdson, "Violence and Historical Authenticity," 254.
13. Simon Coupland, "The Vikings on the Continent in Myth and History," *History* 88 (2003): 196.
14. Coupland, "The Vikings," 196.
15. "The Anglo-Saxon Chronicle—Ninth Century," trans. James Ingram, available at http://avalon.law.yale.edu/medieval/ang09.asp.
16. Anders Winroth, *The Age of the Vikings* (Princeton, NJ: Princeton University Press, 2014), 35.
17. Winroth, *The Age of the Vikings*, 37.
18. http://vikings.wikia.com/wiki/Blood_Eagle.
19. "Odin's Berserks," in *The Viking Age: A Reader*, ed. Angus Somerville and R. Andrew McDonald (Toronto: University of Toronto Press, 2010), 162–163.
20. Neil MacGregor, *A History of the World in 100 Objects* (New York: Penguin, 2010), 395.
21. Winroth, *The Age of the Vikings*, 39.
22. Winroth, *The Age of the Vikings*, 103.
23. MacGregor, *A History of the World in 100 Objects*, 362.
24. Winroth, *The Age of the Vikings*, 108.
25. Nancy Brown, *The Far Traveler* (New York: Harcourt, 2007), 60.
26. Higgins, "Norway again," 2015, available at https://www.nytimes.com/2015/09/18/world/europe/norway-again-embraces-the-vikings-minus-the-violence.html; Jonathan Wynne-Jones, "Vikings Preferred Male Grooming to Pillaging," *The Telegraph*, October 25, 2008, available at http://www.telegraph.co.uk/news/newstopics/howaboutthat/3256539/Vikings-preferred-male-grooming-to-pillaging.html.
27. Philip Grierson, "Commerce in the Dark Ages," in *Transactions of the Royal Historical Society* 5th Series, vol. 9 (London: Cambridge University Press, 1959), 123–140.
28. Winroth, *The Age of the Vikings*, 125.
29. Winroth, *The Age of the Vikings*, 108.

30. "An Arab Description of a Viking Funeral," in *The Viking Age: A Reader*, ed. Angus Somerville and R. Andrew McDonald (Toronto: University of Toronto Press, 2010), 106–110.
31. Christopher Lowe, "Image and Imagination," in *West Over Sea*, ed. Beverly Smith, Simon Taylor and Gareth Williams (Boston: Brill, 2007), 61–62.
32. Jonathan Jarrett, "Once More Mr. Nice Guy: the Vikings and Violence," November 11, 2008, available at https://tenthmedieval.wordpress.com/2008/11/11/once-more-mr-nice-guy-the-vikings-and-violence/.
33. Perry, "White Supremacists," 2017, available at https://www.washingtonpost.com/posteverything/wp/2017/05/31/white-supremacists-love-vikings-but-theyve-got-history-all-wrong/?utm_term=.8864efe6b1a0.

Chapter 10

1. Erich von Däniken, *Chariots of the Gods?* (New York: G.P. Putnam's, 1970), 115.
2. This is the name given to the island by Polynesian sailors in the nineteenth century, and will be used from this point forward unless quoting someone doing otherwise.
3. Jacob Roggeveen quoted in Jared Diamond, *Collapse* (New York: Viking, 2005), 81.
4. Däniken, *Chariots*, 114.
5. Bentley et al., *Traditions and Encounters*, 321.
6. Valerie Hansen and Ken Curtis, *Voyages in World History*, 1st edn (New York: Wadsworth, 2008), 141.
7. Bentley et al., *Traditions and Encounters*, 321.
8. https://www.bighistoryproject.com/chapters/5#the-anthropocene-epoch.
9. Sebastián Englert, *Island at the Center of the World* (New York: Scribner, 1970), 95.
10. Thor Heyerdahl, *The Art of Easter Island* (New York: Doubleday, 1975), 29.
11. von Sivers et al., *Patterns of World History*, 146.
12. *Kon-Tiki*, Official Trailer, 1950, available at https://www.youtube.com/watch?v=bx20hi374as.
13. Patrick Kirch, quoted in John Flenley and Paul Bahn, *The Enigmas of Easter Island* (Oxford: Oxford University Press, 2003), 59.
14. Thor Heyerdahl, *Aku-Aku* (New York: Penguin Books, 1960), 326.
15. Described in Englert, *Island*, 134. The genealogy suggested a survivor of the battle was born in the latter half of the seventeenth century, and a charcoal sample from Poike was dated to 1676.

16. Flenley and Bahn, *The Enigmas*, vii.

17. Englert, *Island*, 93. The word for long ears is *epe*, which caused the problem. Momoko refers to a lizard, which Englert suggests is a reference to a slender build.

18. Flenley and Bahn, *The Enigmas*, 39–40. Note that voyages between Rapa Nui and the South America may have been possible. The presence of sweet potato on Rapa Nui and recent DNA evidence suggests these voyages happened, but the DNA signifiers of Basque ancestry may also have arrived in the nineteenth century. See Lizzie Wade, "Did Early Easter Islanders Sail to South America before Europeans?" *Science*, October 12, 2017, available at http://www.sciencemag.org/news/2017/10/did-early-easter-islanders-sail-south-america-europeans.

19. Terry Hunt and Carl Lipo, *The Statues That Walked* (Berkeley, CA: Counterpoint, 2012), 15–16. Scientists today try to avoid this by drawing samples from short-lived parts of trees, like twigs or seeds.

20. Catherine Orliac, "The Woody Vegetation of Easter Island between the Early 14th and the Mid-17th Centuries AD," in *Easter Island Archaeology*, ed. Christopher Stevenson and William Ayres (Los Osos, CA: Easter Island Foundation, 2000), 218.

21. Steven Fischer, *The Island at the End of the World* (London: Reaktion Books, 2005), 34.

22. Flenley and Bahn, *The Enigmas*, 192–193.

23. Flenley and Bahn, *The Enigmas*, ix.

24. Diamond, *Collapse*, 117.

25. Hunt and Lipo, *The Statues*, 16.

26. Daniel Mann et al., "Drought, Vegetation Change, and Human History on Rapa Nui," *Quaternary Research* 69 (2008): 19.

27. Orliac, "The Woody Vegetation," 218.

28. Hunt and Lipo, *The Statues*, 27.

29. Flenley and Bahn, *The Enigmas*, 83.

30. Flenley and Bahn, *The Enigmas*, 160. Diamond, *Collapse*, 106 notes that every palm nut found on Easter Island shows evidence of gnawing by rats.

31. Hunt and Lipo, *The Statues*, 40.

32. Hunt and Lipo, *The Statues*, 46.

33. Flenley and Bahn, *The Enigmas*, 154.

34. Hunt and Lipo, *The Statues*, 99.

35. Diamond, *Collapse*, 90.

36. Van Tilburg's theories are described here—https://www.pbs.org/wgbh/nova/easter/move/plan.html.

37. Hunt and Lipo, *The Statues*, 92.

38. Hunt and Lipo, *The Statues*, 169.

39. Diamond, *Collapse*, 113.

Chapter 11

1. Tapia cited in Michael Harner, "The Ecological Basis for Aztec Sacrifice," *American Ethnologist* 4, no. 1 (1977): 122.
2. "Aztec Skull Trophy Rack Discovered at Mexico City's Templo Mayor Site," *The Guardian* August 20, 2015, available at https://www.theguardian.com/science/2015/aug/21/aztec-skull-trophy-rack-discovered-mexico-citys-templo-mayor-ruin-site.
3. "Aztec Tower of Human Skulls Uncovered in Mexico City," *BBC* July 2, 2017, available at https://www.bbc.com/news/world-latin-america-40473547.
4. Hernando Cortés, "Letter to Charles V," July 10, 1519. Full text translation included in *Victors and Vanquished*, ed. Stuart Schwartz and Tatiana Seijas, (New York: Bedford St. Martin's, 2018), 65.
5. Quoted in Schwartz and Seijas, *Victors and Vanquished*, 65.
6. Susan Schroeder, *Tlacaelel Remembered* (Norman: Oklahoma University Press, 2016), 11.
7. von Sivers et al., *Patterns of World History*, 533 refers to her as Malinche. Camilla Townsend, *An Indian Woman in the Conquest of Mexico* (Albuquerque: University of New Mexico Press, 2006), 55 and Schwartz and Seijas, *Victors and Vanquished*, 122.
8. Christian et al., *Big History*, 199.
9. Dunn and Mitchell, *Panorama*, 417.
10. Mann, *1491*, 137.
11. Diaz, quoted in Schwartz and Seijas, *Victors and Vanquished*, 190–191.
12. Peter Hassler, "Human Sacrifice among the Aztecs?" *Die Zeit* 1992, available at http://www.elcamino.edu/Faculty/jsuarez/1Cour/H19/WpSacrifice1.htm.
13. Matthew Restall, *Seven Myths of the Spanish Conquest* (New York: Oxford University Press, 2003), 13.
14. Lewis Henry Morgan, "Montezuma's Dinner," *North American Review* 122, no. 2 (1876): 268.
15. Kurly Tlapoyawa, "Did 'Mexika Human Sacrifice' Exist?" available at http://eaglefeather.org/series/Mexican%20Series/Did%20Mexica%20Human%20Sacrifice%20Exist.pdf.
16. Diego Durán, *The Aztecs: the History of the Indies of New Spain* (New York: Orion Press, 1964), 199 claims 80,400 died. Schroeder, *Tlacaelel Remembered*, 120 puts the total at 80,600, citing Chimalpáhin.
17. von Sivers et al., *Patterns of World History*, 454–455.
18. Sahagún from the Florentine Codex, cited in Schwartz and Seijas, *Victors and Vanquished*, 101–102.

19. Eduardo Matos Moctezuma, "Sahagún and the Ceremonial Precinct of Tenochtitlan," in *Representing Aztec Ritual*, ed. Eloise Quiñones Keber, (Boulder: University Press of Colorado, 2002), 51.

20. William Prescott, *The History of the Conquest of Mexico* (London: Chatto & Windus, 1922), 22.

21. Harner, "The Ecological Basis," 131.

22. Bernard R. Ortiz de Montellano, "Counting Skulls," *American Anthropologist* 85, no. 2 (1983): 403–406.

23. Sophie Coe, *America's First Cuisines* (Austin: University of Texas Press, 1994), 97–98.

24. Geoffrey Conrad and Arthur Demarest, *Religion and Empire* (New York: Cambridge University Press, 1984), 38.

25. Durán, *The Aztecs*, 141.

26. Durán, *The Aztecs*, 111–113.

27. Ross Hassig, *Aztec Warfare* (Norman: Oklahoma University Press, 1988), 13.

28. John Ingham, "Human Sacrifice at Tenochtitlan," *Comparative Studies in Society and History* 26, no.3 (1984): 396.

29. Ingham, "Human Sacrifice," 397.

30. Durán, *The Aztecs*, xxx–xxxii.

31. Inga Clendinnen, *Aztecs* (New York: Cambridge University Press, 1991), 289 has a good explanation as to why she feels Sahagún provides more reliable descriptions of everyday rituals than outsiders like Durán.

32. Clendinnen, *Aztecs*, 247.

33. Clendinnen, *Aztecs*, 253.

34. David Carrasco, *City of Sacrifice* (Boston, MA: Beacon Press, 1999), 19.

35. Carrasco, *City of Sacrifice*, 96, 102.

36. Carrasco, *City of Sacrifice*, 7.

37. Wheatley, cited in Carrasco, *City of Sacrifice*, 29.

38. Ximena Chávez Balderas, "Sacrifice at the Templo Mayor of Tenochtitlan and Its Role in Regard to Warfare," in *Embattled Bodies, Embattled Places*, eds. Andrew Scherer and John Verano (Washington DC: Dumbarton Oaks Research Library and Collection, 2014), 190.

39. Clendinnen, *Aztecs*, 90.

40. Lizzie Wade, "Feeding the Gods," *Science* 360 (2018): 1288–1292.

Chapter 12

1. Church of Lukumi Babalu Aye, Inc. v. Hialeah, 508 U.S. 520 at 526 (1993).

2. Church of Lukumi Babalu Aye, Inc. v. Hialeah, 508 U.S. 520 at 541 (1993).

3. Frank James, "Pat Robertson Blames Haitian Devil Pact for Earthquake," *NPR* January 13, 2010, available at http://www.npr.org/sections/thetwo-way/2010/01/pat_robertson_blames_haitian_d.html.

4. Dunn and Mitchell, *Panorama*, 145.

5. Toyin Falola and Ann Genova, "Introduction," in *Orișa*, ed. Falola and Genova (Trenton, NJ: Africa World Press, 2005), 4.

6. Falola and Genova, "Introduction," 5–6.

7. J.D.Y. Peel, *Christianity, Islam, and Orisa Religion* (Oakland: University of California Press, 2016), 218.

8. Peel, *Christianity, Islam, and Orișa*, 216.

9. Cornelius Adepegba, "Associated Place-Names and Sacred Icons of Seven Yorùbá Deities," in *Òrìșà Devotion as World Religion*, ed. Jacob Olupona and Terry Rey (Madison: University of Wisconsin Press, 2008), 120.

10. Peel, *Christianity, Islam, and Orișa*, 48. It is difficult to know how accurate this story is due to the fact that it comes to use primarily through Christian converts in the nineteenth century, who felt this revelation could discredit orisa among the Yoruba.

11. Olabiyi Yai, "Yorùbá Religion and Globalization," in *Òrìșà Devotion as World Religion*, ed. Jacob Olupona and Terry Rey (Madison: University of Wisconsin Press, 2008), 237.

12. Falola and Genova, "Introduction," 5–6; see Peel, *Christianity, Islam, and Orișa*, 218 who claims the priests of Ifa differ from *babalawo* by being predominantly male.

13. Yai, "Yorùbá Religion," 237.

14. Louis Brenner, "Histories of Religion in Africa," *Journal of Religion in Africa* 30, no. 2 (2000): 155. H.O. Danmolé claims the eighteenth century is more accurate. See H.O. Danmolé, "Religious Encounter in Southwestern Nigeria," in *Òrìșà Devotion as World Religion*, ed. Jacob Olupona and Terry Rey (Madison: University of Wisconsin Press, 2008), 203.

15. Peel, *Christianity, Islam, and Orișa*, 157.

16. Brenner, "Histories of Religion," 159.

17. Peel, *Christianity, Islam, and Orișa*, 218.

18. Peel, *Christianity, Islam, and Orișa*, 151.

19. Danmolé, "Religious Encounter," 204.

20. Danmolé, "Religious Encounter," 202–221.

21. Marta Vega, "The Dynamic Influence of Cubans, Puerto Ricans, and African Americans in the Growth of Ocha in New York City," in *Òrìșà Devotion as World Religion*, ed. Jacob Olupona and Terry Rey (Madison: University of Wisconsin Press, 2008), 321. Juan Sosa, "La Santería," in *Òrìșà Devotion as World Religion*, ed. Jacob Olupona and Terry Rey (Madison: University of Wisconsin Press, 2008), 394–395 provides a list of thirty-four orisas with their corresponding saints.

22. Vega, "The Dynamic Influence," 321. See also Church of Lukumi Babalu Aye, Inc. v. Hialeah, 508 U.S. 520 at 524 (1993) for the Supreme Courts definition.
23. José de Barros, "Myth, Memory, and History," in *Òrìṣà Devotion as World Religion*, ed. Jacob Olupona and Terry Rey (Madison: University of Wisconsin Press, 2008), 405.
24. Ijeoma Ndukwe, "Meet the Ooni of Ife, the leader of Nigeria's Yoruba," *Al-Jazeera* September 2, 2017, available at http://www.aljazeera.com/indepth/features/2017/08/meet-ooni-ife-leader-nigeria-yoruba-170808123223824.html.
25. Peel, *Christianity, Islam, and Oriṣa*, 221.
26. F.O Ajose, "Some Nigerian Plants of Dermatologic Importance," *International Journal of Dermatology* 46 (2007): 48–55.
27. Funlayo Wood, "Sacred Healing and Wholeness in Africa and the Americas," *Journal of Africana Religion* 1, no. 3 (2013): 378.
28. Soyinka, *Of Africa*, 166.
29. Soyinka, *Of Africa*, 134.
30. Tomoko Masuzawa quoted in Jacob Olupona and Terry Rey, "Introduction," in *Òrìṣà Devotion as World Religion*, ed. Olupona and Rey (Madison: University of Wisconsin Press, 2008), 7.
31. Wole Soyinka, "The Tolerant Gods," in *Òrìṣà Devotion as World Religion*, ed. Jacob Olupona and Terry Rey (Madison: University of Wisconsin Press, 2008), 36.

Chapter 13

1. Lévesque, *Thinking Historically*, 140–141. He based this account on excerpts contained in Primo Levi, *The Drowned and the Saved* (New York: Simon and Schuster, 2017).
2. A typical example quotes Antonio Vazquez de Espinosa, a Catholic missionary, who observed in 1616 that indigenous laborers were at extreme risk of mercury poisoning. See Dunn and Mitchell, *Panorama*, 520.
3. Dennis Flynn and Arturo Giráldez, "Cycles of Silver: Global Economic Unity through the Mid-Eighteenth Century," *Journal of World History* 13, no. 2 (2002): 391–427.
4. Bentley et al., *Traditions and Encounters*, 403.
5. Peter Bakewell, *Miners of the Red Mountain* (Albuquerque, NM: University of New Mexico Press, 2010), 45.
6. Jeffrey Cole, *The Potosi Mita* (Palo Alto, CA: Stanford University Press, 1985), 3.

7. Bakewell, *Miners of the Red Mountain*, 54.
8. Cole, *The Potosi Mita*, 5. Note that Pope Pius V was concerned that abuses by Spanish colonists might impede conversions of Andeans. See Jeremy Mumford, *Vertical Empire* (Durham, NC: Duke University Press, 2012), 80.
9. Cole, *The Potosi Mita*, 12–14.
10. Bakewell, *Miners of the Red Mountain*, 142.
11. Nicholas Robins, *Mercury, Mining, and Empire* (Bloomington, IN: Indiana University Press, 2011), 81–90.
12. Jeffrey Cole, "An Abolitionism Born of Frustration," *Hispanic American Historical Review* 63, no. 2 (1983): 312.
13. Aquinas quoted in Orlando Bentancor, *The Matter of Empire* (Pittsburgh, PA: Pittsburgh University Press, 2017), 7.
14. *The New Laws of the Indies*, trans. Henry Stevens (London: Chiswick Press, 1893), iii–xvii.
15. Bentancor, *The Matter of Empire*, 101.
16. Mumford, *Vertical Empire*, 99.
17. Mumford, *Vertical Empire*, 103.
18. Mumford, *Vertical Empire*, 109–110.
19. Bakewell, *Miners of the Red Mountain*, 81–82.
20. Bentancor, *The Matter of Empire*, 208.
21. Bentancor, *The Matter of Empire*, 170–171.
22. Bentancor, *The Matter of Empire*, 242.
23. Bentancor, *The Matter of Empire*, 276.
24. Bentancor, *The Matter of Empire*, 307.
25. Cited in Bentancor, *The Matter of Empire*, 308.
26. Ed Stavig, *The World of Túpac Amaru* (Lincoln, NE: University of Nebraska Press, 1999), 201.
27. Stavig, *The World of Túpac Amaru*, 204.
28. Mumford, *Vertical Empire*, 54.
29. Stavig, *The World of Túpac Amaru*, 20.
30. Stavig, *The World of Túpac Amaru*, 181.
31. Rossana Barragán, "Working Silver for the World," *Hispanic American Historical Review* 97, no. 2 (2017): 193–222.

Chapter 14

1. "Paris City Guide," *Lonely Planet* February 22, 2013, available at https://www.youtube.com/watch?v=5XYUHJ13KHM.
2. "Paris City Guide."
3. Stephane Kirkland, *Paris Reborn* (New York: Picador, 2014), 238.

4. Joan DeJean, *How Paris Became Paris* (New York: Bloomsbury, 2014), 123.
5. DeJean, *How Paris Became Paris*, 145.
6. Germain Brice, *A New Description of Paris...* (London: Henry Bonwicke, 1687), unnumbered page.
7. Nicolas de Blégny quoted in DeJean, *How Paris Became Paris*, 4.
8. Leon Bernard, *The Emerging City* (Durham, NC: Duke University Press, 1970), vi.
9. Karen Newman, *Cultural Capitals* (Princeton, NJ: Princeton University Press, 2007), 58.
10. Newman, *Cultural Capitals*, 37–38.
11. The image is available at https://art.rmngp.fr/fr/library/artworks/nicolas-guerard_l-embarras-de-paris-le-pont-neuf_eau-forte_burin-estampe.
12. DeJean, *How Paris Became Paris*, 30–31.
13. Brice, *A New Description of Paris*, 187–188.
14. Newman, *Cultural Capitals*, 38–39.
15. Newman, *Cultural Capitals*, 46.
16. DeJean, *How Paris Became Paris*, 35.
17. Bernard, *The Emerging City*, 13.
18. DeJean, *How Paris Became Paris*, 113.
19. DeJean, *How Paris Became Paris*, 115.
20. DeJean, *How Paris Became Paris*, 38.
21. DeJean, *How Paris Became Paris*, 156.
22. DeJean, *How Paris Became Paris*, 167.
23. Bernard, *The Emerging City*, 57–58.
24. Bernard, *The Emerging City*, 59.
25. DeJean, *How Paris Became Paris*, 131.
26. Bernard, *The Emerging City*, 66.
27. DeJean, *How Paris Became Paris*, 134.
28. DeJean, *How Paris Became Paris*, 134.
29. DeJean, *How Paris Became Paris*, 136.
30. Bernard, *The Emerging City*, 53.
31. Bernard, *The Emerging City*, 160.
32. DeJean, *How Paris Became Paris*, 139.
33. DeJean, *How Paris Became Paris*, 138.
34. DeJean, *How Paris Became Paris*, 181.
35. DeJean, *How Paris Became Paris*, 187.
36. Bernard, *The Emerging City*, 130.
37. Bernard, *The Emerging City*, 131.
38. Jan de Vries, *European Urbanization, 1500–1800* (Cambridge, MA: Harvard University Press, 1984), 5.
39. de Vries, *European Urbanization*, 150.

Chapter 15

1. J.R. McNeill, *Mosquito Empires* (New York: Cambridge University Press, 2010), 2. He defines the Greater Caribbean as the Atlantic coastal regions of North, Central, and South America capable of supporting a plantation economy (generally Surinam to Chesapeake Bay), along with the islands of the Caribbean.
2. McNeill, *Mosquito Empires*, 5.
3. Elizabeth Fenn, *Pox Americana* (New York: Hill and Wang, 2001), 275.
4. Strayer and Nelson, *Ways of the World*, 709–711; Bentley et al., *Traditions and Encounters*, 479.
5. Lester Langley, *The Americas in the Age of Revolution, 1750–1850* (New Haven, CT: Yale University Press, 1996), 119, 132.
6. Laurent Dubois, *Avengers of the New World* (Cambridge, MA: Belknap Press of Harvard University Press, 2004), 141.
7. Jerome Greene, *Guns of Independence* (New York: Savas Beatie, 2005), 8, 111, 129.
8. Sarah Schuetze, "Carrying Home the Enemy," *Early American Literature* 53, no. 1 (2018): 97–98.
9. McNeill, *Mosquito Empires*, 7.
10. Rachel Carson, *Silent Spring* (New York: Houghton Mifflin, 1962) is often considered pivotal in this regard.
11. Fernand Braudel, *The Mediterranean and the Mediterranean World in the Age of Philip II*, 2 vols. (New York: Harper and Row, 1972), 1238–1244.
12. Alfred. Crosby, *Ecological Imperialism*, 2nd edn (New York: Cambridge University Press, 2004), xviii.
13. William Cronon, *Changes in the Land*, 1st edn (New York: Hill and Wang, 1983), 156.
14. John Schwaller, "Environmental Historian: An Interview with Alfred W. Crosby," *The Americas* 72, no. 2 (2015): 312.
15. Fenn, *Pox Americana*, 9.
16. Fenn, *Pox Americana*, 27–28.
17. Fenn, *Pox Americana*, 89.
18. Fenn, *Pox Americana*, 67.
19. Fenn, *Pox Americana*, 46.
20. Fenn, *Pox Americana*, 92.
21. Greene, *Guns of Independence*, 136.
22. McNeill, *Mosquito Empires*, 203–207.
23. McNeill, *Mosquito Empires*, 208.
24. McNeill, *Mosquito Empires*, 211.
25. McNeill, *Mosquito Empires*, 219.

26. McNeill, *Mosquito Empires*, 224.
27. McNeill, *Mosquito Empires*, 226.
28. McNeill, *Mosquito Empires*, 234.
29. McNeill, *Mosquito Empires*, 47–52.
30. J. Erin Staples and Thomas Monath, "Yellow Fever: 100 Years of Discovery," *Journal of the American Medical Association* 300, no. 8 (2008): 960–962.
31. McNeill, *Mosquito Empires*, 33–34.
32. McNeill, *Mosquito Empires*, 51–52.
33. McNeill, *Mosquito Empires*, 5.
34. McNeill, *Mosquito Empires*, 240–242.
35. McNeill, *Mosquito Empires*, 244–247.
36. Dubois, *Avengers*, 260 reveals that the expedition was sent to arrive at a time when the climate was not "dangerous to European troops."
37. McNeill, *Mosquito Empires*, 251–260.
38. McNeill, *Mosquito Empires*, 253.
39. William Cronon, "The Uses of Environmental History," *Environmental History Review* 17, no. 3 (1993): 13.

Chapter 16

1. George Feifer, *Breaking Open Japan* (New York: Smithsonian Books, 2006), 6.
2. Feifer, *Breaking Open Japan*, 1.
3. Kazushi Ohkawa and Henry Rosovsky, "Capital Formation in Japan," in *The Economic Emergence of Modern Japan*, ed. Kozo Yamamura (New York: Cambridge University Press, 1997), 205.
4. Christian et al., *Big History*, 252.
5. Ohkawa and Rosovsky, "Capital Formation in Japan," 208.
6. Mark Ravina, *To Stand with the Nations of the World* (New York: Oxford University Press, 2017), 27–28.
7. Strayer and Nelson, *Ways of the World*, 2nd edn, 950.
8. Strayer and Nelson, *Ways of the World*, 2nd edn, 967; see also Tignor et al., *Worlds Together Worlds Apart*, 659.
9. James Bradley, *Flyboys* (Boston, MA: Little and Brown, 2003), 36.
10. Ravina, *To Stand*, 62.
11. Feifer, *Breaking Open Japan*, 84–87.
12. Feifer, *Breaking Open Japan*, 66.
13. Ravina, *To Stand*, 88.
14. Ravina, *To Stand*, 67–68.

15. Sydney Crawcour, "Economic Change in the 19th Century," in *The Economic Emergence of Modern Japan*, ed. Kozo Yamamura (New York: Cambridge University Press, 1997), 19.

16. Ohkawa and Rosovsky, "Capital Formation in Japan," 211.

17. Ravina, *To Stand*, 69.

18. Peter Duus, *Modern Japan*, 2nd edn (New York: Houghton Mifflin, 1998), 69.

19. Duus, *Modern Japan*, 72.

20. Ravina, *To Stand*, 85.

21. Ravina, *To Stand*, 108.

22. Conrad Totman, *A History of Japan*, 2nd edn (Malden, MA: Blackwell, 2013), 299.

23. Ravina, *To Stand*, 134.

24. Duus, *Modern Japan*, 88.

25. Yokoi Shonan, quoted in Huffman, *Japan and Imperialism* (Ann Arbor, MI: Association for Asian Studies, 2010), 67.

26. Huffman, *Japan and Imperialism*, 17.

27. Byron Marshall, *Capitalism and Nationalism in Prewar Japan* (Palo Alto, CA: Stanford University Press, 1967), 3.

28. Osamu Saito and Masahiro Sato, "Japan's Civil Registration Systems Before and After the Meiji Restoration," in *Registration and Recognition*, ed. Keith Breckenridge and Simon Szreter (New York: Cambridge University Press, 2012), 124–125.

29. Strayer and Nelson, *Ways of the World*, 858; John P. McKay et al., *Understanding World Societies*, (New York: Beford St. Martin's, 2013), 709.

30. Ohkawa and Rosovsky, "Capital Formation in Japan," 217.

31. Kenichi Ohno, "The Industrialization and Global Integration of Meiji Japan," in *Globalization of Developing Countries: Is Autonomous Development Possible?* (Tokyo: Toyo Keizi Shinposha, 2000): 45.

32. Sydney Crawcour, "Industrialization and Technological Change," in *The Economic Emergence of Modern Japan*, ed. Kozo Yamamura (New York: Cambridge University Press, 1997), 95.

33. Peter Stearns, *The Industrial Revolution in World History*, 4th edn (New York: Routledge, 2012), 139–140.

34. Crawcour, "Industrialization and Technological Change," 85.

35. Misaka Nakabayashi, "The Rise of a Factory Industry: Silk Reeling in Suwa District," in *The Role of Tradition in Japan's Industrialization*, ed. Masayuki Tanimoto (New York: Oxford University Press, 2006), 183–216.

36. Jun Sasaki, "Factory Girls in an Agrarian Setting circa 1910," in *The Role of Tradition in Japan's Industrialization*, ed. Masayuki Tanimoto (New York: Oxford University Press, 2006), 121–139.

37. E.P. Thompson, "Time, Work-Discipline, and Industrial Capitalism," *Past and Present* 38 (1967): 56–97.
38. Thomas Smith, "Peasant Time and Factory Time in Japan," in *Native Sources of Japanese Industrialization, 1750–1920* (Berkeley: University of California Press, 1988), 199–235.
39. Niall Ferguson, *Civilization: The West and the Rest* (New York: Penguin, 2012), 221–222.
40. McKay et al., *Understanding World Societies*, 711.
41. Helen Hopper, *Fukuzawa Yukichi* (New York: Pearson Longman, 2005), 107.

Chapter 17

1. Henry Spiller, *Javaphilia* (Honolulu: University of Hawai'i Press, 2015), 42.
2. I have followed Laurie Sears's preferred spelling. *Dalang* is also acceptable.
3. Jennifer Goodlander, "Gender, Power, and Puppets," *Asian Theatre Journal* 29, no. 1 (2012): 55.
4. Benedict Anderson, *Mythology and the Tolerance of the Javanese* (Ithaca, NY: Cornell University Press, 1996), 23–37; Jeune Scott-Kemball, *Javanese Shadow Puppets* (London: British Museum, 1970), 32–33.
5. Sadiah Boonstra, "Negotiating Heritage: Wayang Puppet Theatre and the Dynamics of Heritage Formation," in *The Heritage Theatre*, ed. Marlite Halbertsma, Patricia van Ulzen, and Alex van Stipriaan (Newcastle: Cambridge Scholars Publishing, 2011), 31.
6. Spiller, *Javaphilia*, 54.
7. Tignor et al., *Worlds Together Worlds Apart*, 648; Cornelis Fasseur, *The Politics of Colonial Exploitation*, trans. R.E. Elson and Ary Kraal (Ithaca, NY: Cornell University Press, 1992).
8. Bentley et al., *Traditions and Encounters*, 552–553.
9. Ann Stoler and Fred Cooper, "Between Metropole and Colony," in *Tensions of Empire*, ed. Stoler and Cooper (Berkeley: University of California Press, 1997), 6.
10. Ann Stoler and Fred Cooper, "Preface," in *Tensions of Empire*, ed. Stoler and Cooper (Berkeley: University of California Press, 1997), ix.
11. Dunn and Mitchell, *Panorama*, 544–545.
12. Neil Chanock, *Law, Custom and Social Order* (New York: Cambridge University Press, 1987).
13. Laurie Sears, *Shadows of Empire* (Durham, NC: Duke University Press, 1996), 36.

14. Soemarsaid Moertono, *State and Statecraft in Old Java* (Ithaca, NY: Cornell University Press, 1968), 60–61.

15. Marzanna Poplawska, "Wayang wahyu as an Example of Christian Forms of Shadow Theatre," *Asian Theatre Journal* 21, no. 2 (2004): 196.

16. Kathy Foley, "The *Ronggeng*, the *Wayang*, the *Wali*, and Islam," *Asian Theatre Journal* 32, no. 2 (2015): 365–366.

17. Sears, *Shadows of Empire*, 200.

18. Anderson, *Mythology*, 14.

19. Sears, *Shadows of Empire*, 55.

20. Sears, *Shadows of Empire*, 101.

21. Sears, *Shadows of Empire*, 13–15.

22. Sears, *Shadows of Empire*, 97, 180–185.

23. Sears, *Shadows of Empire*, 107–108.

24. *On Thrones of Gold*, ed. James Brandon (Cambridge, MA: Harvard University Press, 1970), 7.

25. Sears, *Shadows of Empire*, 89–91.

26. Sears, *Shadows of Empire*, 151.

27. Sears, *Shadows of Empire*, 204.

28. Sears, *Shadows of Empire*, 243.

29. Sears, *Shadows of Empire*, 262.

30. Boonstra, "Negotiating Heritage," 30.

31. Boonstra, "Negotiating Heritage," 35, 42.

32. Boonstra, "Negotiating Heritage," 36–38.

33. Boonstra, "Negotiating Heritage," 28.

34. Dahlan Abdul Bin Ghani, "Dissemination of 'Seri Rama' Shadow Play Puppet as a Cultural Heritage through Capcom's Street Fighter IV," Proceedings of the 9th International Conference on ubiquitous information management and communication, January 2015.

Chapter 18

1. "Jedwabne—Timeline of Remebrance [*sic*]," *Polin: The Museum of the History of Polish Jews* July 10, 2016, available at http://www.polin.pl/en/news/2016/07/09/jedwabne-timeline-of-remebrance.

2. Wasersztajn remembers eight Gestapo members who were consulted by the town council. Jan Gross, *Neighbors* (Princeton, NJ: Princeton University Press, 2001), 18.

3. Gross, *Neighbors*, 21.

4. Gross, *Neighbors*, 7.

5. Gross, *Neighbors*, 123. Elsewhere he notes a pogrom that took place in 1934.
6. Gross, *Neighbors*, 140.
7. Anna Bikont, *The Crime and the Silence* (New York: Farrar, Straus and Giroux, 2015), 278.
8. Gross, *Neighbors*, 29.
9. Gross, *Neighbors*, 23.
10. Gross, *Neighbors*, 81–82.
11. Gross, *Neighbors*, 78.
12. Bogdan Musiał, "The Pogrom in Jedwabne," in *The Neighbors Respond*, ed. Antony Polonsky and Joanna Michlic (Princeton, NJ: Princeton University Press, 2004), 339.
13. Jan Gross, "Critical Remarks Indeed," in *The Neighbors Respond*, ed. Antony Polonsky and Joanna Michlic (Princeton, NJ: Princeton University Press, 2004), 363.
14. Bikont, *The Crime*, 516–517.
15. Bikont, *The Crime*, 7.
16. Antoni Macierewicz, "The Revolution of Nihilism," in *Thou Shalt Not Kill*, ed. William Brand (Warsaw: Więź, 2001), 207.
17. Tomasz Strzembosz, "Covered-up Collaboration," in *Thou Shalt Not Kill*, ed. William Brand (Warsaw: Więź, 2001), 180.
18. Strzembosz, "Covered-up Collaboration," 173.
19. Bikont, *The Crime*, 408.
20. Strzembosz, "Covered-up Collaboration," 176.
21. Jasiewicz in *Thou Shalt Not Kill*, ed. William Brand (Warsaw: Więź, 2001), 130.
22. Richard Lukas, "Jedwabne and the Selling of the Holocaust," in *The Neighbors Respond*, ed. Antony Polonsky and Joanna Michlic (Princeton, NJ: Princeton University Press, 2004), 434.
23. Bikont, *The Crime*, 195.
24. Antony Polonsky and Joanna Michlic, "Introduction," in *The Neighbors Respond*, ed. Antony Polonsky and Joanna Michlic (Princeton, NJ: Princeton University Press, 2004), 44; Bikont, *The Crime*, 135 includes an account of Bishop Stefanek telling Jedwabne residents that "there's going to be an attack on Jedwabne, and it's all about money."
25. "A Roundtable: Jedwabne—Crime and Memory," in *Thou Shalt Not Kill*, ed. William Brand, (Warsaw: Więź, 2001), 263–264.
26. Czesław Milosz, quoted in Abraham Brumberg, "Poles and Jews," *Foreign Affairs* September-October 2002: 174.
27. Bikont, *The Crime*, 28–29.
28. Bikont, *The Crime*, 46.
29. Gross, *Neighbors*, 40; Antony Polonsky and Joanna Michlic, "Introduction: The Initial Reporting," in *The Neighbors Respond*,

ed. Antony Polonsky and Joanna Michlic (Princeton, NJ: Princeton University Press, 2004), 58.

30. Brumberg, "Poles and Jews," 174.
31. Bikont, *The Crime*, 37.
32. Bikont, *The Crime*, 45.
33. Bikont, *The Crime*, 23.
34. Bikont, *The Crime*, 180.
35. Bikont, *The Crime*, 120.
36. Bikont, *The Crime*, 178–179.
37. Gross, *Neighbors*, 109.
38. Bikont, *The Crime*, 118–119.
39. Gross, *Neighbors*, 119–120.
40. Bikont, *The Crime*, 500–501.
41. Gross, *Neighbors*, 148.
42. Bikont, *The Crime*, 150.
43. "Interview with the Primate of Poland, Cardinal Józef Glemp, on the Murder of Jews in Jedwabne," in *The Neighbors Respond*, ed. Antony Polonsky and Joanna Michlic (Princeton, NJ: Princeton University Press, 2004), 180–185.
44. "Ritual Murder Painting of Jew's Killing Christian's," *Huffington Post* January 14, 2014, available at https://www.huffingtonpost. com/2014/01/14/ritual-murder-painting_n_4596940.html.
45. Tamara Zieve, "This Week in History: The Jedwabne Pogrom," *The Jerusalem Post* July 8, 2012, available at http://www.jpost.com/Features/ In-Thespotlight/This-Week-In-History-The-Jedwabne-Pogrom. The text reads "In memory of Jews from Jedwabne and environs, men, women, and children, co-owners of this land, murdered and burned alive at this spot on July 10th, 1941."
46. Antony Polonsky and Joanna Michlic, "Introduction: Voices of the Inhabitants of Jedwabne," in *The Neighbors Respond*, ed. Antony Polonsky and Joanna Michlic (Princeton, NJ: Princeton University Press, 2004), 196.
47. Omer Bartov, *Anatomy of a Genocide* (New York: Simon and Schuster, 2018).
48. "Jedwabne—Timeline of Remembrance [*sic*]."
49. Manuela Tobias, "Understanding Poland's 'Holocaust law,'" *Polifact* March 9, 2018, available at https://www.politifact.com/truth-o-meter/ article/2018/mar/09/understanding-polish-holocaust-law/.
50. Jon Henley, "Poland Provokes Israeli Anger with Holocaust Speech Law," *The Guardian* February 1, 2018, available at https://www.theguardian. com/world/2018/feb/01/poland-holocaust-speech-law-senate-israel-us.
51. Brumberg, "Poles and Jews," 174.

Chapter 19

1. Quinton Fortune, "South Africa Spent £2.4bn to Host the 2010 World Cup. What Happens Next?" *The Guardian* September 23, 2014, available at https://www.theguardian.com/football/2014/sep/23/south-africa-2010-world-cup-what-happened.
2. Francis Fukuyama, "The End of History," *The National Interest* 16 (1989): 4.
3. Fukuyama, "The End," 18.
4. Thomas Friedman, *The World Is Flat* (New York: Picador, 2007).
5. Barber, "Jihad vs McWorld," https://www.theatlantic.com/magazine/archive/1992/03/jihad-vs-mcworld/303882/.
6. Naomi Klein, *The Shock Doctrine* (New York: Metropolitan Books, 2007), 216.
7. Bentley et al., *Traditions and Encounters*, 662.
8. von Sivers et al, *Patterns of World History*, 994. See also p.854 which includes the three forms of modernity the author feels vied for supremacy in the twentieth century, with liberal democracy winning out. The final chapter mentions the "exuberant" faith in democracy and its spread beyond its "culturally specific, western European" origins.
9. Dunn and Mitchell, *Panorama*, 833–836; Strayer and Nelson, *Ways of the World*, 1044–1050; Bentley et al., *Traditions and Encounters*, 664–665.
10. Phyllis Martin, *Leisure and Society in Colonial Brazzaville* (New York: Cambridge University Press, 2002), 99–126.
11. Peter Alegi, *African Soccerscapes* (Athens: Ohio University Press, 2010).
12. Simon Kuper and Stefan Szymanski, *Soccernomics* (New York: Nation Books, 2009), 107–108.
13. Alegi, *African Soccerscapes*, 93–97.
14. Kushatha Ndibi, "SA Soccer Stars among the Worst Paid," *Cape Argus* November 25, 2005, available at https://www.iol.co.za/capeargus/sport/sa-soccer-stars-among-the-worst-paid-551777.
15. Wayne Veysey, "Steven Pienaar Rejected Chelsea," *Goal.com* January 20, 2011, available at http://www.goal.com/en-gb/news/2896/premier-league/2011/01/20/2313876/steven-pienaar-rejected-chelsea-after-tottenham-offered.
16. Available at https://www.youtube.com/watch?v=1mVd4V_BOVY.
17. "Marine Le Pen: Les résultats des Bleus, conséquence de 'l'ultralibéralisme,'" *Le Point* November 18, 2013, available at http://www.lepoint.fr/politique/marine-le-pen-les-resultats-des-bleus-consequence-de-l-ultra-liberalisme-18-11-2013-1758152_20.php.

18. Laurent Dubois, "Afro-Europe in the World Cup," February 20, 2014, available at http://roadsandkingdoms.com/2014/afro-europe-in-the-world-cup/.

19. Dubois, "Afro-Europe."

20. Michael Ralph, "'Crimes of History': Senegalese Soccer and the Forensics of Slavery," *Souls* 9, no. 3 (2007): 201.

21. Ralph, "'Crimes of History,'" 201–202.

22. Devesh Kapur and John McHale, *Give Us Your Best and Brightest* (Washington, DC: Center for Global Development, 2005), 207.

23. Rafaelle Poli, "Africans' Status in the European Football Players' Market," *Soccer and Society* 7, no. 2 (2006): 289.

24. Duncan White, "Match-Fixing: Fear and Loathing in Lapland," *The Telegraph* May 7, 2011, available at https://www.telegraph.co.uk/sport/football/news/8499679/Match-fixing-Fear-and-loathing-in-Lapland-one-clubs-nightmare.html.

25. "South Africa Living with Mixed Legacy of 2010 World Cup," *Agence France Presse* July 19, 2018, available at https://www.capitalfm.co.ke/sports/2018/07/19/south-africa-living-with-mixed-legacy-of-2010-world-cup/.

26. Derina Holtzhausen and Jami Fullerton, "The 2010 World Cup and South Africa," *Journal of Marketing Communications* 21, no. 3 (2015): 185–193.

27. Omar Mohammed, "South Africa Paid Millions of Dollars in Bribes to Host the 2010 World Cup, Says FIFA," *Quartz Africa* March 16, 2016, available at https://qz.com/africa/640707/south-africa-paid-millions-of-dollars-in-bribes-to-host-the-2010-world-cup-fifa-says/.

28. Shaheed Tayob, "The 2010 World Cup in South Africa: A Millennial Capitalist Moment," *Journal of Southern African Studies* 38, no. 3 (2012): 735.

29. Alegi, *African Soccerscapes*, 131.

30. Sophie Nakueira, "Power, Profit and Sport: The Real Legacy of the World Cup," *Review of African Political Economy* July 16, 2018, available at http://roape.net/2018/07/16/power-profit-and-sport-the-real-legacy-of-the-football-world-cup/.

31. Alex Smith, "The Empty Stadiums," *Monocle* October 21, 2010, available at https://monocle.com/monocolumn/business/the-empty-stadiums-south-africa-s-white-elephants/.

32. Albert Grundlingh and John Nauright, "Worlds Apart," in *Africa's World Cup*, ed. Peter Alegi and Chris Bolsmann (Ann Arbor: University of Michigan Press, 2013), 196.

33. Scarlet Cornelisson, "Our Struggles Are Bigger Than the World Cup," *British Journal of Sociology* 63, no. 2 (2012): 329.

34. Tayob, "The 2010 World Cup," 734.
35. Meg Vandermerwe, "South Africa Welcomes the World," in *Africa's World Cup*, ed. Peter Alegi and Chris Bolsmann, (Ann Arbor: University of Michigan Press, 2013), 207.
36. Kuper and Szymanski, *Soccernomics*, 291–306; Darby cited in Alegi, *African Soccerscapes*, 79.
37. Alegi, *African Soccerscapes,* 79–80.

Chapter 20

1. Paul Collier, *The Bottom Billion* (New York: Oxford University Press, 2007), xii.
2. Collier, *The Bottom Billion*, 11–12.
3. Tamara Shreiner and David Zwart, "It's Just Different," *The History Teacher*, forthcoming.
4. Simon Kuznets did include government spending in his initial formula, but spent much of his professional career fighting to exclude them since he didn't consider this type of spending productive. See Ehsan Masood, *The Great Invention* (New York: Pegasus Books, 2016), 16–17.
5. Lorenzo Fioramonti, *Gross Domestic Problem* (New York: Zed Books, 2013), 6.
6. Elizabeth Dickinson, "GDP: A Brief History," *Foreign Policy* January 3, 2011, available at https://foreignpolicy.com/2011/01/03/gdp-a-brief-history/.
7. Firoamonti, *Gross Domestic Problem*, 8.
8. "Maddison Historical Statistics," available at https://www.rug.nl/ggdc/historicaldevelopment/maddison/.
9. Patrick Manning, "The Maddison Project: Historical GDP Estimates Worldwide," *Journal of World Historical Information* 1, no. 3–4 (2016–2017): 36–37.
10. Fioramonti, *Gross Domestic Problem*, 26.
11. Jim Lacey, *Keep from All Thoughtful Men* (Annapolis, MD: Naval Institute Press, 2011), 7.
12. Masood, *The Great Invention*, 35.
13. Arturo Escobar, *Encountering Development* (Princeton, NJ: Princeton University Press, 2012), 24.
14. Escobar, *Encountering Development*, 24.
15. Cited in Escobar, *Encountering Development*, 171.
16. Escobar, *Encountering Development*, 173.
17. Fioramonti, *Gross Domestic Problem*, 51.

18. Fioramonti, *Gross Domestic Problems*, 145.
19. Robert F. Kennedy, "Remarks at the University of Kansas," March 18, 1968, available at https://www.jfklibrary.org/Research/Research-Aids/Ready-Reference/RFK-Speeches/Remarks-of-Robert-F-Kennedy-at-the-University-of-Kansas-March-18-1968.aspx.
20. Rachel Carson, "Silent Spring," *The New Yorker* (1962), available at https://www.newyorker.com/magazine/1962/06/16/silent-spring-part-1.
21. *The Limits of Growth* (New York: Universe Books, 1972), 23.
22. Richard Easterlin, "Does Economic Growth Improve the Human Lot," in *Nations and Households in Economic Growth*, ed. Paul David and Melvin Reder (New York: Academic Press, 1974), 89–125.
23. Mahbub ul Haq, *The Poverty Curtain* (New York: Columbia University Press, 1976), 32–33.
24. Masood, *The Great Invention*, 49–50.
25. Morten Jerven, *Poor Numbers* (Ithaca, NY: Cornell University Press, 2013), 43.
26. Douglas Rimmer, "Learning about Economic Development from Africa," *African Affairs* 102 (2003): 471.
27. Fioramonti, *Gross Domestic Problem*, 58.
28. Jerven, *Poor Numbers*, 41.
29. Kean Ng, "Ugandan Borders: Theatres of Life and Death," *Journal of Borderland Studies* 33, no. 3 (2018): 465–486.
30. Jerven, *Poor Numbers*, 51.
31. Jerven, *Poor Numbers*, x.
32. Jerven, *Poor Numbers*, 97.
33. Jerven, *Poor Numbers*, 12.
34. Jerven, *Poor Numbers*, 27.
35. Fioramonti, *Gross Domestic Problem*, 106.
36. Fioramonti, *Gross Domestic Problem*, 107.
37. Fioramonti, *Gross Domestic Problem*, 79.
38. Crystal Biruk, *Cooking Data* (Durham, NC: Duke University Press, 2018), 187.
39. Masood, *The Great Invention*, 108.
40. Masood, *The Great Invention*, 120–121.
41. Joseph Stiglitz, "The Great GDP Swindle," *The Guardian* September 13, 2009, available at https://www.theguardian.com/commentisfree/2009/sep/13/economics-economic-growth-and-recession-global-economy.

Index